My Life in Photography

Behind the Scenes— How the Photographs Were Made

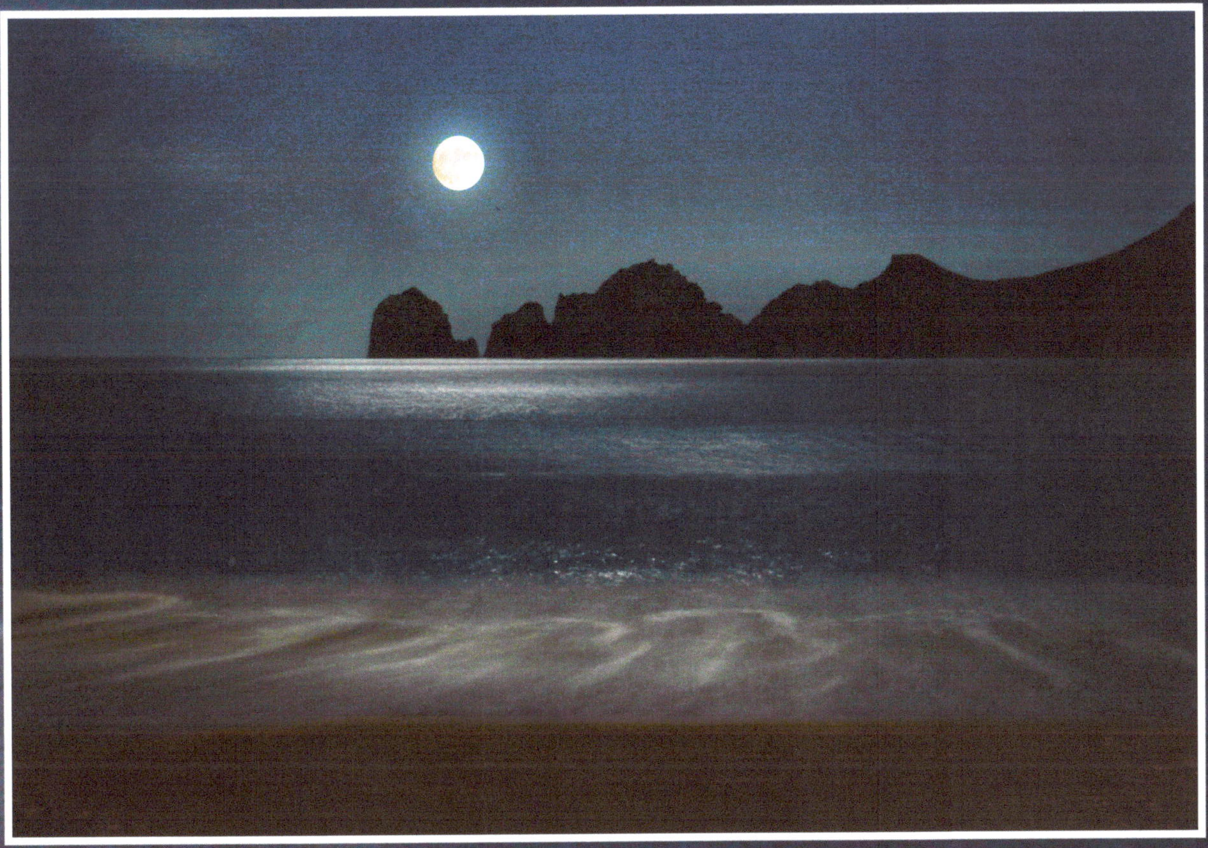

Will Chubb

Many dates as given for the photographs are approximate.

My Life in Photography
Behind the Scenes - How the Photographs Were Made

v3.0

New Times Bay Area Publishing

Paperback ISBN: 978-0-578-23566-0
Hardback ISBN: 978-0-578-23565-3

PRINTED IN THE UNITED STATES OF AMERICA

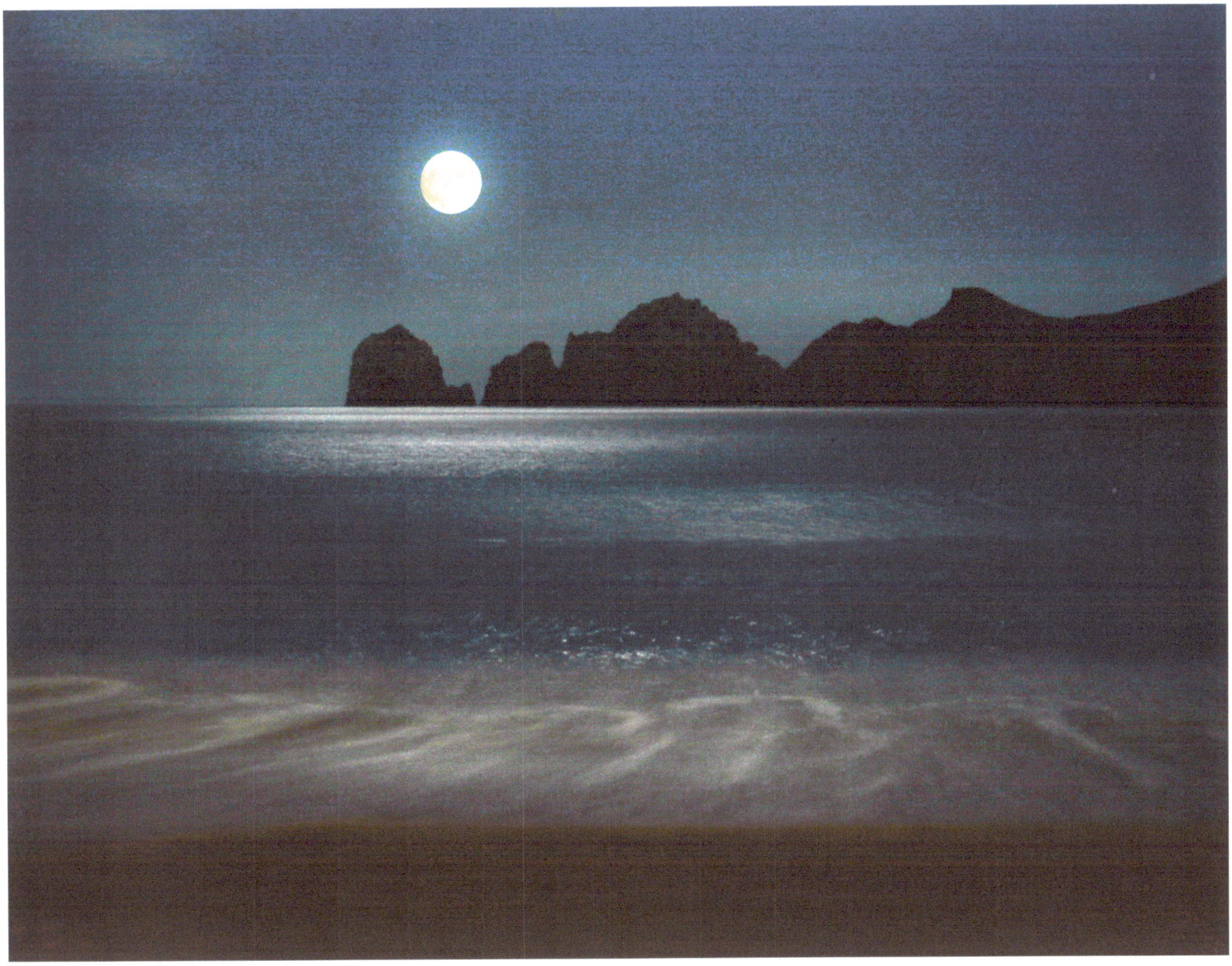

June 2005 147 Cabo Romance

Acknowledgment

MY DEEPEST GRATITUDE TO THE EDITOR OF THIS BOOK: GAIL TERRY GRIMES. THIS BOOK WOULD NOT HAVE BEEN POSSIBLE WITHOUT HER INCREDIBLE HELP AND EXPERTISE.

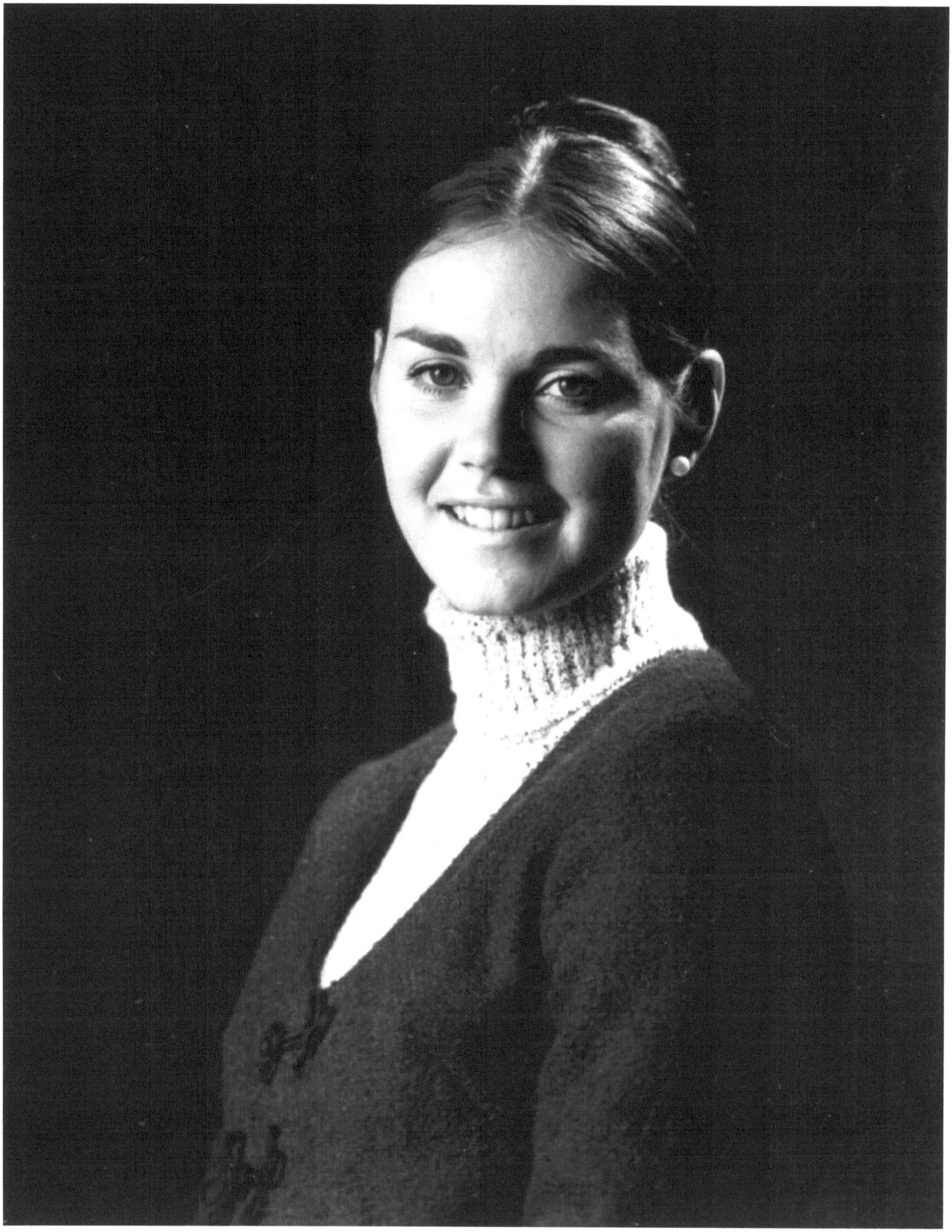

September 1966 **Linda Chubb**

My Book Dedication

This book is dedicated to my lovely wife, Linda, to whom I was blessed to be married for 32 years. Linda died of cancer at the age of 52 on January 27, 1998. A huge loss for me and my boys.

I thank God we had our two boys, Bryan and William. They have been such a great comfort to me in all these years without Linda, a real stabilizing force in my life.

I did have an epiphany even before meeting Linda, but it was a glimpse into what I later would come to know as merely a reason for my life. That reason is love. I certainly had it with Linda, and later my two boys and finally with my dear dog, Teddy. He is such a kind soul on this planet. Love is absolutely the best thing on the planet and the reason we are here.

I am going to have my first grandchild, a grandson, who is due to be born in mid-July of this year. Love is ever-expanding! I've had a remarkable life, full of love and creativity. I've been truly blessed to have been able to see and capture the world through my eyes. I'm hoping my book will be an inspiration to others to be kind in your actions and treat the planet and your fellow man with love and compassion, and to see the extraordinary in the ordinary.

Table of Contents

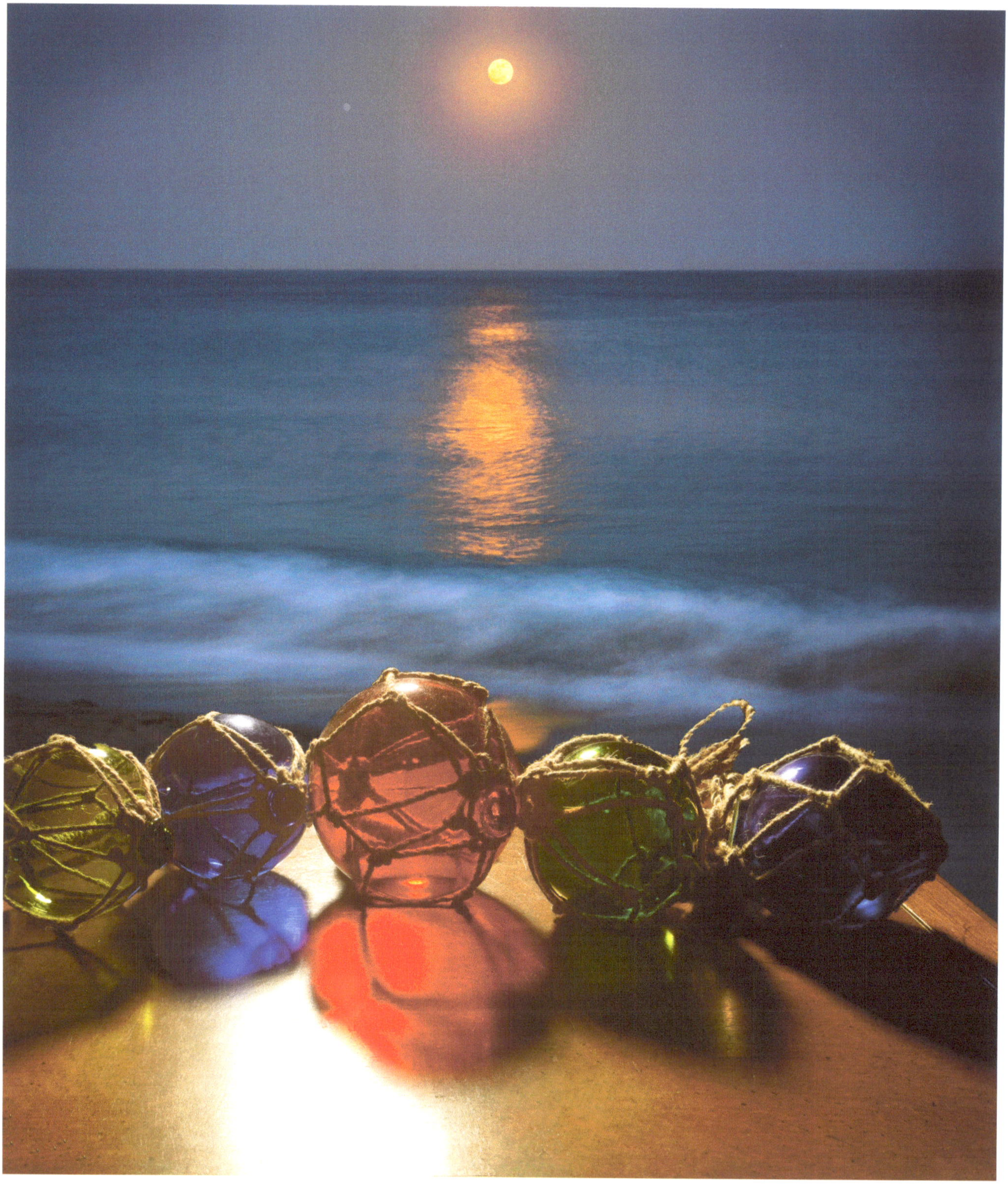

August 1963

365 My Epiphany

My Epiphany
How I entered my photography career

After high school I thought I'd follow my dad's footsteps and pursue a career as a physicist. I entered San Diego State College and did pretty well in most of the science classes until I took calculus. I hit the wall and flunked out!! As it turns out Dad is left-brained and I'm right-brained.

I needed a breather from it all to figure out what I was going to do in my life. I talked to a couple of my body surfing buddies and we planned a trip to Mexico to meet up with a mutual friend who was an exchange student in Guadalajara, Mexico. When we arrived we asked the family he was staying with to point out a non-tourist place on the coast where we could body surf. They pointed out a sleepy little town (which it was in 1963) called Manzanillo, Mexico, where we found a villa on the beach. It was built by a retired Canadian who only charged us each $2.50 a night, which included a huge breakfast. The best thing was that the waves were fabulous.

After several weeks; we were finally down to the last few days. We spent the entire day surfing, I was getting tired and told my buddies I was going back to the villa to relax on the veranda. The sun was getting lower in the sky and the soft warm wind filled the air with the scent of the ocean before me. The palm trees were swaying in the wind. I had several cervezas and some smooth jazz was playing. To say the least, I was in the zone--the creative zone.

On the coffee table in front of me were glass balls of different sizes and colors, which were used as floats for the fishing nets. The sunlight was casting beautiful shapes on the table and I thought if only I had a set of paints I'd paint this beautiful scene. Then I remembered my dad had offered me a camera to take on the trip. I told him I didn't want to look like a "tourista," but he insisted and included a few rolls of film.

By the time my buddies returned from surfing I was lying on the floor shooting up through the colored glass balls with the sun and palm trees in the background. I was in heaven. I thought what a wonderful way this was to capture the beauty of life around me. For the rest of the trip, and until this day, I've had a camera in front of me. It was truly an epiphany.

When I returned to San Diego, I met with five different photographers. They all shot weddings or portraits and I just wanted to shoot beautiful, creative imagery. Well, the fifth photographer I met with said, "You know, Will, you need to go up to LA and take a look at a place called the Art Center College of Design." So, another buddy and I took off in my little Austin Healy sports car to take a look.

When I walked in through the doors, I couldn't believe my eyes. There on the walls were the most creative images I'd ever seen; like you'd see in the best high-end magazines.

I submitted my images from my trip to Mexico and was rejected. It turns out that you have to be *really good* at photography before they will accept you! So, for the next year and a half I attended San Diego City College and took photography courses. I was determined to get in. A second portfolio was rejected after a year at City College. Finally, my third portfolio was accepted! I was admitted on probation in a class of 43 people. After four grueling years, twelve of us graduated and I graduated with honors. It is one of the best design schools in the world–somewhat like Julliard is to music, design is to Art Center.

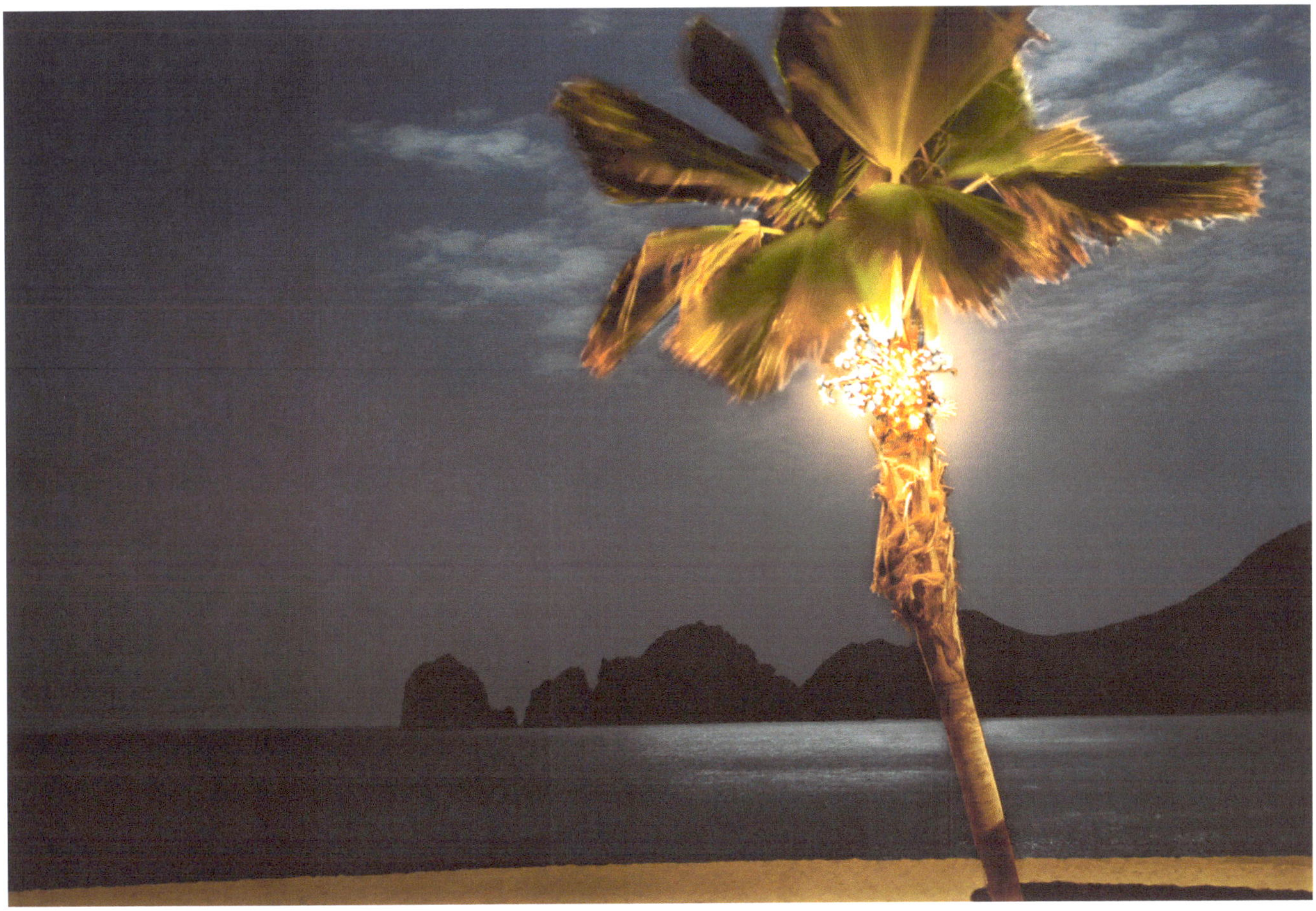

June 2005

148 Cabo Palm

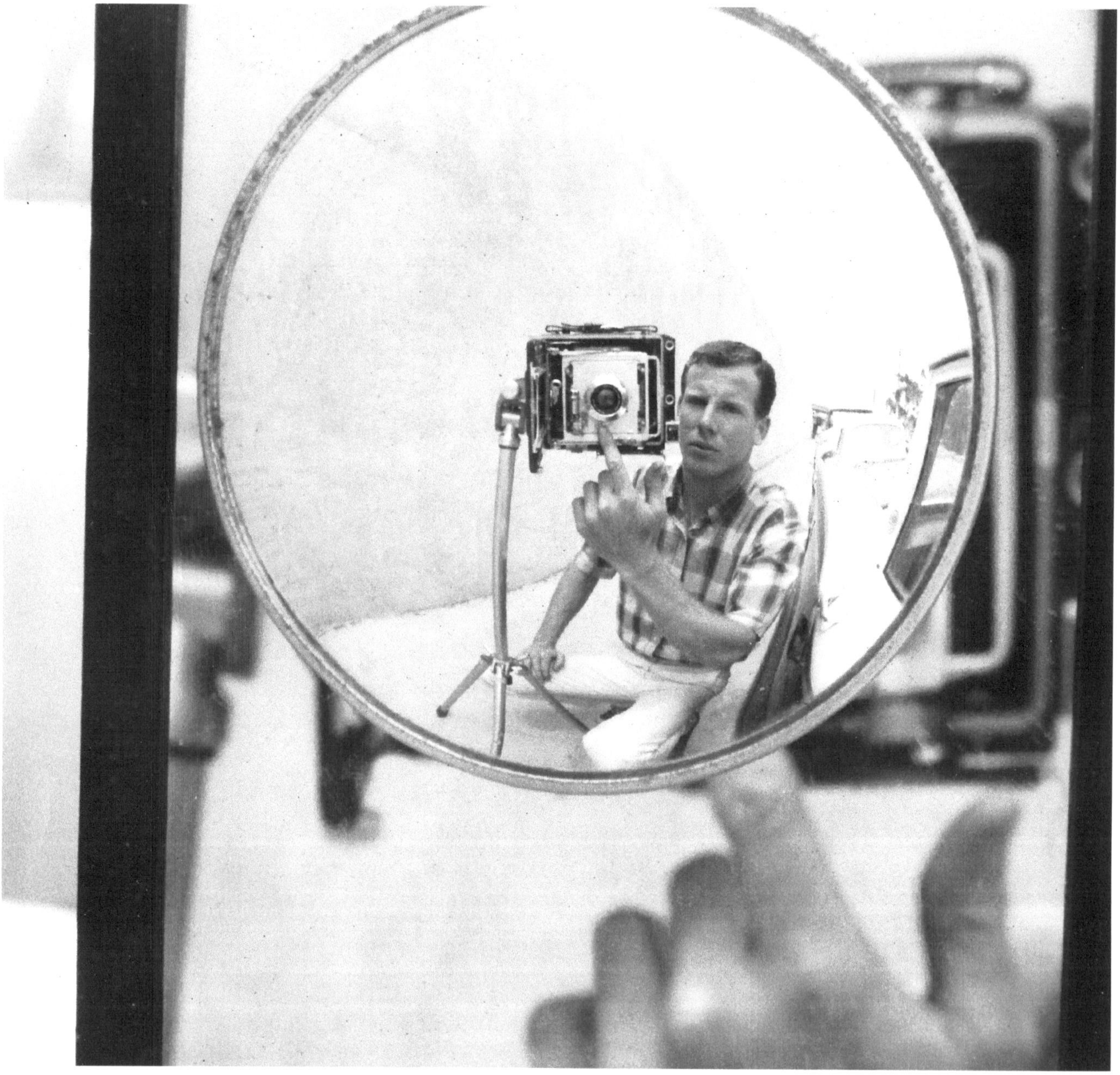

September 1965 Semester 1 Art Center Self Portrait

My First Day at Art Center

Now Art Center College of Design is in Pasadena, California. Back in 1964, when I entered the school, it was in the Wilshire District of Los Angeles at 5353 W Third Street. It had previously been a private girls' school.

On our first day the 43 of us gathered in the auditorium. We sat on the wooden steps leading up to the stage. Behind us was a keg light (spotlight) and no other lights were on. It was set to shine a narrow beam of light and was illuminating the director of the photography department, Charles Potts, who was sitting behind a wooden table. The sharply focused light was illuminating white wooden objects, like cubes, pyramids, balls which Charles would hold up one by one and show us how the light defined the shape of each object. The light was very theatrical on old Charlie Potts. With his deep wrinkles and enormous eyebrows, he looked like a character out of an old black and white mystery movie.

I'm kind of a front row center kind of guy and I was so excited to finally be attending Art Center. So, there I was right in front of old Charlie. As he finished showing us the objects, he stared right at me, leaned forward, pounded the wooden table with his fist and with a booming voice said, "Light is a Law." It scared the hell out of me and I almost peed my pants. This was my first day and I was thinking I'm not sure I can take this.

Charlie was ever so right; light is everything in a photograph or a movie. It sets the entire tone. Looking back, I really think my epiphany was greatly influenced by the light, and of course the alcohol!

I'm extremely careful to make sure the light in my images captures the essence of what I'm trying to say. If I'm shooting outdoors, I won't waste my time unless the quality of light is exactly right. Usually this is the "golden hour" just before sunrise or shortly after sunset when the light is softer and warmer than when the sun is high in the sky. I kid you not, I hear Charlie's voice all the time! He made quite a lasting impression on me!

Living in Los Angeles

Not only was Art Center a learning experience, but just living in L.A. was quite an experience, as well. Art Center was very expensive so both Linda and I worked extra jobs to make ends meet. One such job I had was working at Beverly Hills Camera store on Rodeo Drive. Many famous people shopped there. One, although not necessarily famous, was an elderly lady that came in with an old creased black and white photo of her grandfather. We had a darkroom lab in the back of the store, along with a retouch artist. The lady asked if we could retouch her photo to make it look better. I said no problem. Then she added, "Can you take my grandfather's top hat off?" I again said, "No problem but first let me get some information from you."

I asked if her grandfather had thinning hair and what side did he have a part. At that point she stood back from the counter with her hands on her hips and said, "I don't know why you're asking me all these silly questions; you'll find out when you take the hat off!" Truth is stranger than fiction.

Another interesting experience was showing Carl Reiner a camera. He came in the store smoking a big thick cigar, which you could do in those days. As I was explaining the details of the camera he drew a big drag on his cigar and blew a huge cloud of smoke directly in my face! I've never figured out why he did this other than to get my reaction in order to try a similar reaction for an actor in one of his films.

A lady came in and said in her English accent, "Good afternoon." It was Alfred Hitchcock's wife and she sounded just like Alfred saying good afternoon.

It was a full-service camera store. We served tea and coffee and would project the client's 8mm or 16mm home movies for them in our projection room.

Linda had several jobs. The first one was working at Beverly Hills Pharmacy on the corner of Rodeo Drive and Santa Monica Boulevard, just down the street from the camera store. She worked in the cosmetic department. One lady named Ann Margret rode her motorcycle in and parked it on the sidewalk. She always asked for Linda's help. After they got to know each other, Ann Margret trusted Linda to recommend a hair color for her, and that's when she became a redhead!

Mickey Rooney came in almost every afternoon and bought a fudge bar and a newspaper.

Linda went out for lunch one day and saw Fred Astaire doing some window shopping. She told me that night that she skipped lunch and just followed him because he moved so gracefully and smoothly she couldn't get enough!

Linda's next job was working for Ed Handler, a portrait photographer on Rodeo Drive. Lots of famous people came in to be photographed. One group was Paul Revere & the Raiders. They were pretty crass and sat around Ed's desk in the reception room with their feet up on his desk. Well, one of them told Linda, "Hey babe, watch the parking meter for me." When he was in the back having his picture taken, Linda was delighted when the parking meter lady placed a ticket on his Lamborghini parked out front.

One day Linda, Ed Handler and I were standing out front of Ed's studio. Ed suddenly said "look, it's Howard Hughes." He was entering a custom clothing store across the street to have a suit made. He was dressed in grey sweats. In Beverly Hills you never knew who you were going to see!

Linda studied cosmetics with some of the greats in Hollywood like the Westmores, who created makeup for the motion picture industry, Estee Lauder, Ben Nye, and Lili Dache. She went a long way from the cosmetic counter at the drug store. Linda did makeup on Rodeo Drive and her clients included Agnes Moorhead, Bette Davis, Stephanie Powers, and Cheryl Tiegs, just to name a few. She worked at the Beverly Hills Hotel during the Academy Awards. One story was about a rather loud woman yelling and cursing in the back of the salon. She asked what was going on and as it turns out it was Elizabeth Taylor. She usually traveled with her own makeup artist but she was sick and couldn't be there. So, Elizabeth Taylor had to lower herself and come down to the salon herself, which made her very unhappy!

Another time an unknown haircutter, Vidal Sassoon, showed up and was enamored with Linda's thick and beautiful long auburn hair. He asked if he could use her as a model and cut her hair in his new style that he became noted for. Linda said OK. Well, it was the most amazing cut I've ever seen. She could mess up her hair and shake her head and it would fall into place without brushing it. Linda came home that night and said, "I hope you're not mad but I got my long hair cut off today." Wow, she was even more beautiful than ever!

...more to the story

I was involved in the beginning stages of a newly developing department at Art Center: the film department; it has really developed into an amazing major.

As it turns out I did one of the first films at Art Center. It was a visualization of Simon and Garfunkel's "The Sound of Silence," a lot like the style of MTV but much sooner. The film gained some recognition and was shown at my commencement ceremony.

I was actually drawn to be a DP, a "director of photography" in the motion picture industry. After graduating, I applied for and was accepted to the Universal Studios director's apprenticeship program. That is when Steven Spielberg first arrived at Universal Studios. Who knows what may have developed if I'd stayed! I decided to accept a job at an AD Agency in San Francisco, which paid a lot more than Universal's apprenticeship program. For the next three years I was shooting brochures, magazine advertising and TV commercials.

While at the AD Agency my wife, Linda, and I lived in Marin County's City of San Anselmo. Here is where I met a firefighter named Pat Williams. We became good friends and have been for 50 years. Pat talked me into becoming a volunteer firefighter with his department. So, during the time I was at the AD agency I was also a volunteer firefighter.

One of the AD agency shoots was a short film for Schilling Spice to be used at their annual sales meeting to introduce new products. We showed the products and then cut back to a pretty model to keep their interest up. The model was an unknown lady raising a twelve-year old son by herself in Mill Valley; her name was Suzanne Somers. The theme of the film was something that couldn't be done today, it involved Suzanne dressed as a cheerleader and we would cut back to her to keep the sales staff interested. At the end of the film she raised her pom poms and said "go Shilling Spice" and exposed her bare breasts.

After three years I left the agency to become a rich and famous photographer on my own. Well, it didn't work out. After all, I had so few clients and money was tight because Linda was taking courses at College of Marin in dental assisting. But one notable client I had on my own was Maharaja Water Skis. They hired me to do a brochure and a poster. They wanted a blond wearing a tee shirt with their logo on it but wearing no bra. I said let's wet the tee shirt and they went crazy, It really hadn't been done in those days. They asked me if I knew of a model and I said I had the perfect model, Suzanne Somers. I went home and told Linda that I got the job and mentioned the concept. Linda said "Why have the tee shirt on at all, just paint the Maharaja logo on her bare chest." I called the client and they went crazy again. So, that's what we did, and it was a poster that was printed for over twenty years.

Shortly after this, Suzanne made a film with a new director named George Lucas, and the film was American Graffiti. After that, Suzanne met a wealthy Canadian producer and television host named Alan Hamel and the rest is history!

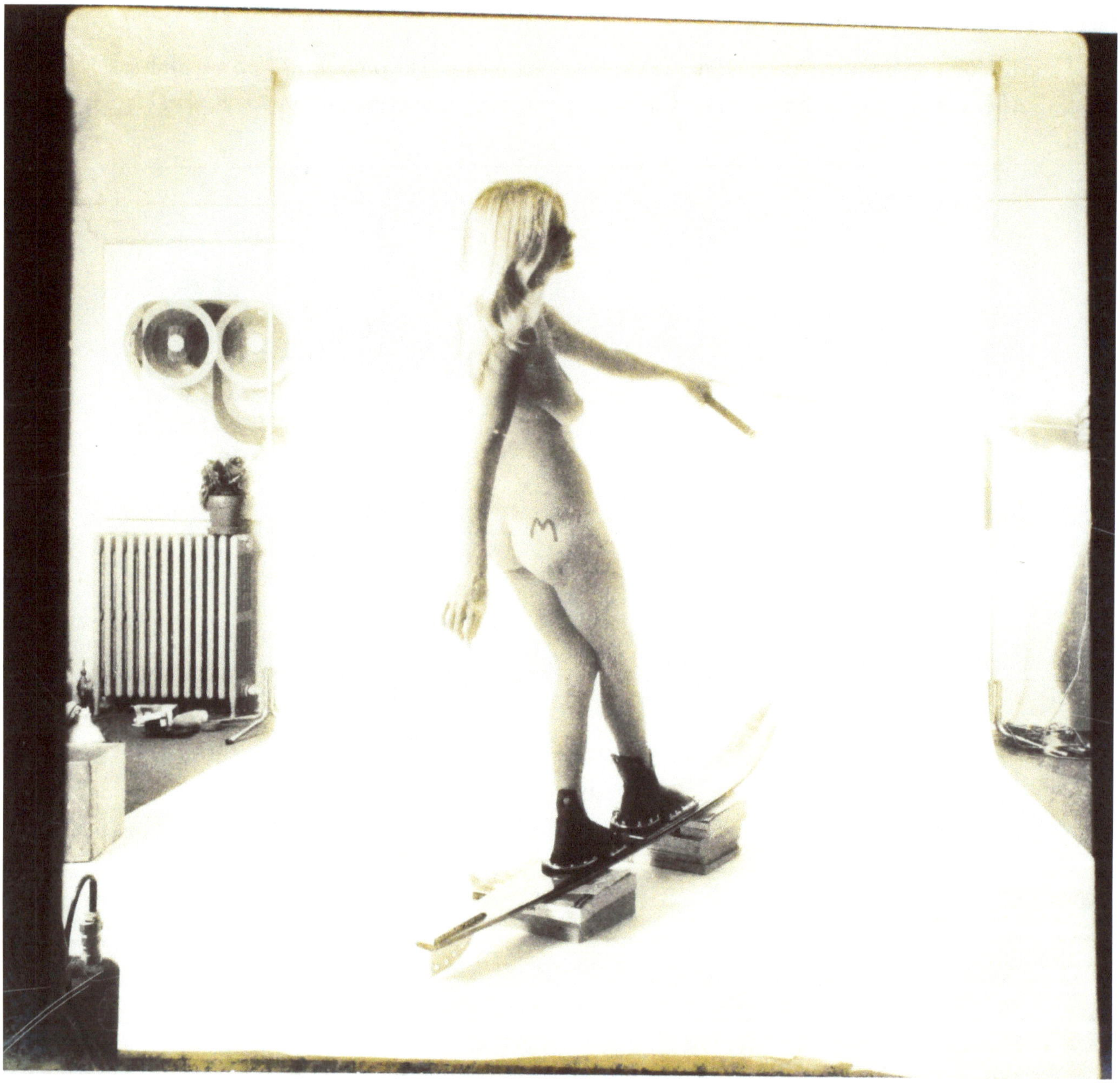

A polaroid test shot of Suzanne on the set. The plan was to cut her out and place her on water. It never materialized.

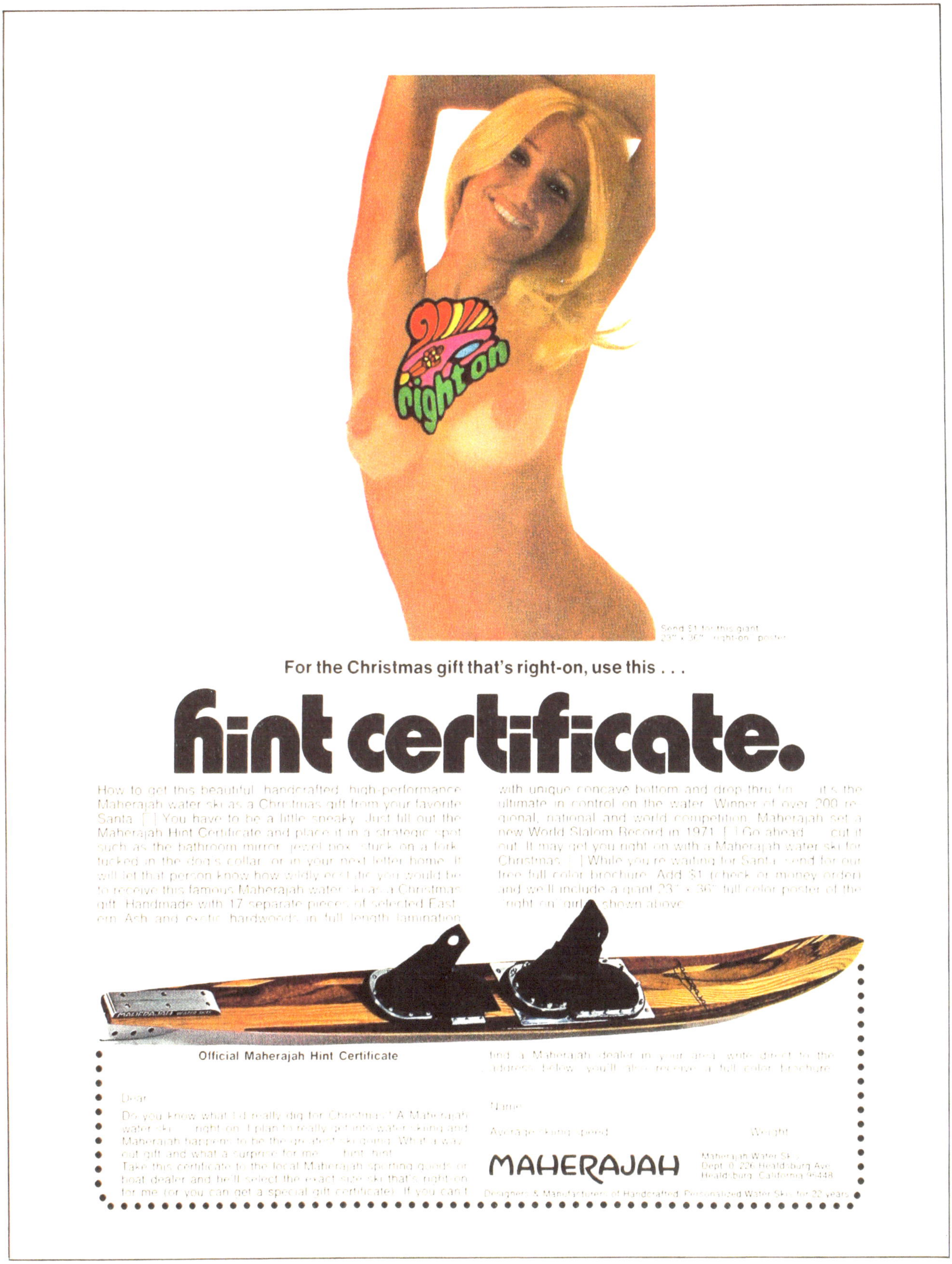

November 1972 **NFS Suzanne Somers**

So here I am in beautiful San Francisco at my first job out of college.

My first assignment at the AD Agency was to do an image that depicted San Francisco for KFRC, a local radio station. I thought it really worked well for them. This was before there were a million photos of the Golden Gate Bridge. I gave the print to Tom, one of my three bosses. He didn't like it at all and told me he was meeting with the client in an hour but was very embarrassed to show him such poor work. That was late Friday afternoon. I spent the weekend disheartened because I wanted to do a great job for him. I got to the office early on Monday morning to face the music. The front desk girl gave me a FedEx letter from the president of KFRC. The letter exclaimed that he was so excited that I was hired by the AD Agency and that he was thrilled with the image.

I just finished reading the letter when in walked Tom, who said, "In my office now!" In his office he repeated what he told me on Friday--how embarrassed he was to show such poor work. I showed Tom the letter and that shut him up!

Tom's brother was a very talented illustrator and Tom didn't have any artistic talent that I could see. All I could figure out is that he was jealous of me and was putting me in my place. Anyway, I worked there for three long years.

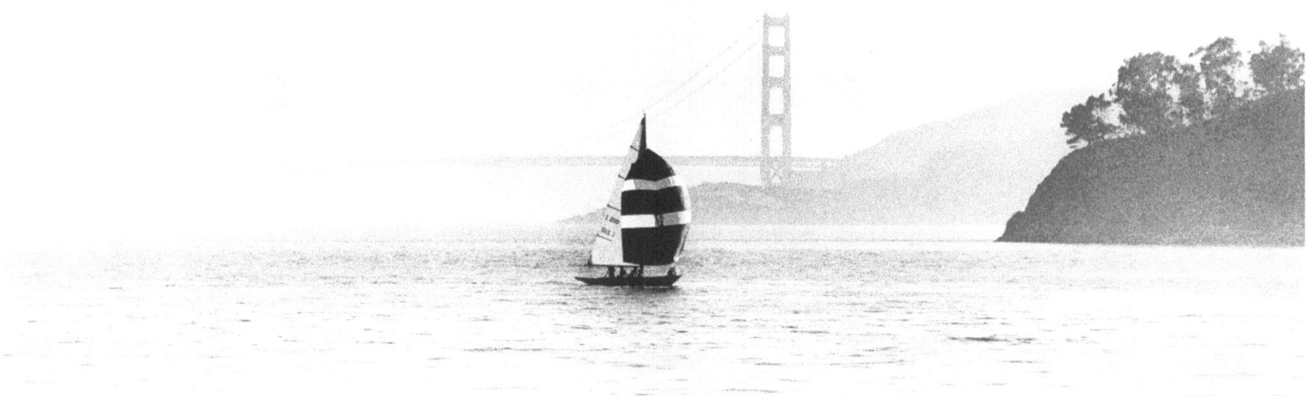

August 1968 **366 My First Photo Assignment in SF**

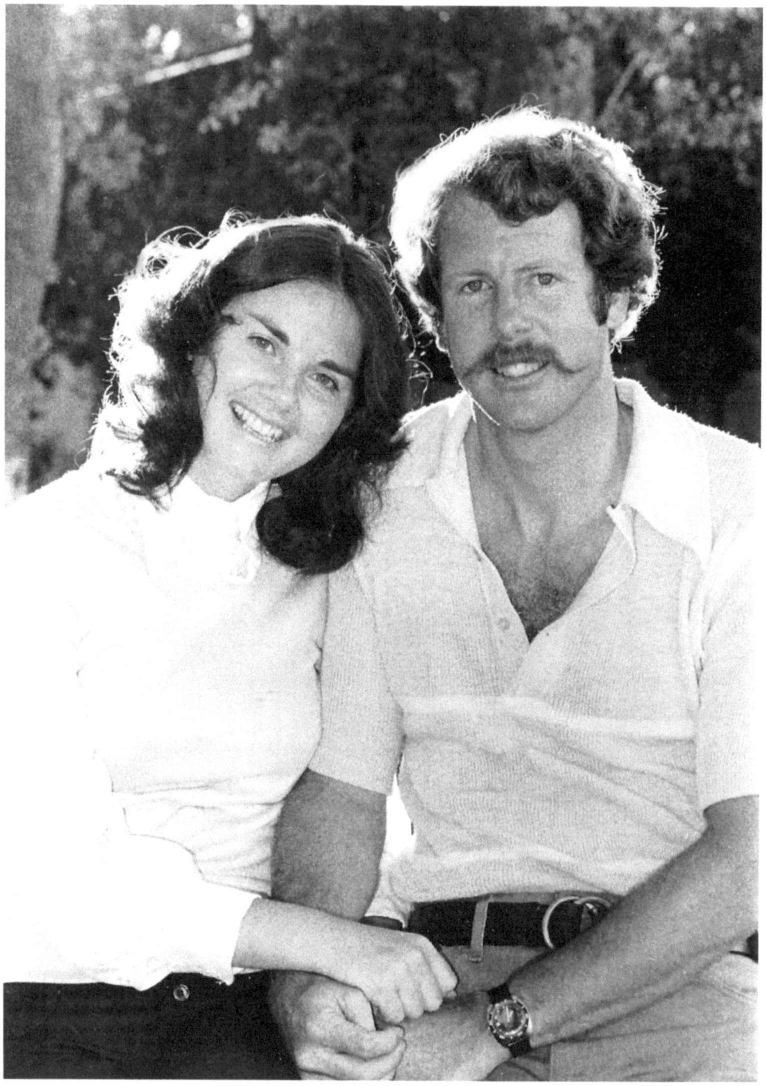

This was taken shortly after we moved to the San Francisco Bay area.

Linda and I were settling in nicely to our new life in the San Francisco bay area.

Los Angeles was fun but really hectic and high energy for four years. It was nice to know we had made a decision on where to live that suited us. We would wait a total of ten years before having kids. I'm glad we waited but I'm *really* glad we had our two boys. We never know what life has in store for us as humans. I would be doubly at a loss to lose Linda and be alone without my boys. Family is so important.

Life was grand; we might go into the city and see a great play, then go out to eat. San Francisco is, to me, one of the greatest cities in the world.

When the boys were old enough we bought a 32' power boat which we could sleep on. We docked it in Sausalito and we went into the city on our boat. Instead of paying hundreds for a hotel room, we could dock it near Fisherman's Wharf for about $32 a night. Of course, owning a boat is very expensive, but what a bonding experience it was for our family.

Before taking this image, I had spent two hours on the edge of SF Bay waiting for the full moon to come up. It finally did but it wasn't in the location I wanted. I had just skipped dinner to get what I thought was going to be a fantastic image with the moon shining on the water. I had listened to Wolf Man Jack on the car radio the whole time so I guess it wasn't a complete waste. I had been so excited and filled with anticipation to get my shot that I couldn't just give up and go home. I remember I was starving but you have to sacrifice for your craft, and I certainly wasn't going home empty-handed. I drove up over the hills of Sausalito to see if I could get the vantage point I wanted of the fog flowing so gracefully over the hills toward Sausalito. I finally came upon this scene and took the photograph under a full moon. I hadn't seen the little house with smoke coming out of the chimney until I processed the film and made a proof sheet. This was, of course the pre-digital days. Unlike instant digital, I didn't make my discovery until the next afternoon.

October 1968 **367 Fog over Mt. Tamalpais**

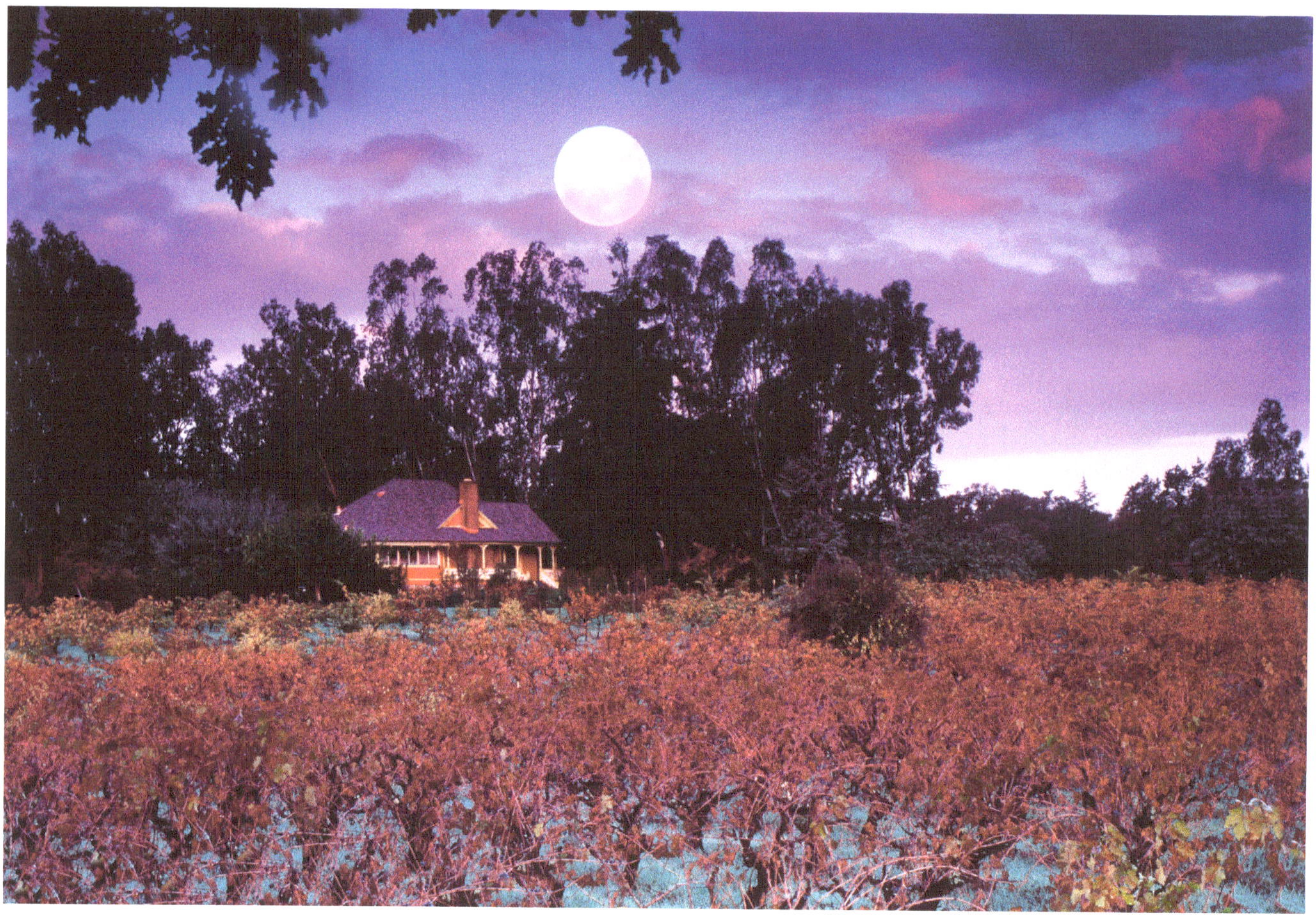

November 1973 119 Harvest Moon

Meeting Ansel Adams

In March 1972 I called directory assistance (you could do that in those days!) and asked for the number of Ansel Adams. To my surprise he was listed. I called him and he actually picked up the phone.

I told him that I loved his work and I would love to meet him anytime and anyplace. He responded, "Friday after next for cocktails at my house." I about fell over. Linda and I drove to Carmel, went into a wine shop and asked if Ansel Adams shopped there and what wine he liked. It was starting to get dark when we arrived. Ansel's wife answered the door and invited us in to sit by a fire roaring in the big stone fireplace. She said he was out shooting tests for polaroid. Bear in mind this was a cold March afternoon and it was drizzling, not to mention Ansel was in his late '70s. When Ansel showed up, we offered him the wine and he said he was going to have bourbon and would we join him? So, there we were, the three of us having bourbon in Ansel Adams's living room.

We had a pleasant conversation but the thing I remember most was a story he told about an opening show of his work he had at a gallery in San Francisco. He was talking to me but his eyes never left my pretty wife, Linda. At his opening a pretty but arrogant older woman came in and took a whirlwind tour of his images. She came up to Mr. Adams and said, "I don't know what the problem is but your photographs don't do a thing for me."

Ansel replied, "Don't worry. I think it's the same problem that I have when I look at you: I can't get an erection!"

Well, he was on his third bourbon at this point and he asked me if I had any images I'd like to show him. I said I had one image in the car that I would like to share with him. I had been working on the image for a couple of months to make it perfect. Bear in mind these were the pre-digital days. I had used a roll of Kodachrome film to shoot a series of full moons. I then wound the film back to the mark I had made on the start of the film and double exposed a series of vineyards.

Upon showing him the image it seemed to have touched a nerve and he replied robustly, "Was the moon really there?"

I told him I had double exposed the images in the camera. At this point he abruptly got up, went into his darkroom and slammed the door closed. Ansel Adams was a purist and if the moon wasn't actually there he wouldn't take the picture. His wife entered the living room and announced, "The evening is over!"

When we were walking back to the car, I noticed a tear coming down Linda's cheek. I said, "Are you upset that I angered Ansel Adams?" and she said, "No, I'm just taken to have had this meeting with such a master."

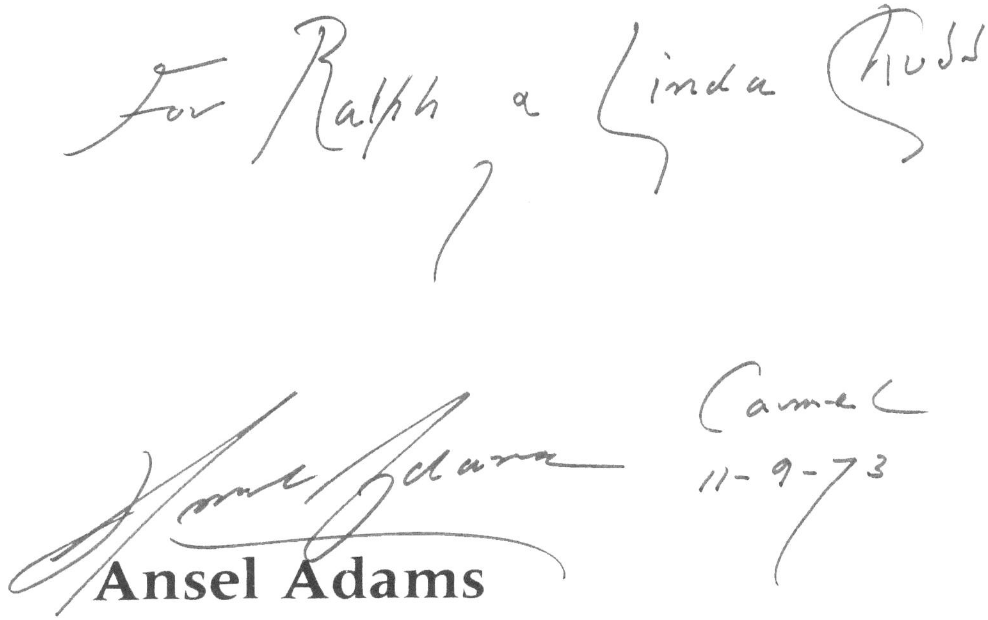
For Ralph & Linda Chubb

Ansel Adams Carmel 11-9-73

Ansel Adams

We had Ansel Adams sign a copy his book on photography during our visit.

Laguna Morning

During my morning meditation I often get an inspiration for a photograph. One particular morning I saw that I should go to the Laguna de Santa Rosa, a watershed in Sonoma County, at midnight under a full moon.

That evening my wife and I went out to dinner. As we were driving home I noticed a giant full moon. I hadn't realized tonight was going to be the night. I dropped my wife off and gathered my photo gear.

I drove to the Laguna and had to climb over a barbed wire fence with all my photographic gear and tripod. Then, I had to walk about a half mile in the dark over uneven ground to get to the right spot.

I envisioned this image to be in the early morning. To accomplish this, I had to set the exposure to about 30 seconds. Exposing for such a long time turned the dark night into a tranquil morning, it's all a matter of exposure.

The "before" shot shows what the scene actually looked like at midnight.

The moon was incredibly bright. The fragrance of new mown hay filled the air. It was a magical evening. If I wasn't involved so passionately in my craft, I never would have experienced standing alone in the middle of this remote field at midnight! When I got home I was too excited to sleep. I loaded my images into the computer to see what I had. The results were exceptional but not to my standard; something was missing. I decided to let it simmer overnight and tackle it again in the morning.

In the spring I had photographed a series of egrets flying to their nesting trees on West Ninth Steet in Santa Rosa. I went through my files and found the perfect image. The challenge was to find a photo that matched the lighting I wanted; it had to be backlighted to illuminate the wings properly to look authentic.

The next step was to photoshop the image into the scene. It didn't look natural until I duplicated the image, flipping it over and putting it into the water to look like a reflection. To further add realism, I added a ripple in the water to suggest the egret had just taken flight.

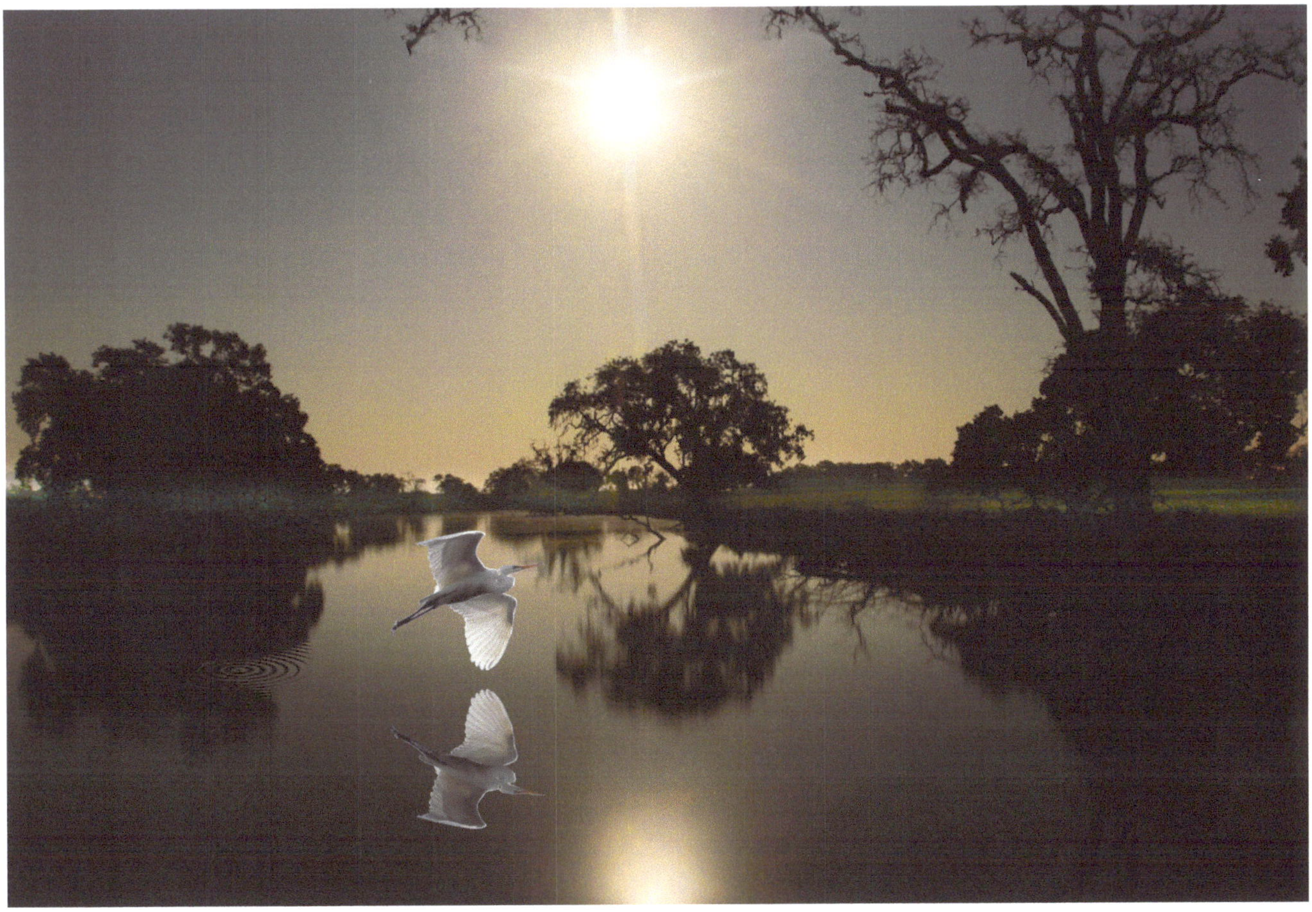

August 2006 235 Laguna Morning

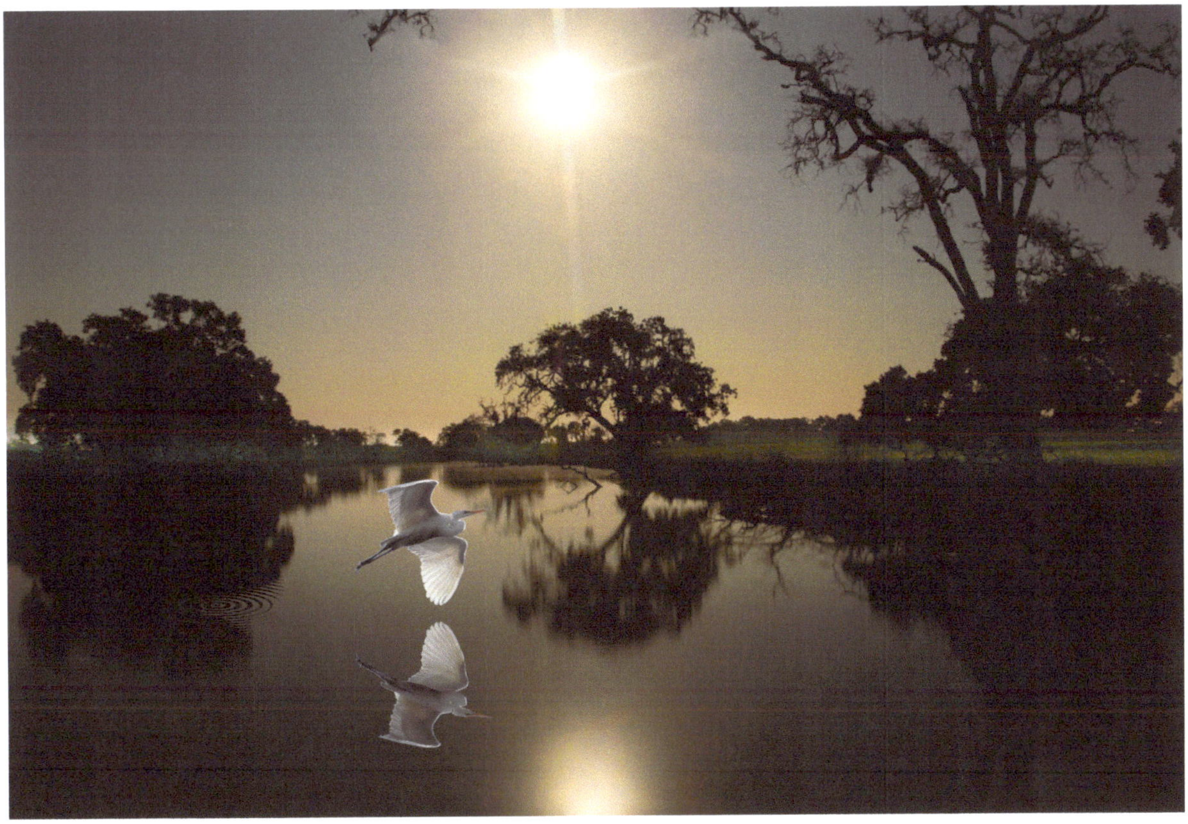

Image taken at midnight with a long exposure, turning it into morning

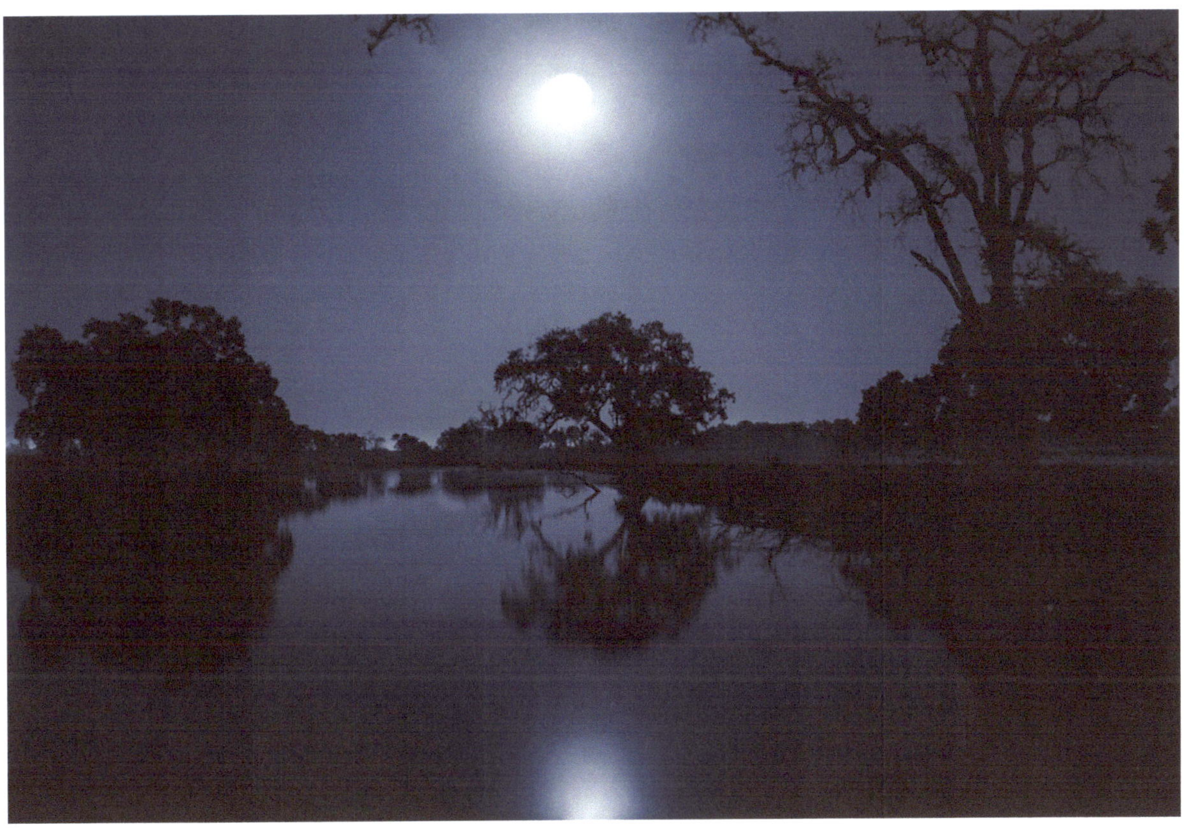

Image taken at midnight with a normal shorter exposure

After Sonoma County fires, retired firefighter offers his iconic image of Round Barn for free

DIANNE REBER HART Sonoma County Press Democrat

TOWNS CORRESPONDENT | November 13, 2017

Retired firefighter, Will Chubb, was leaving a holiday party near the Fountaingrove Round Barn a few years ago when he glanced toward the historic structure and was moved by the beauty of the moment.

It was sunset and the December sky was striking against the red of the iconic barn, a treasured Santa Rosa landmark built in 1899.

A longtime commercial photographer, Chubb, 73, grabbed his camera and walked out to a grassy knoll where he framed his shot, clicked the shutter and went on with his evening.

"It was getting dark and the moon was coming up," he said. "I saw that scene. It was the right time and the right place."

He had no idea the image would later bring comfort to hundreds of people — those who loved the barn and were saddened that it was among the prominent structures destroyed by the prior month's deadly firestorm.

Chubb thought that perhaps by sharing his image, he could bring a bit of relief to those in the county who had fond memories of the Round Barn.

He spent 30 years as a firefighter with the San Rafael Fire Department, retiring as an engineer/driver. He's continuously worked as a commercial photographer, with a camera always at the ready, and also volunteers as a photographer with the nonprofit Make-A-Wish Foundation, which grants wishes to children with life-threatening medical conditions.

He credits his firefighting career with developing his desire to help others.

Chubb has been moved by the gratitude and appreciation of those who've ordered his photo. One note in particular, from a woman who lost her home and collection of California art, also expresses his belief.

"Art heals," she wrote, saying that Chubb's photo of the Round Barn will be the first piece of artwork in her new collection.

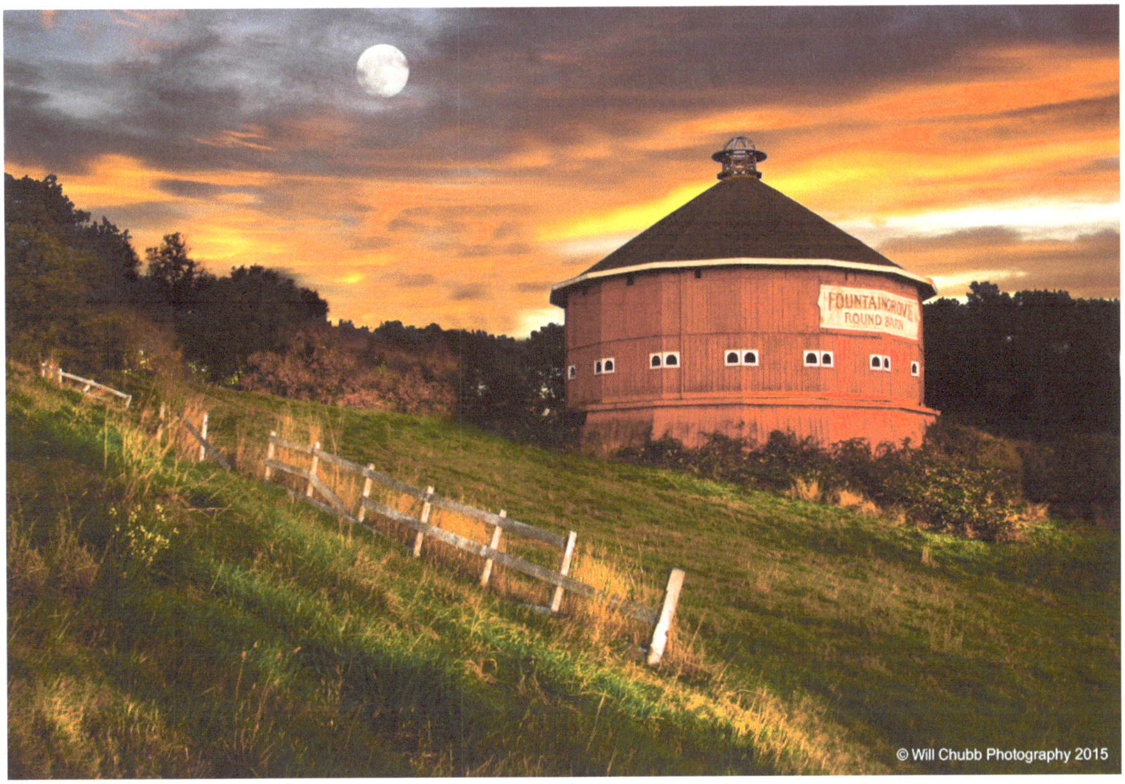

November 2014 317 Round Barn Santa Rosa, CA

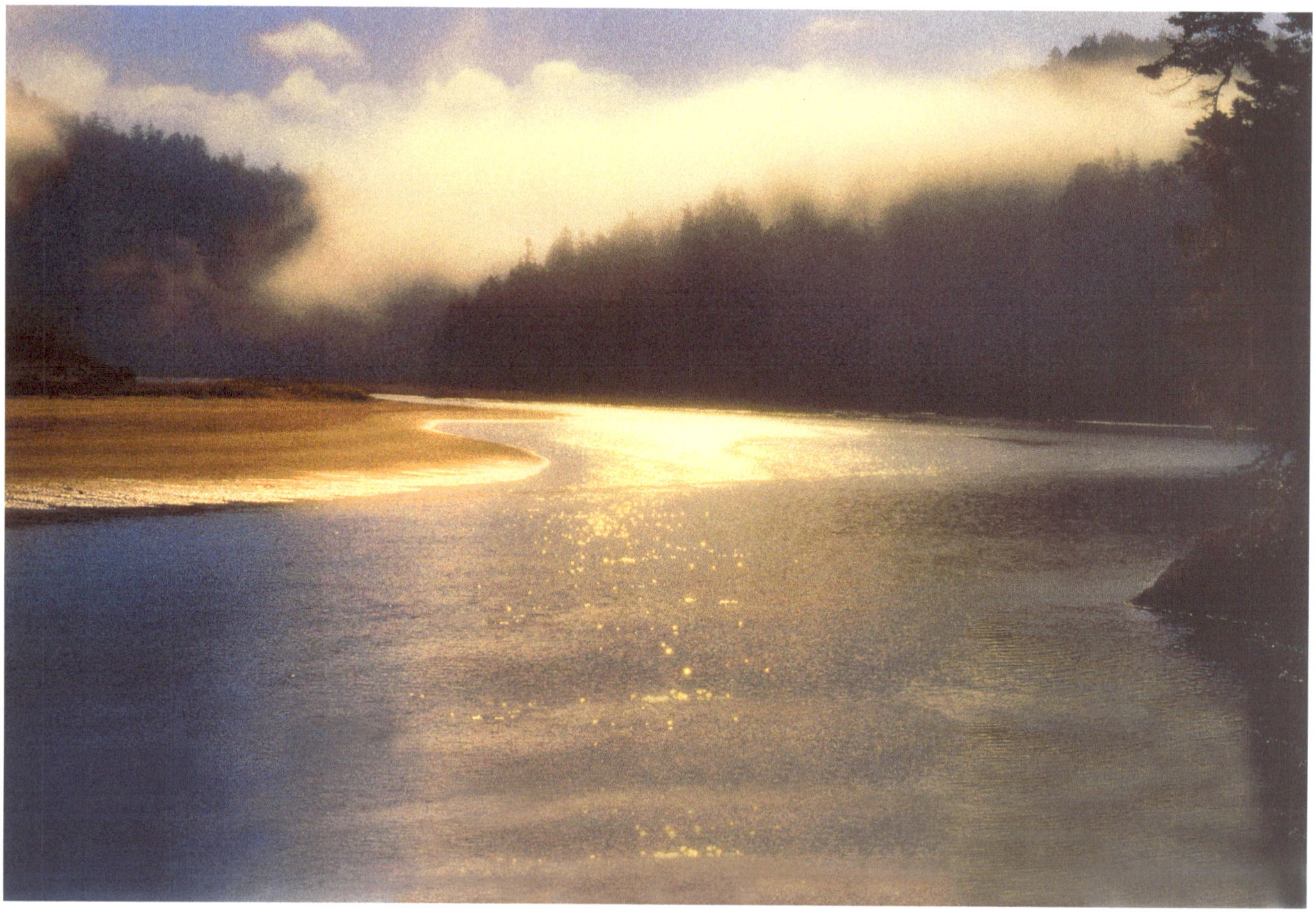

July 1995 145 Mystical River

The Quality of Light is Crucial to My Work

Like Charlie Potts said, “Light is everything.”

To me it’s as much Spiritual as it is the essence in photography. I often try to include the sun, the moon or a source of light that to me represents the Divine in my photographs.

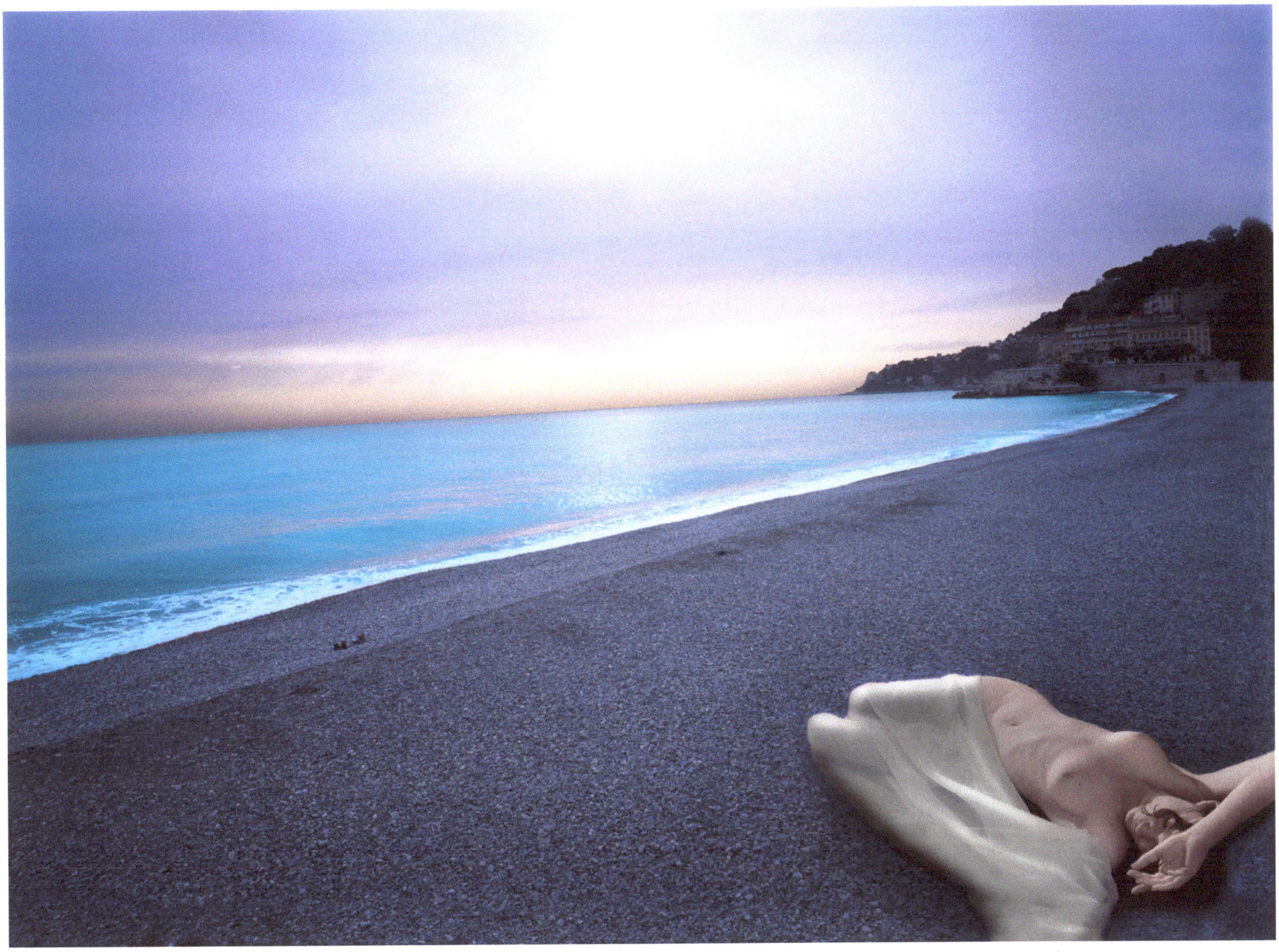

August 2005 161 The Beach at Nice, France

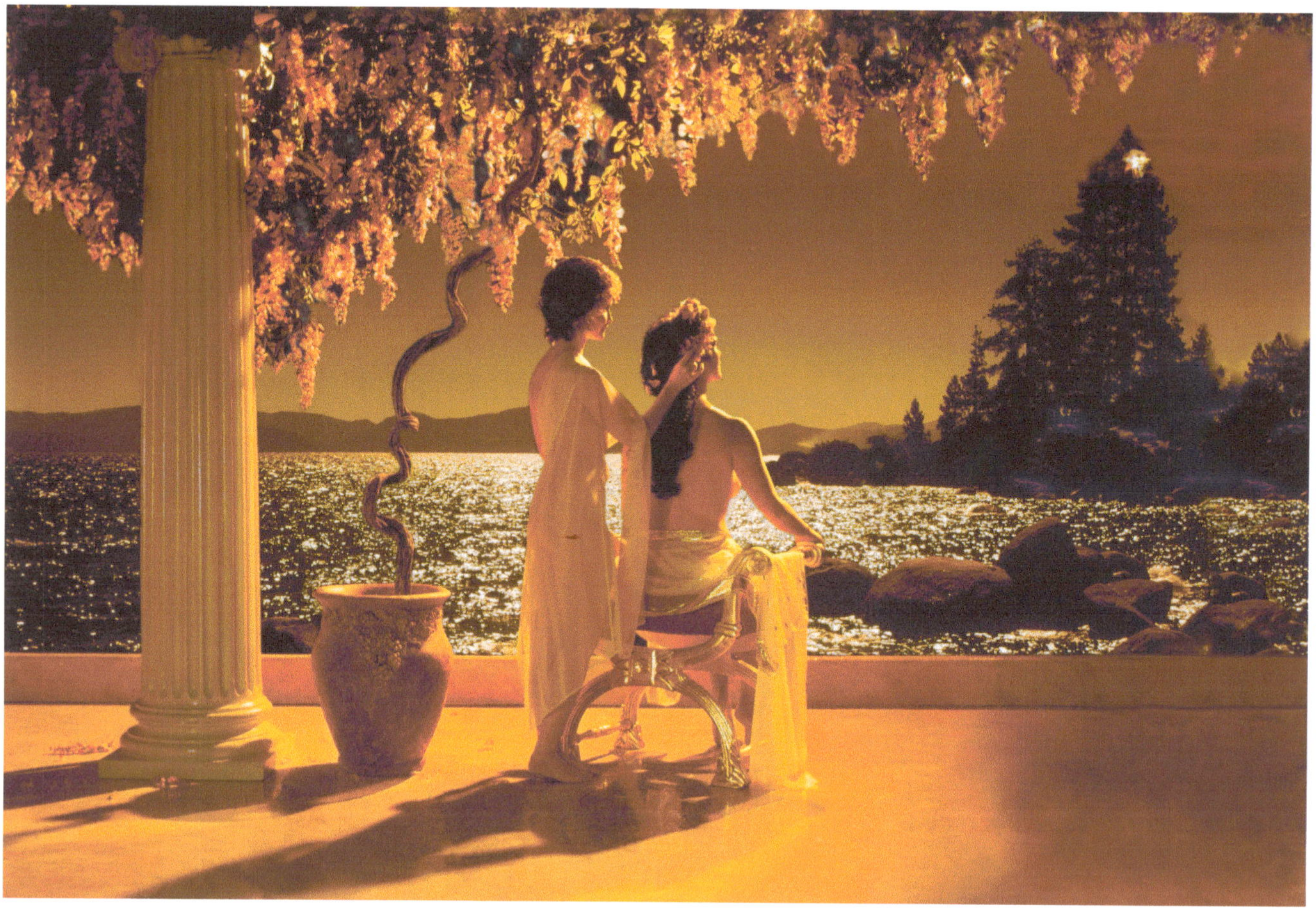

1999

172 Atlantis Sunrise

In 1999 I got this idea of shooting a photograph of a fanciful mystical era like Atlantis and I call this Atlantis Sunrise. I really needed to busy my mind with a distraction, because my wife, Linda, had died after 32 wonderful years of marriage.

I used Maxfield Parrish as a guide. I love his work and especially his warm luminous saturated color palette. I really jumped into building this set with both feet. I kind of went crazy and spent too much money, the pillar alone was $1,000. I was fortunate to be able to build the set in a warehouse that one of my clients wasn't going to move into for some time. I had a whole month to build the set and make my fantasy come true.

The floor looks like marble but it's linoleum. The flowers were purchased at the San Francisco Flower Mart and are silk wisteria. I found the stool at an antique store. The model's clothes were made to look Grecian or something that would look like it was from Atlantis. It was all just a fantasy I was inventing, distinct from the reality in which I was currently living.

After the set was completed, I hung black fabric where I would bring in the image of Lake Tahoe I had in my files.

I filtered the camera with a warming filter and used strobes to look like the setting sun.

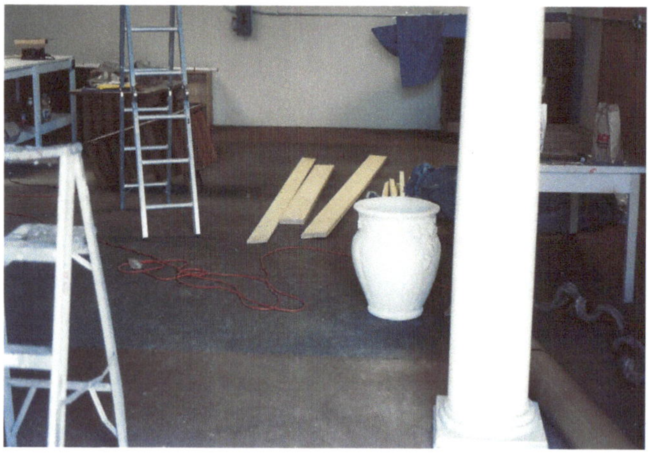

Building the set 1

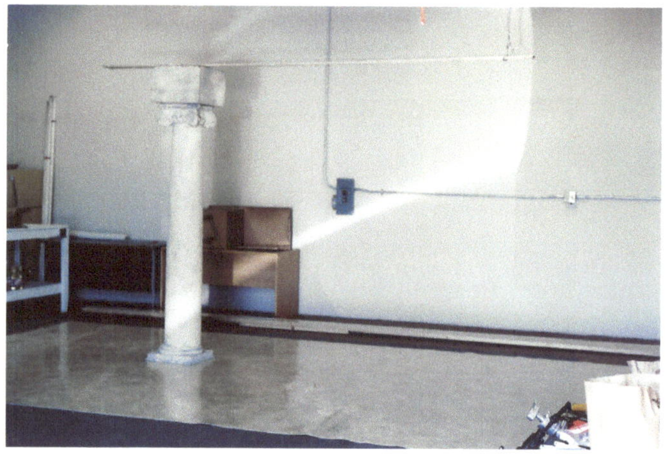

Building the set 2

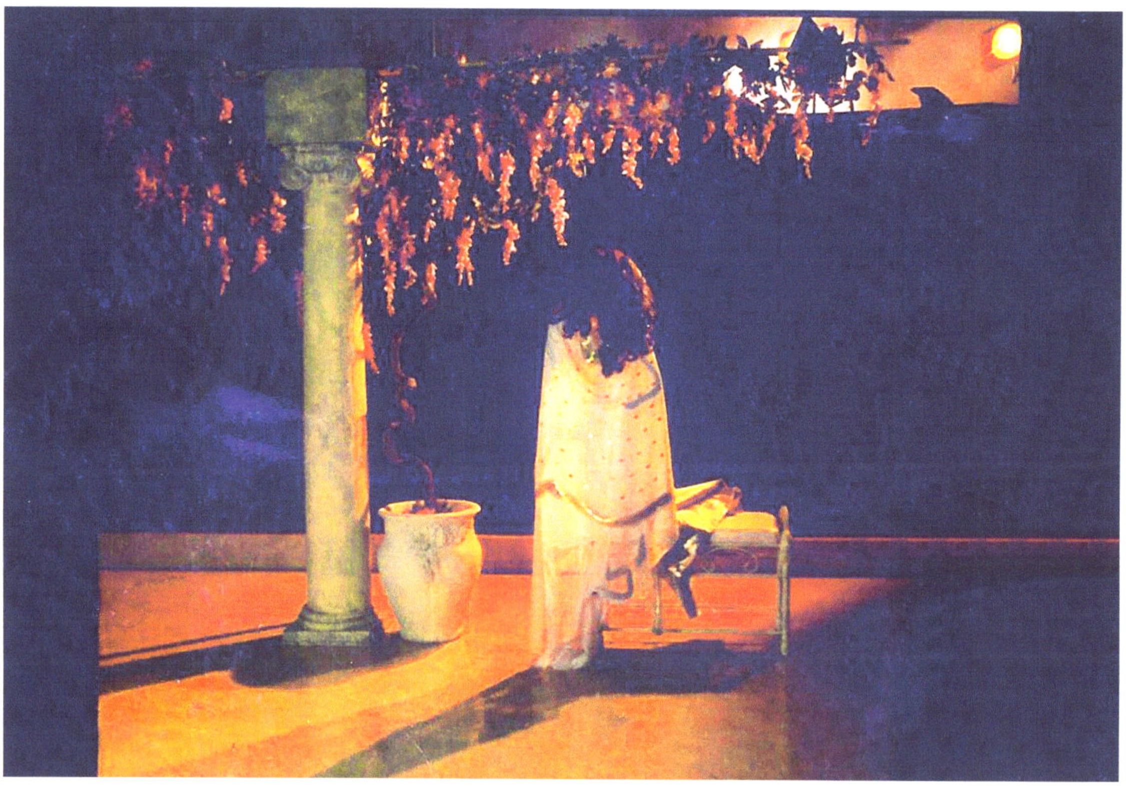

Building the set 3

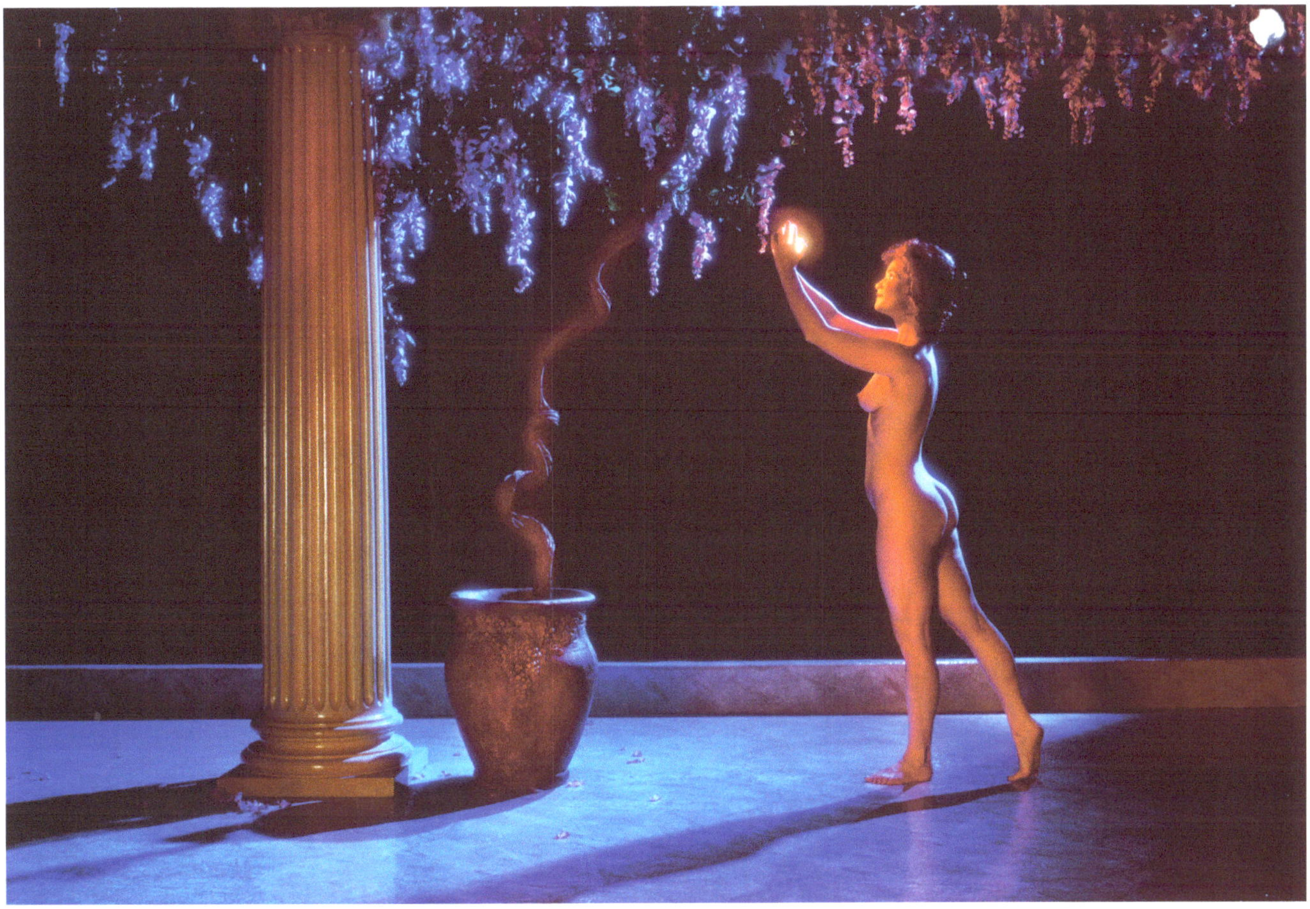

September 2005 **173 Illumination**

Harvest Sunrise

This photo was printed as a poster for Seghesio Winery to celebrate their 100-year-old zinfandel vines. As it turns out, they were going to dig up a very small section of the vineyard so I used this opportunity to dig up one of the vines myself. In honor of its age I said a prayer during the process. I brought the vine into the studio, along with some top soil and a few of the fallen leaves. It was wintertime so it was just a bare vine. By bringing the vine into the studio, I had full control of the lighting.

After I completed the photo for my client, I moved the set to a corner of the studio, out of the way. I knew I would eventually use it to do my own version. For months I walked by the setup thinking about what to do. I decided to do an image in the style of the painter, Maxfield Parish. By this time many months had gone by and it was summer. This was to my advantage because I had the opportunity to go to a vineyard, cut some clumps of grapes and leaves and hang them on the bare vine.

To illuminate the vine, I used a technique called "Light Painting". To do this the studio has to be completely dark, the camera is mounted on a tripod, and the lens is left open. I then use a special lighting tool with a fiber optic hose to paint the vine with light. The end result is an effect that looks more like a painting than a photograph. Maxfield Parish is known for his warm tone colors. So, I used warm colored gels to make the setting look like the early morning sunrise, thus the name "Harvest Sunrise."

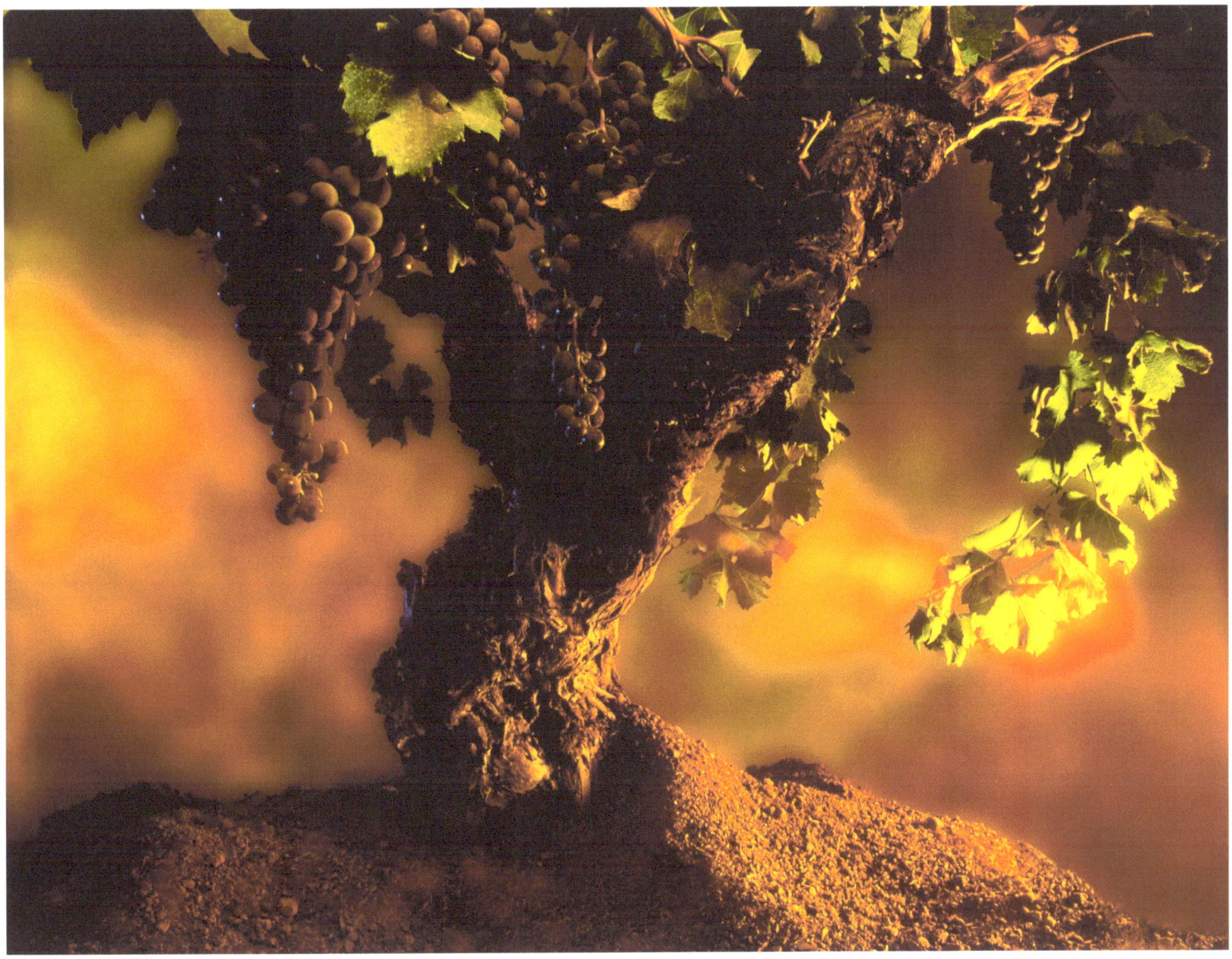

September 2005 112 Harvest Sunrise

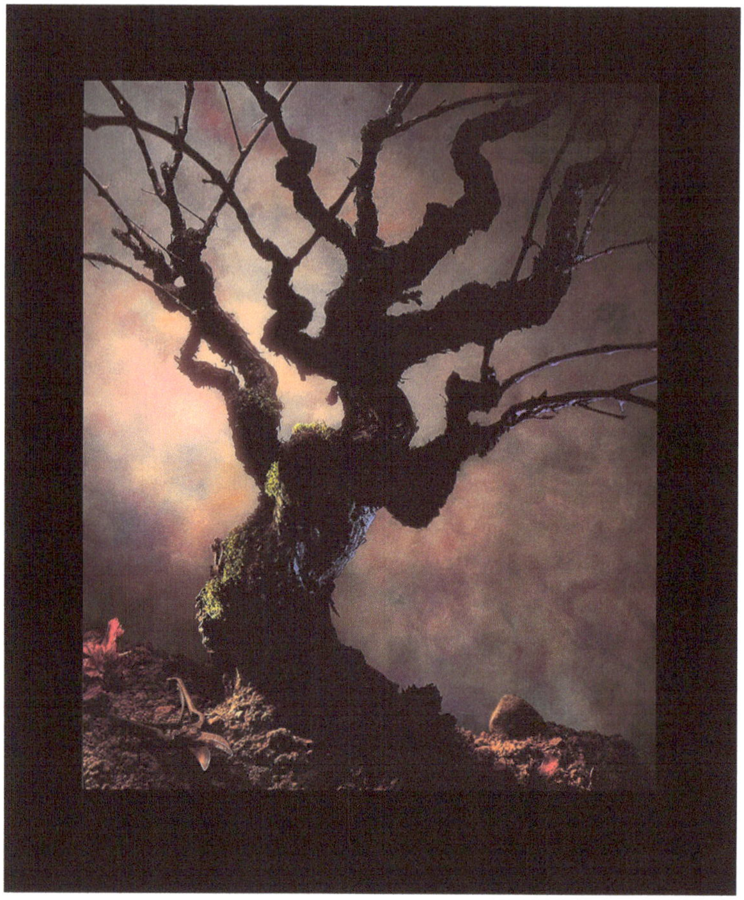

Seghesio Winery Poster – the same vine without leaves and grapes

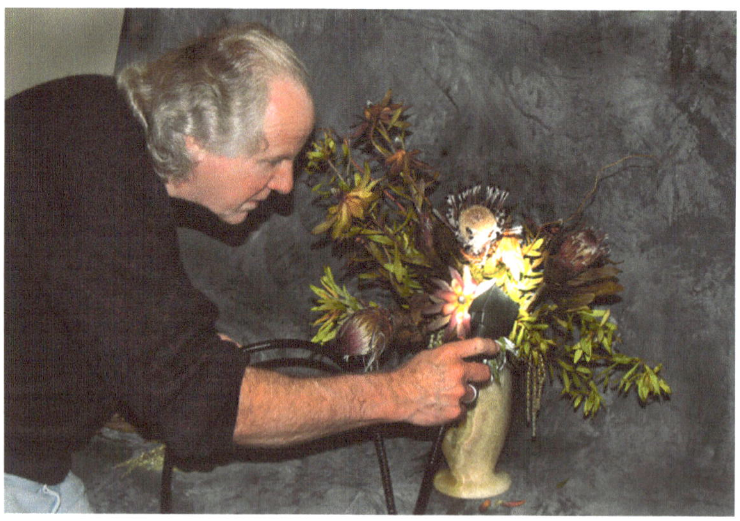

"Lightpainting" another subject

The small photo here (lighting a different subject) shows how I paint with the light. This would normally be done in total darkness if I was actually taking the photograph. The exposure can take anywhere from a few minutes to as long as thirty minutes. It takes a lot of trial and error until you get the feel for moving the light over the subject to bring out the effect you want.

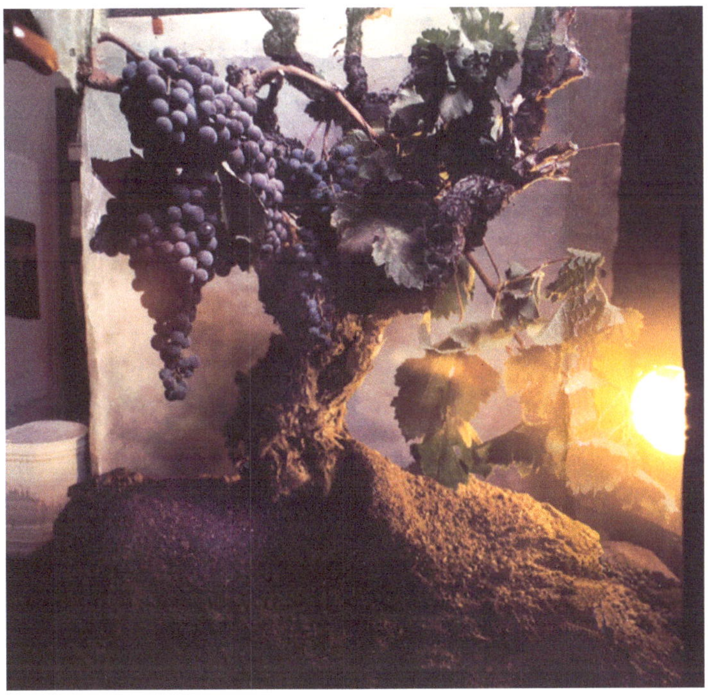

September 2005 The Set of Harvest Sunrise in the Studio

My favorite uncle was a lepidopterist or butterfly collector. When I was nine years old, Uncle Bud gave me this particular Swallowtail butterfly. Not long after this, he passed away, and the butterfly became even more precious to me. I kept it preserved in a cigar box for 51 years! I knew I would someday come up with a way of capturing it with the camera to do it justice. I enjoy photographing things in unique ways. The image had to be unusual. One day the idea hit me. I decided to do the photograph from a different perspective, from underneath the leaf, primarily showing the butterfly's shadow, with only a little of its wings showing. I got permission from a grape grower in Sebastopol to use his vineyard. I needed to use photo light stands and clamps to hold the leaves and grapes in just the right position to get the sun shining from behind. I wanted the grapes to have the right luminosity. It took about an hour to set up the shot, and about 30 minutes to capture it with my digital camera. (Digital is so great to use because you can see exactly what you've got.) Just as I got the last and final shot a gust of wind came up and the fragile butterfly blew apart, the pieces scattered everywhere. The wind could have just as easily come up five minutes earlier. Maybe Uncle Bud was looking over my shoulder, because at least now his Swallowtail butterfly will be preserved forever in this photo.

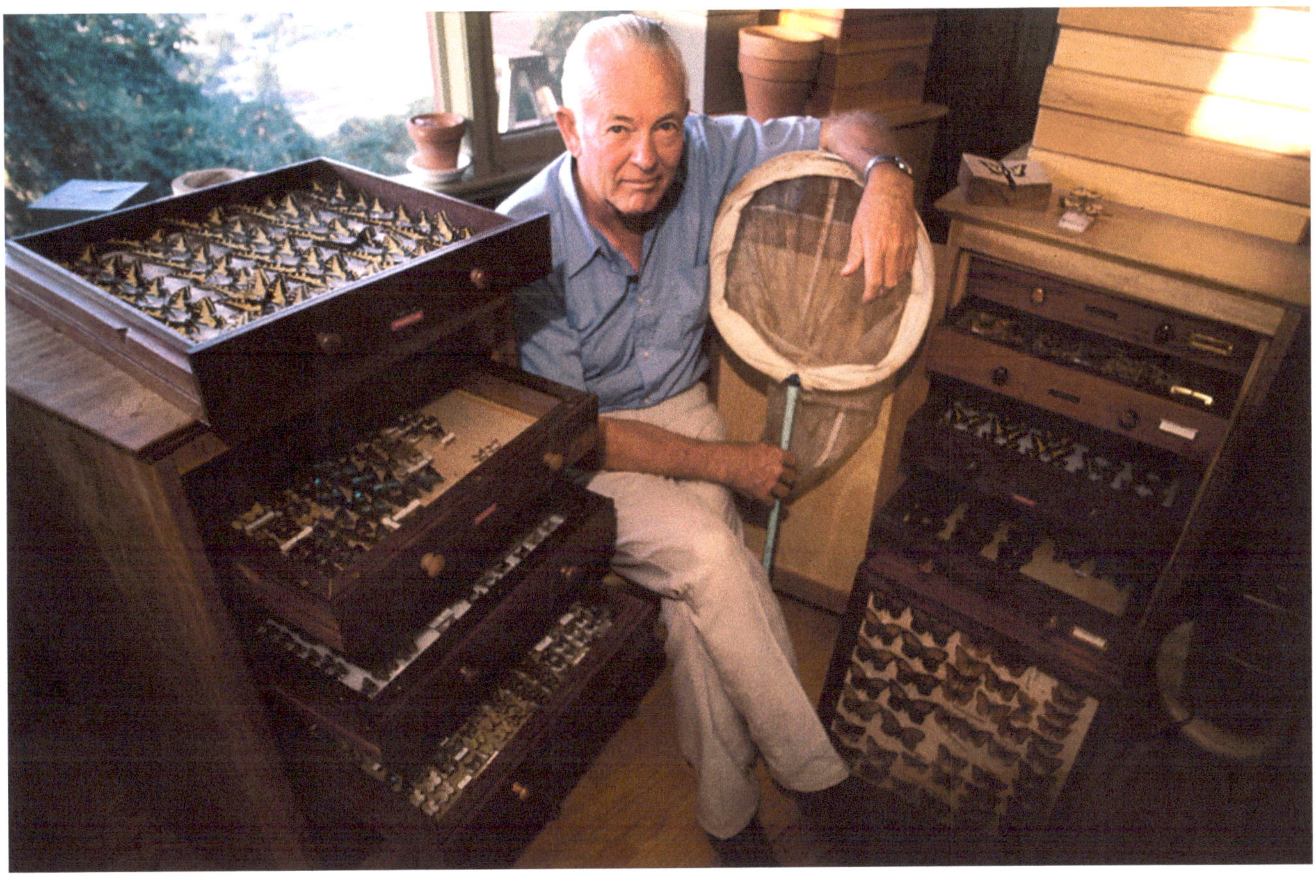

July 1968 My Uncle Bud

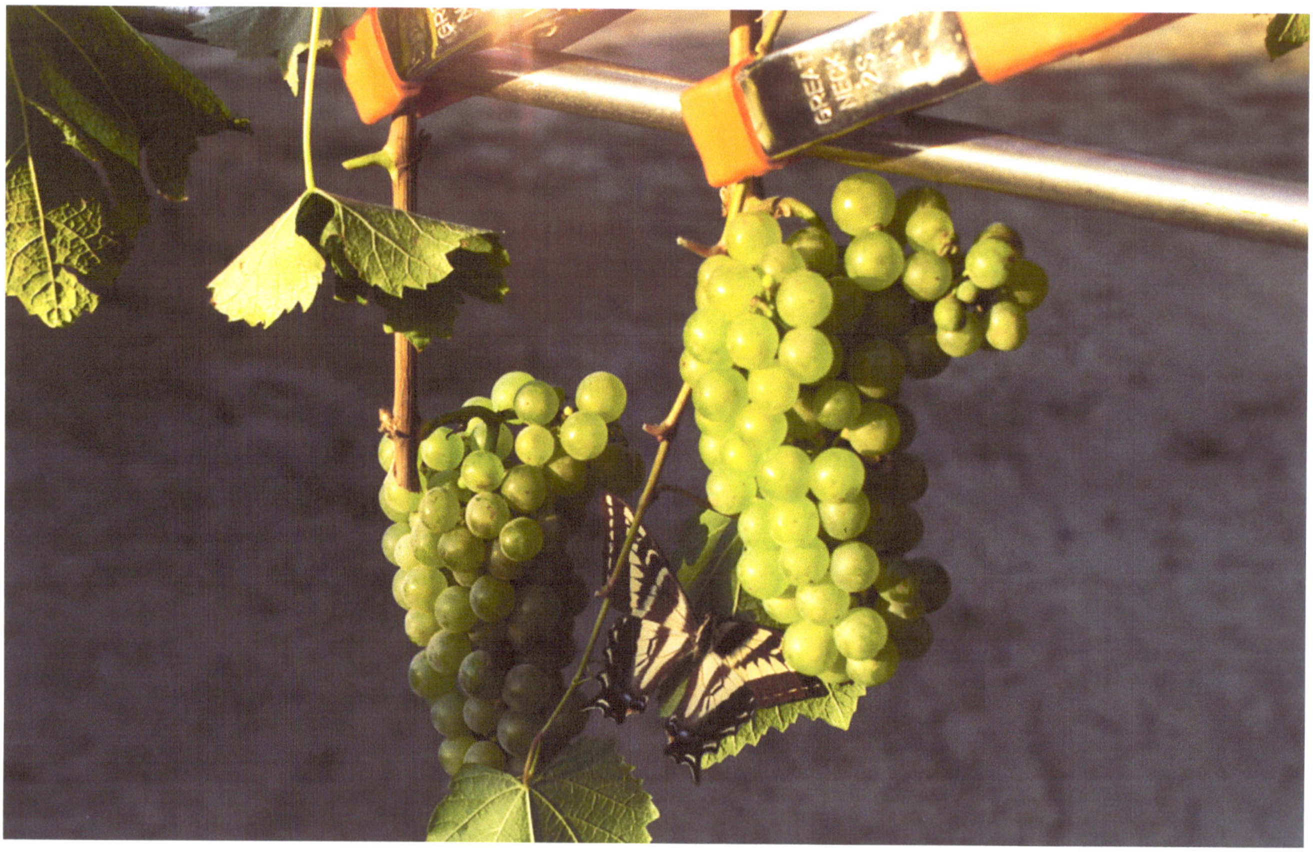

The Setup in the Vineyard

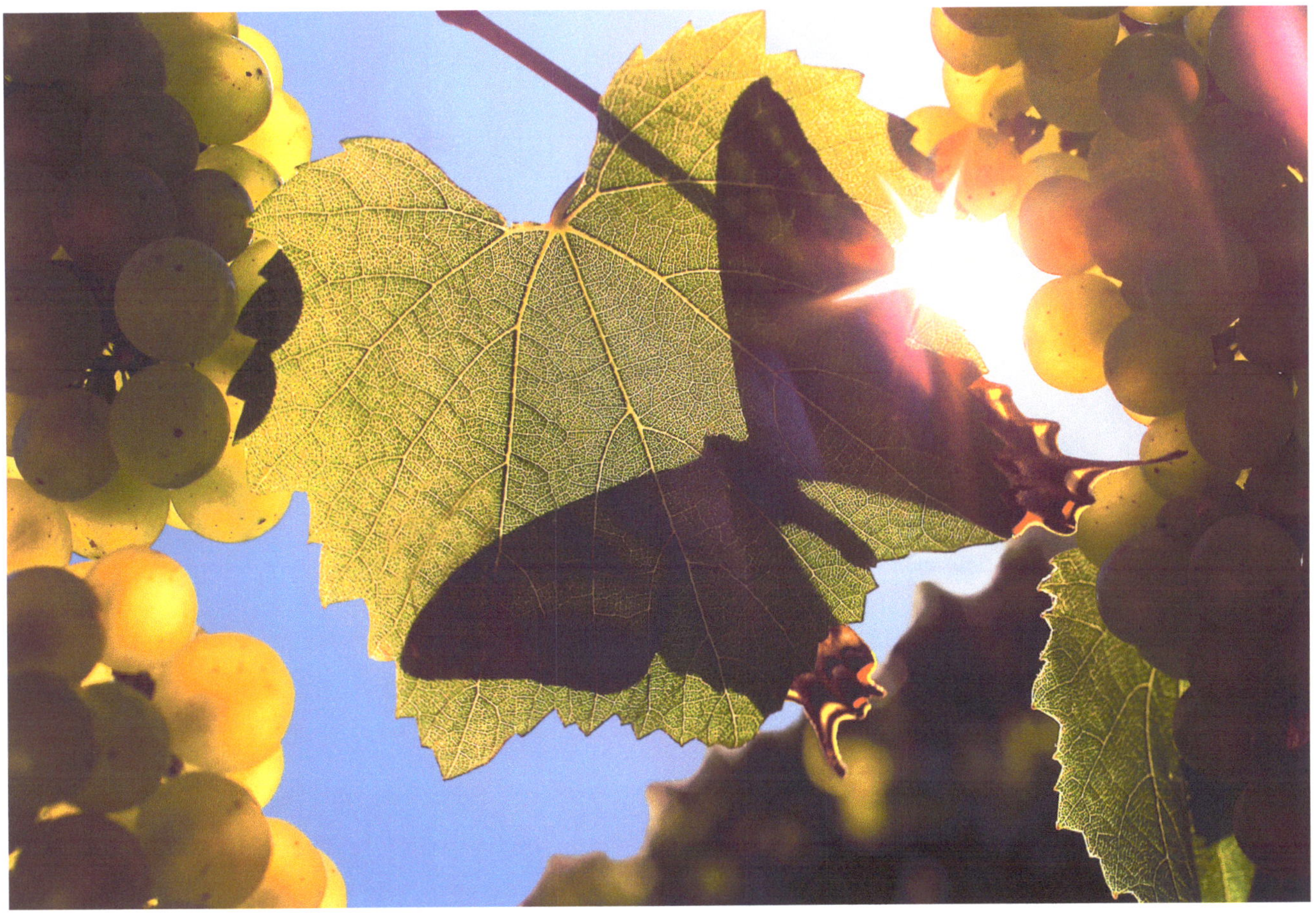

August 2003 140 Butterfly in the Vineyard

Kenwood Train Depot

We raised our two boys in Kenwood and I've always been fascinated by the old train depot there. Trains haven't been in Kenwood for decades. Originally the train carried cobblestones from the Kenwood quarries to be used for the cobblestone streets in San Francisco.

Some "old timers" thought the train was somewhere in the Bay Area. After making inquiries, rumors started to fly about my new photo project--you know, small towns. I was approached by the managers of the Fourth of July planning committee to come up with a new image to promote the festivities. I decided that if I could locate the train, I'd create an image using the actual train in front of the depot. After some research, I found the train across the Bay in Richmond. With permission I was able to use a smoke generating machine under the train to simulate steam. Then I used the same technique in front of the depot.

Combining the two images in photoshop produced the final image. This was the early days of photoshop in about 1984. To add a final touch I changed the black & white image to sepia tone for that old time feel of the era.

The image was used on Tee shirts and for publicity purposes on the Fourth of July Pillow Fights in Kenwood. Tommy Smothers and Robin Williams would announce the Pillow Fights and keep everyone laughing!

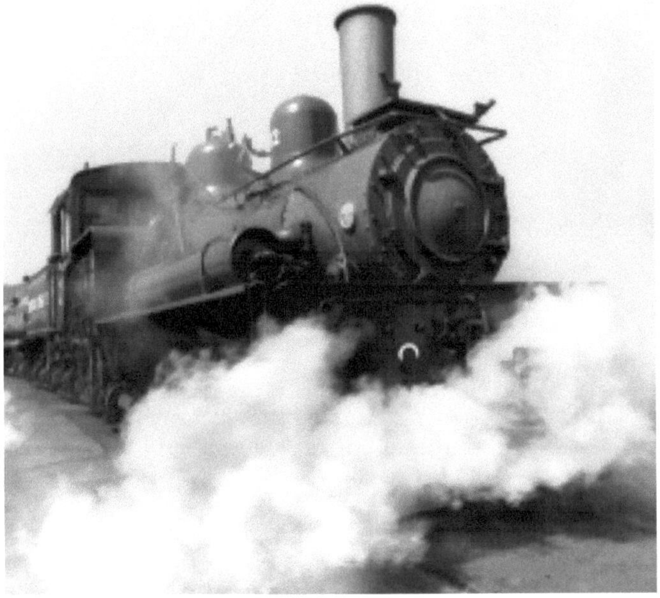

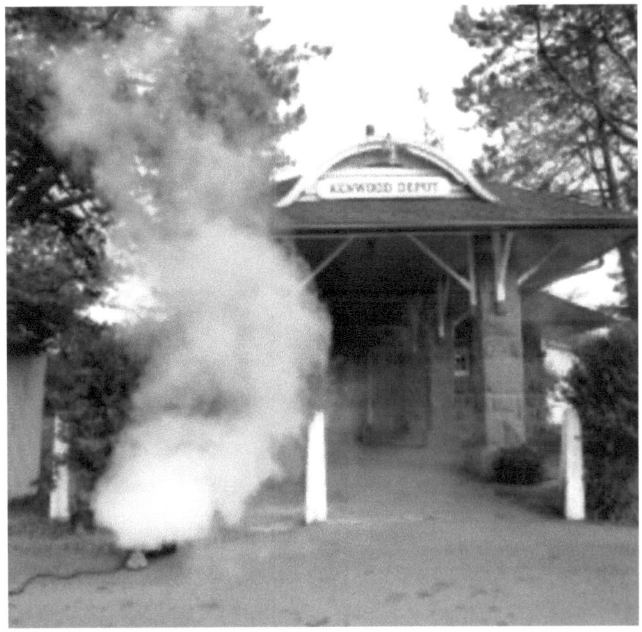

Smoke generators under the train and in front of the Kenwood Depot

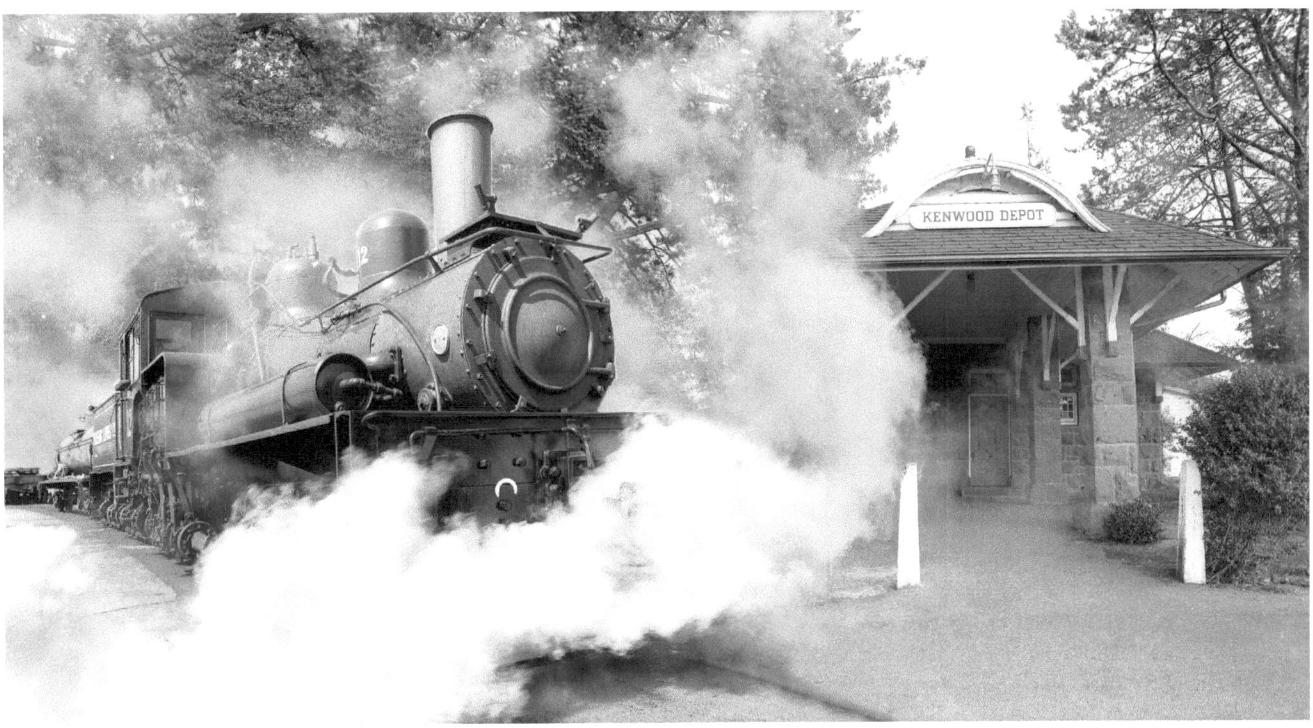

June 1979 368 Train in Front of Kenwood Depot

In the Spotlight

Now that I had my dream studio, Linda decided to open her own business within the studio. She called it "In the Spotlight." Her advertising stated, "There is star quality in all of us, let yours shine today! Let's put you in the spotlight!" We would pamper our clients with champagne, Godiva chocolates, and romantic music, and Linda would do magical makeup, transforming the ladies into movie stars. They loved it!!

It was wonderful working together, each doing what we loved to do best. We were magical, producing beautiful images for our clients and ourselves. It was a wonderful time.

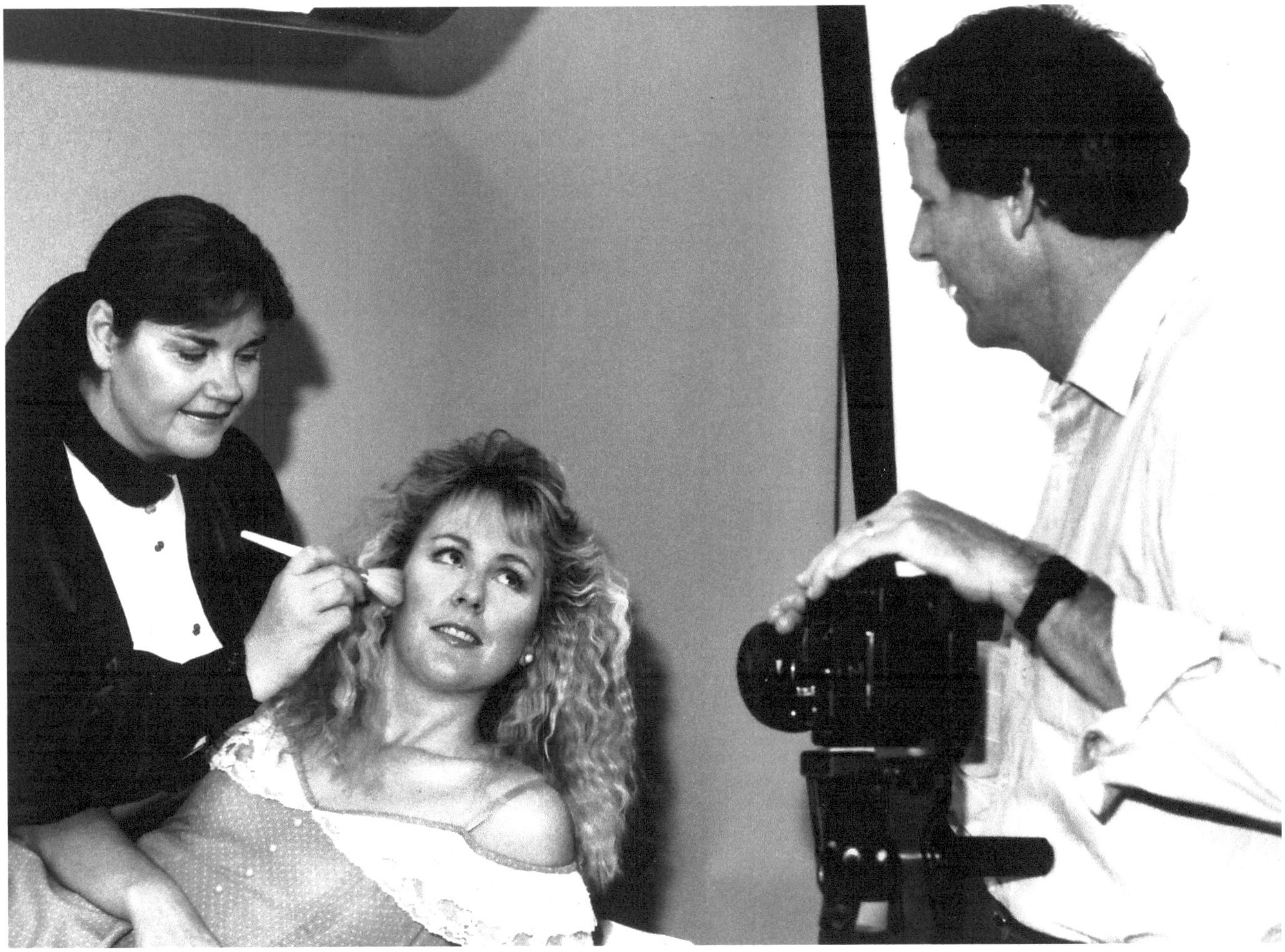

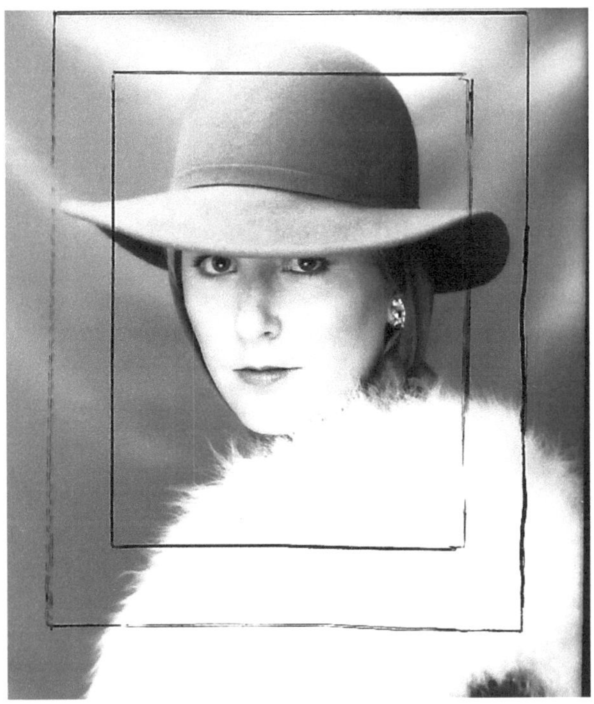

Mystery Girl

I owe this image to my wife, Linda, who was my makeup artist and stylist. The model actually had long blond hair and Linda put one of our black short haired wigs on her and did the appropriate makeup to look like the "pulp fiction" novels from the 1950s.

Linda and I would discuss the look we wanted before the shoot.

Meanwhile, I set up the props and lighting. I didn't have a gobo setup so I had to use actual venetian blinds in front of the strobe. Now, 30 years later I have a gobo setup with all sorts of patterns to project like venetian blinds or ferns or about anything you can think of. They are used primarily for the motion picture industry.

Usually, in the studio we would have the appropriate music playing, not only for us but for the model to get in the mood.

During this shoot we played music from the 1950s movies to get everyone on the same page.

I call this image "Mystery Girl" because you don't know what's on her mind, except there is definitely an air of mystery on her face.

The original photo didn't have the letter, rose and glass of wine, I put those in digitally 30 years later! I must be crazy but I'm really into authenticity and I shopped in antique stores until I found a letter that was dated about 1953!

You can't tell that in the photo, but I wanted it to be perfect. The one thing that stands out is that it is written by hand which gives you an idea of the date. Who nowadays writes a letter and puts it in the mail!

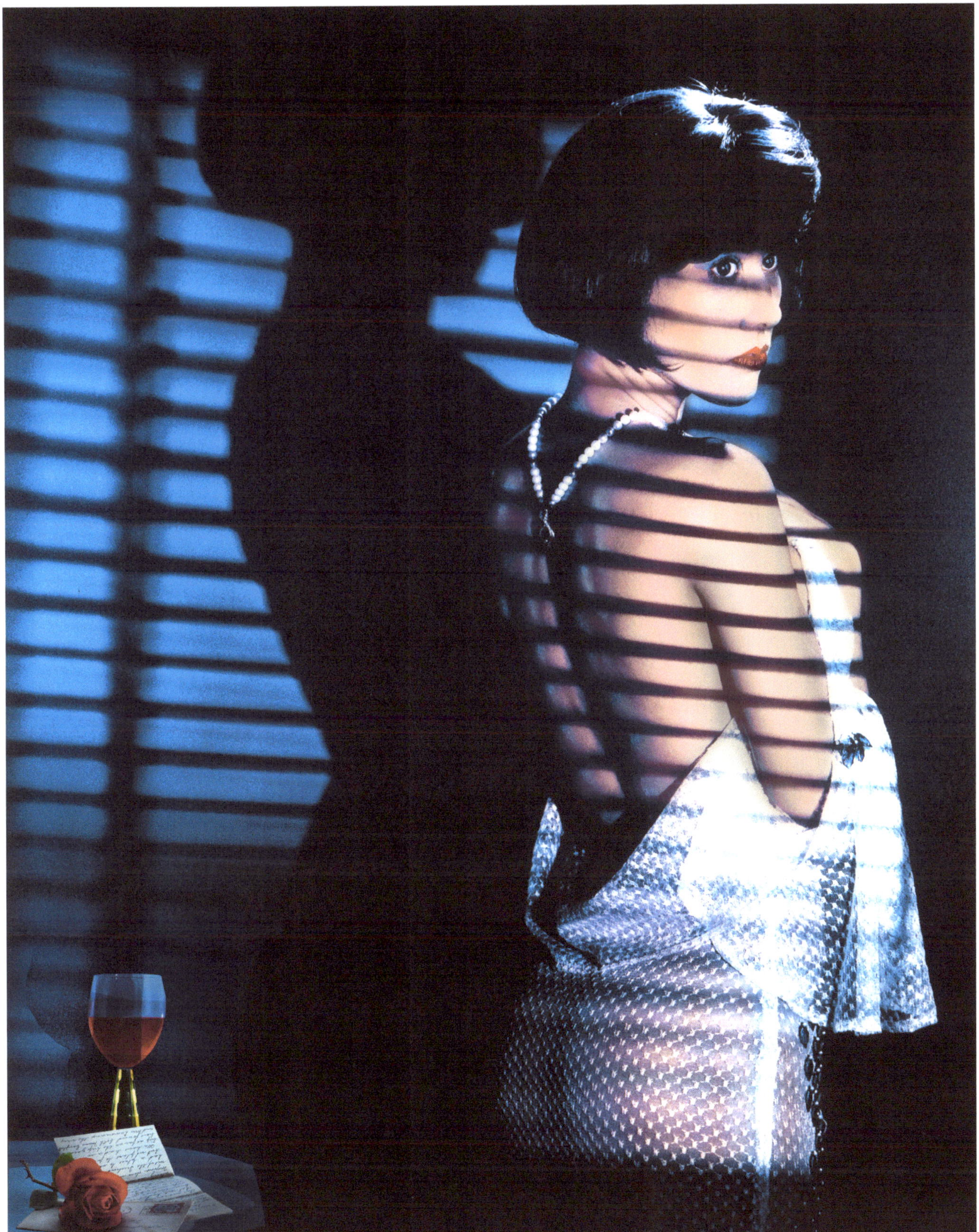

1988

124 Mystery Girl

Thirty's Girl

Produced in my Santa Rosa dream studio. I had finally acquired a nice big studio where I had plenty of room, I could shoot anything. I could even drive a car in through the roll up door.

This was in the 1980s.

The 30's girl was produced in 1988. Once again Linda, my wife and excellent makeup artist and stylist, did her part in making this a wonderful piece of art. I recall this was not a model. She showed up with frizzy long hair.

I looked at Linda and she saw my shock. Linda responded, "No worries; just relax and go set up your lighting."

I kept coming back to see how she was doing with the makeup. She would say, "Stop obsessing; it's going to be perfect." At one point the model went into the bathroom, saw herself in the mirror and let out a screech! Linda repeated, "Stop worrying; it will be perfect."

I had the model come onto the set. Linda had done her makeup like a Japanese actress. It was essentially all white except for the eyes. She said take your test shots and you'll see. I was using strobes and they pretty much wash out the facial skin. Her makeup was perfect, it looked porcelain, which was the look I was hoping for!

This was, again, back in the film days. The Polaroids were perfect.

Linda knew what she was doing, I just had to stop worrying because it was perfect. Now it was up to me to get the shot I was after. I did a lot of shooting. Both the model and Linda kept saying, "You've got it, we're hungry. Let's have lunch."

I kept saying, "I'm almost there, just a couple more shots.

Finally, I got the shot I was after with the model's eye just barely showing under the brim of her hat. "Bingo," I yelled out, "I've got it, now let's have lunch!"

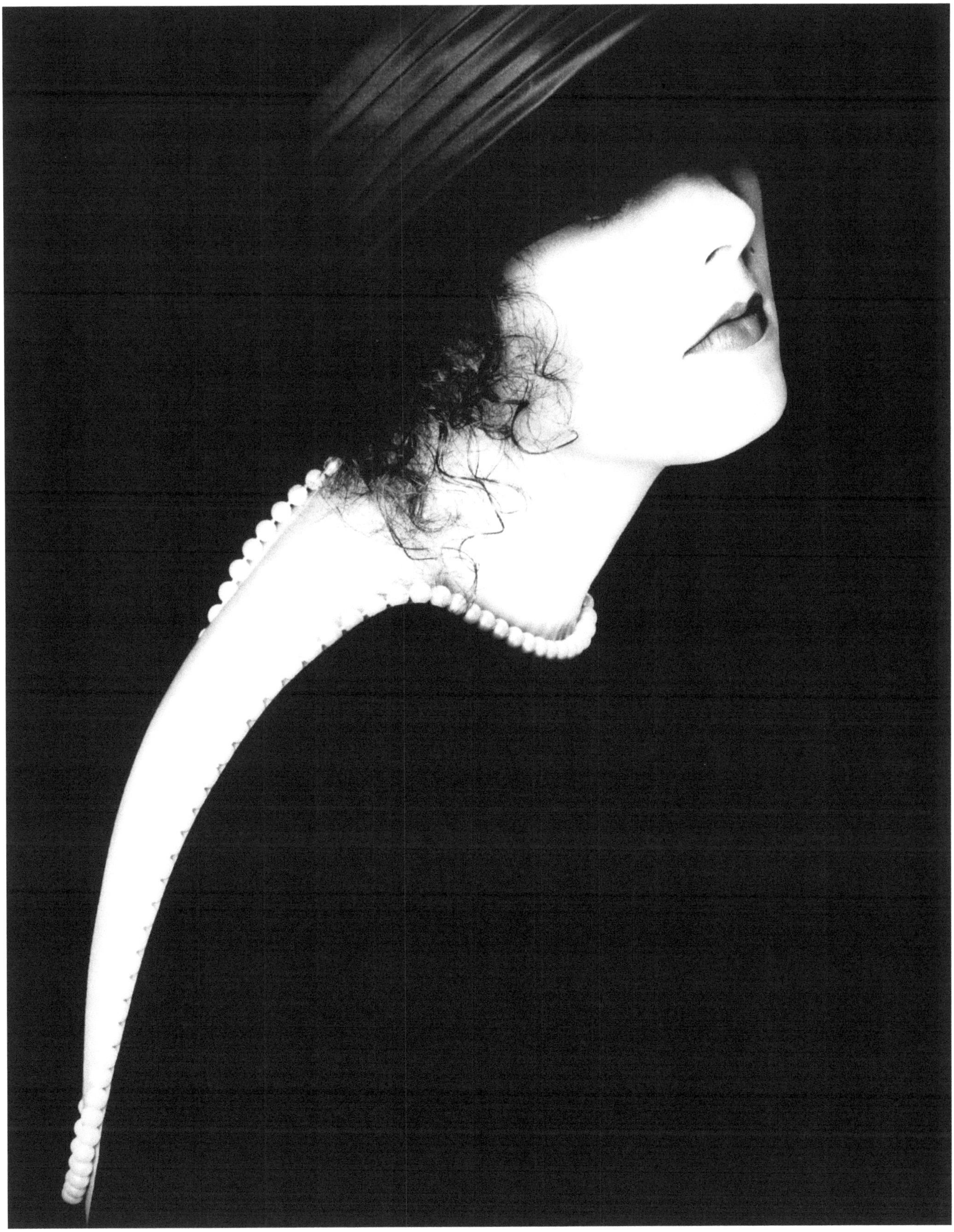

1988 125 Thirty's Girl

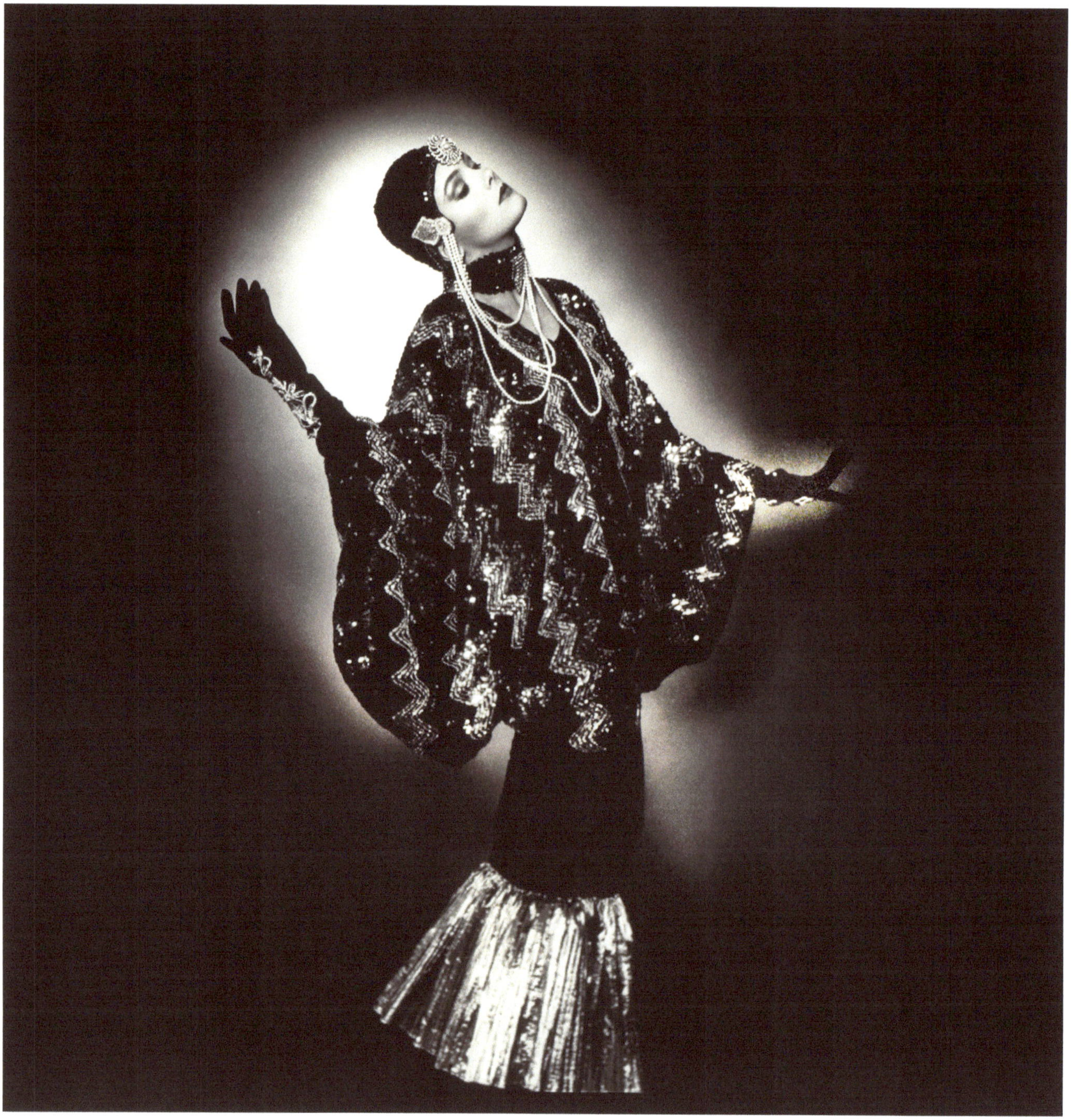

1987 278 Art Deco Lady

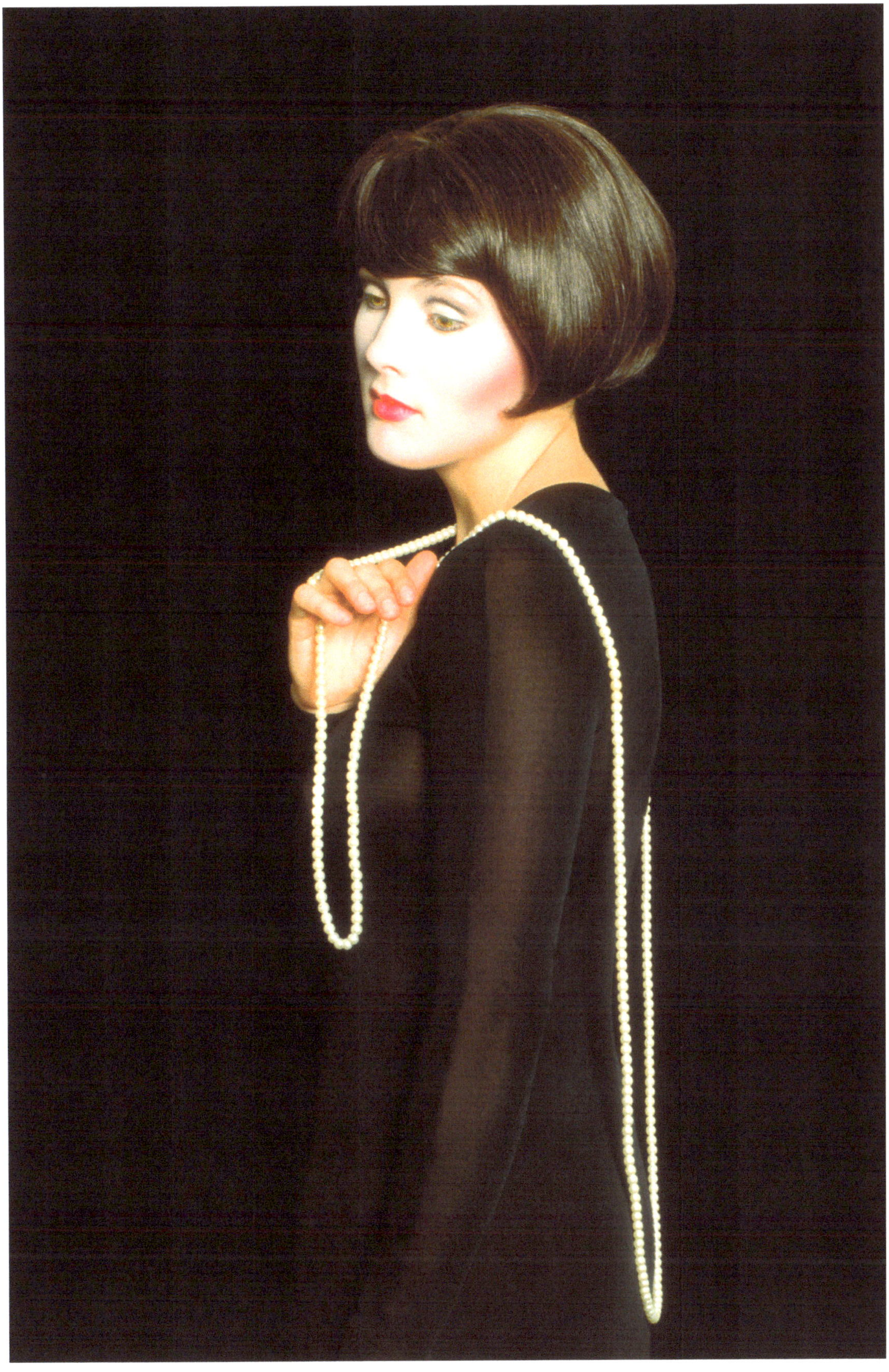

1988 246 Woman with Pearls

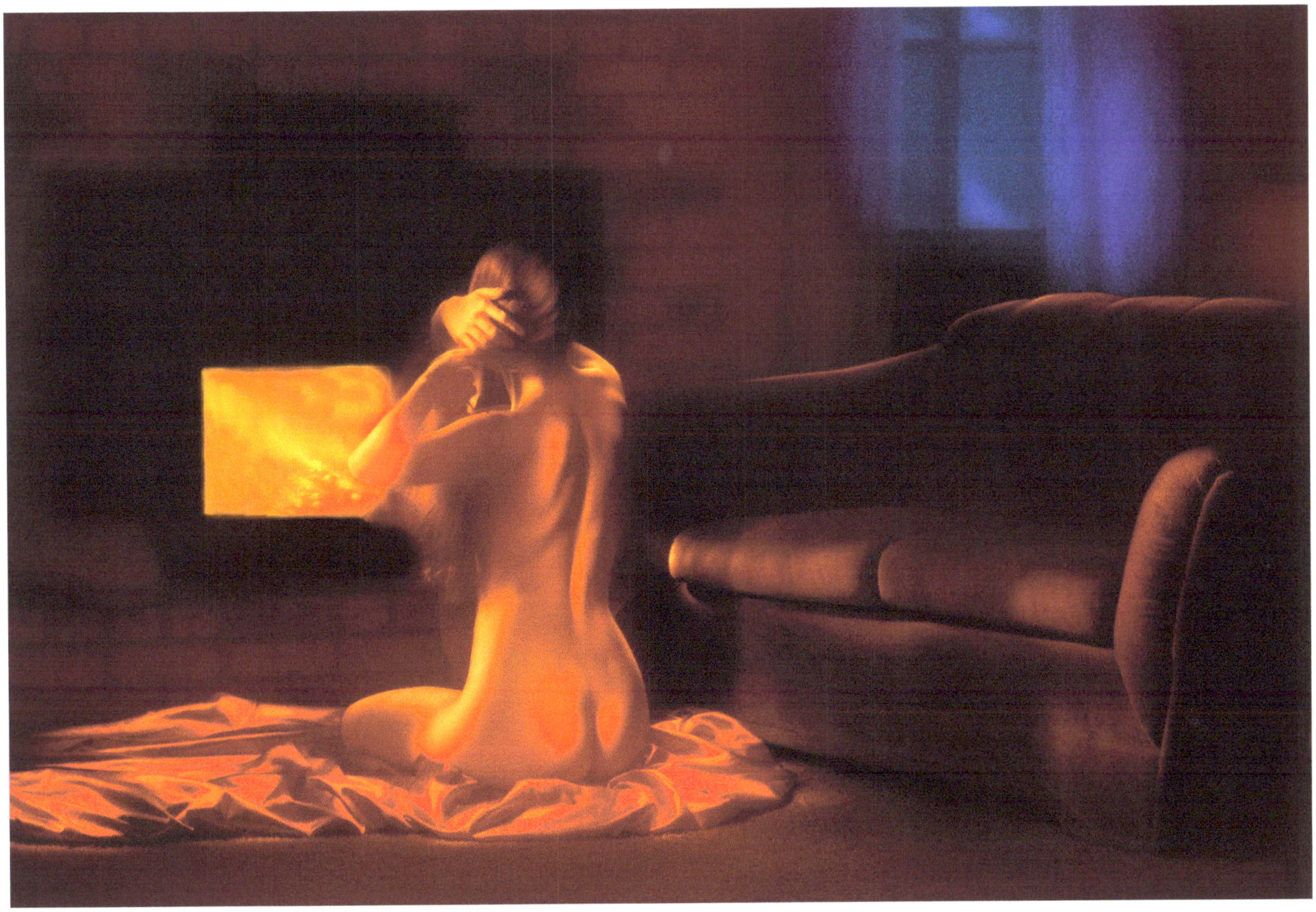

December 1997 **116 Warmth by the Fireside**

This was done by using my Aaron Jones Hosemaster light painting system. Basically, I burned one piece of newspaper in the wood burning stove which only lasted fifteen seconds or so, but that's all I needed. I then started light painting the model, after which she was free to get up and move out of the set. I spent the rest of the time light painting the rest of the set, in the dark, of course. There wasn't a window to the right of the fireplace, but I felt it needed something to infer the cold outside. I used snow in an aerosol can to spray on the window. The window itself was a prop I had, along with the curtains. I used blue jells over the light to further emphasize the cold.

A Pinhole Camera

This homemade pinhole camera was made out of a cigar box. (see photo). A 1" hole is made in the end of the box, and a thin piece of metal (aluminum foil) taped inside. A pin or needle is used to make a small hole in the metal. Next take the box into a dark room and load a piece of film inside the box, taping the film to the opposite end of the box. Then using black tape, tape the lid shut. Be sure to place a piece of tape over the pin hole. Now you're ready to take a picture. Place the cigar box on a flat rock or secure it to a tripod. Aim the box at your subject and peel off the tape from the pin hole. The exposure varies, but try 20 seconds. Then place the tape back over the hole. Now develop your film...Good luck!!

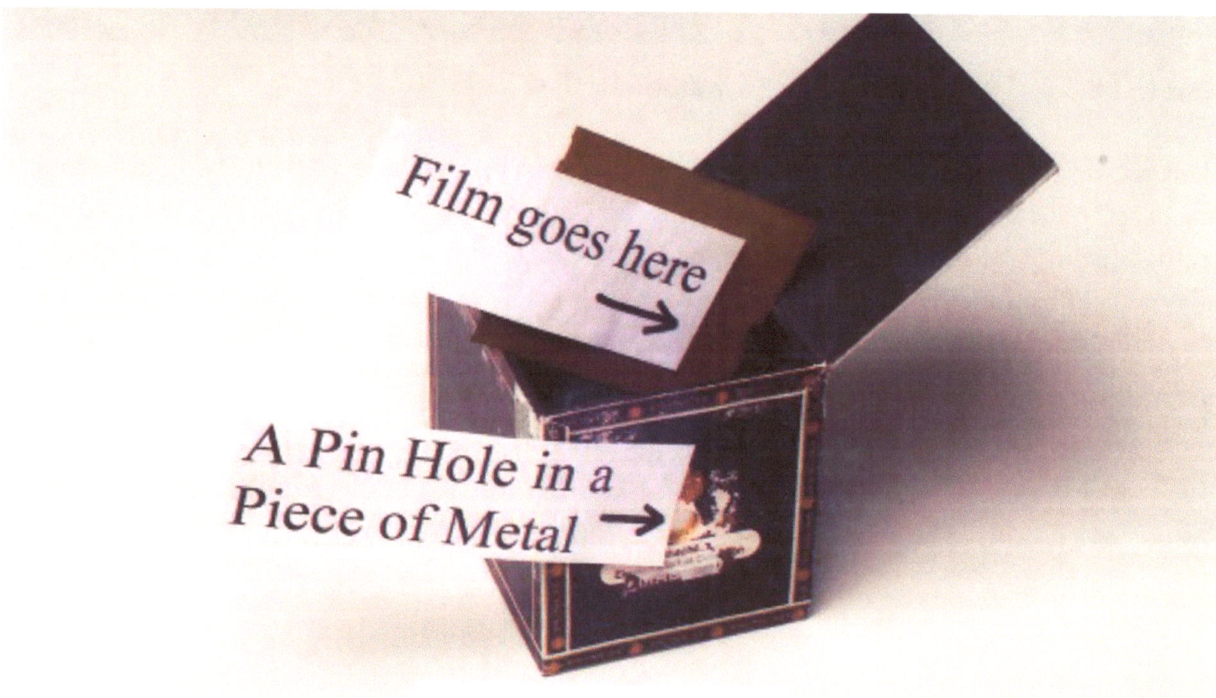

An Ordinary
Cigar Box

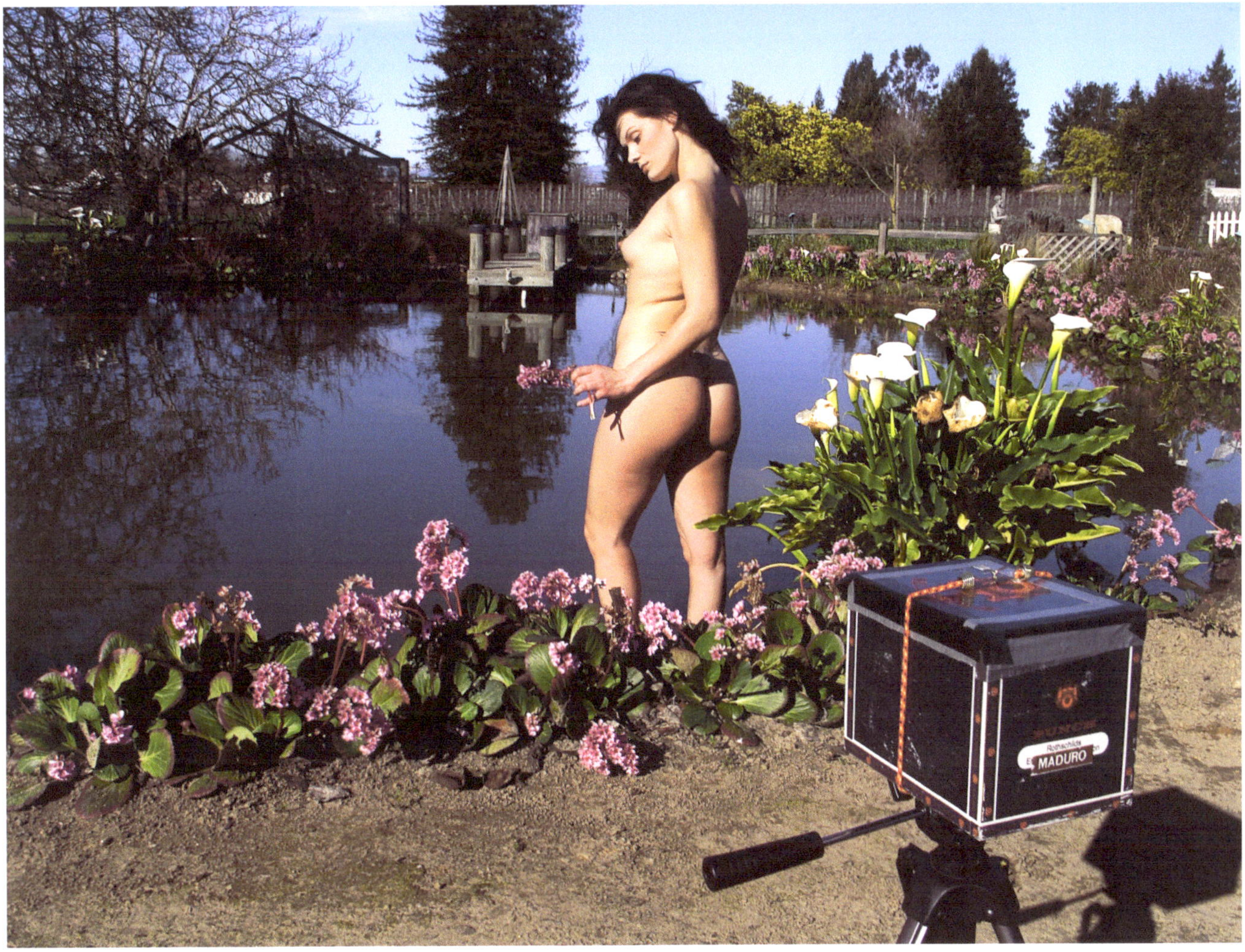
Rothschilds
MADURO

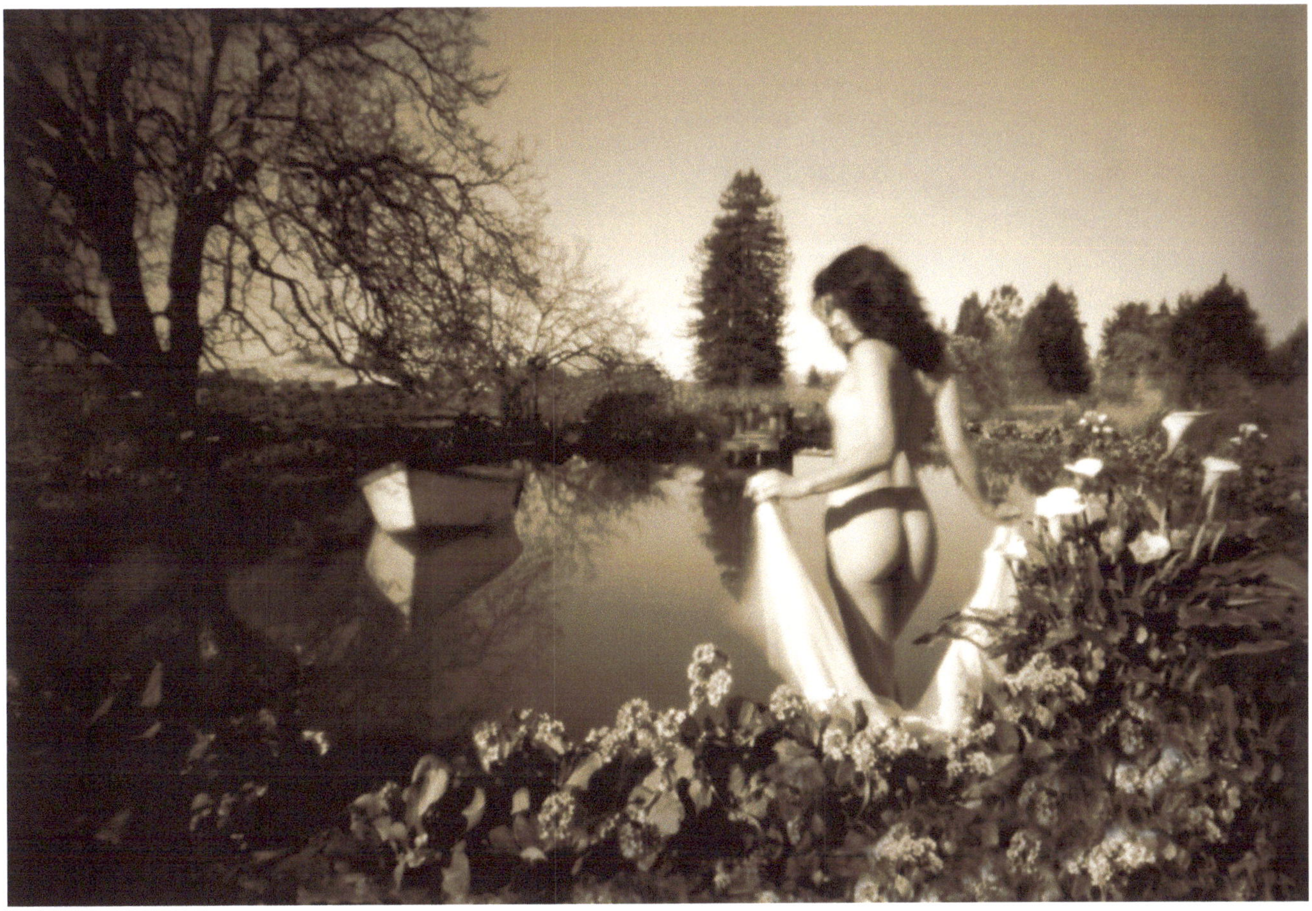

May 2011 137 Morning at the Pond

This unique wine glass came from a wonderful store in Tiburon, California called "Junella's Hidden Treasures." The glass was indeed a treasure that I couldn't live without! For days it was on my mind; I was constantly thinking about ways to photograph it to do it justice.

During a meditation the vision came to me. The creative process is stimulating; it's a huge part of my life. One of the hardest things in the whole process is to actually produce the images that come to mind. On the other hand, it can be one of the most rewarding aspects of the creative process.

The image you see here is exactly what came to me in my meditation.

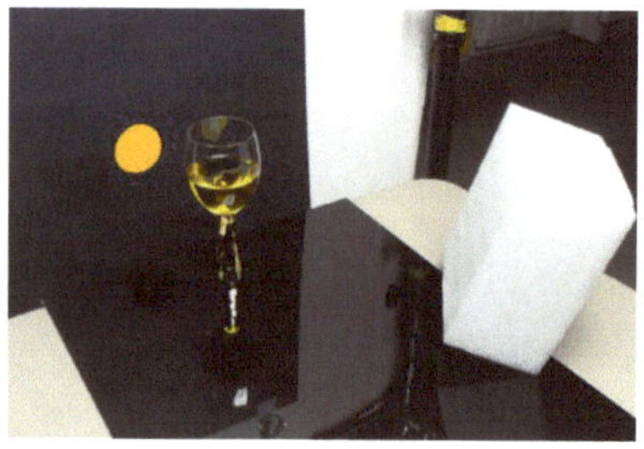

The first step was to cut a hole in black paper. The second step was to hang the black paper behind the glass. The white foam square is to bounce light into the glass.

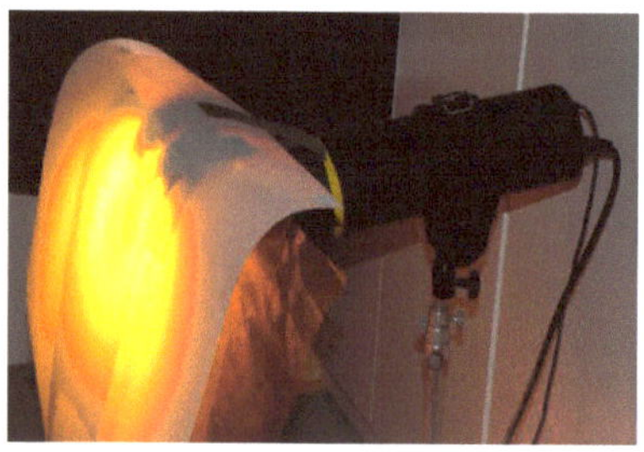

The orange sun was made by aiming a strobe behind the cutout hole from behind. Colored jells were used in front of the strobe.

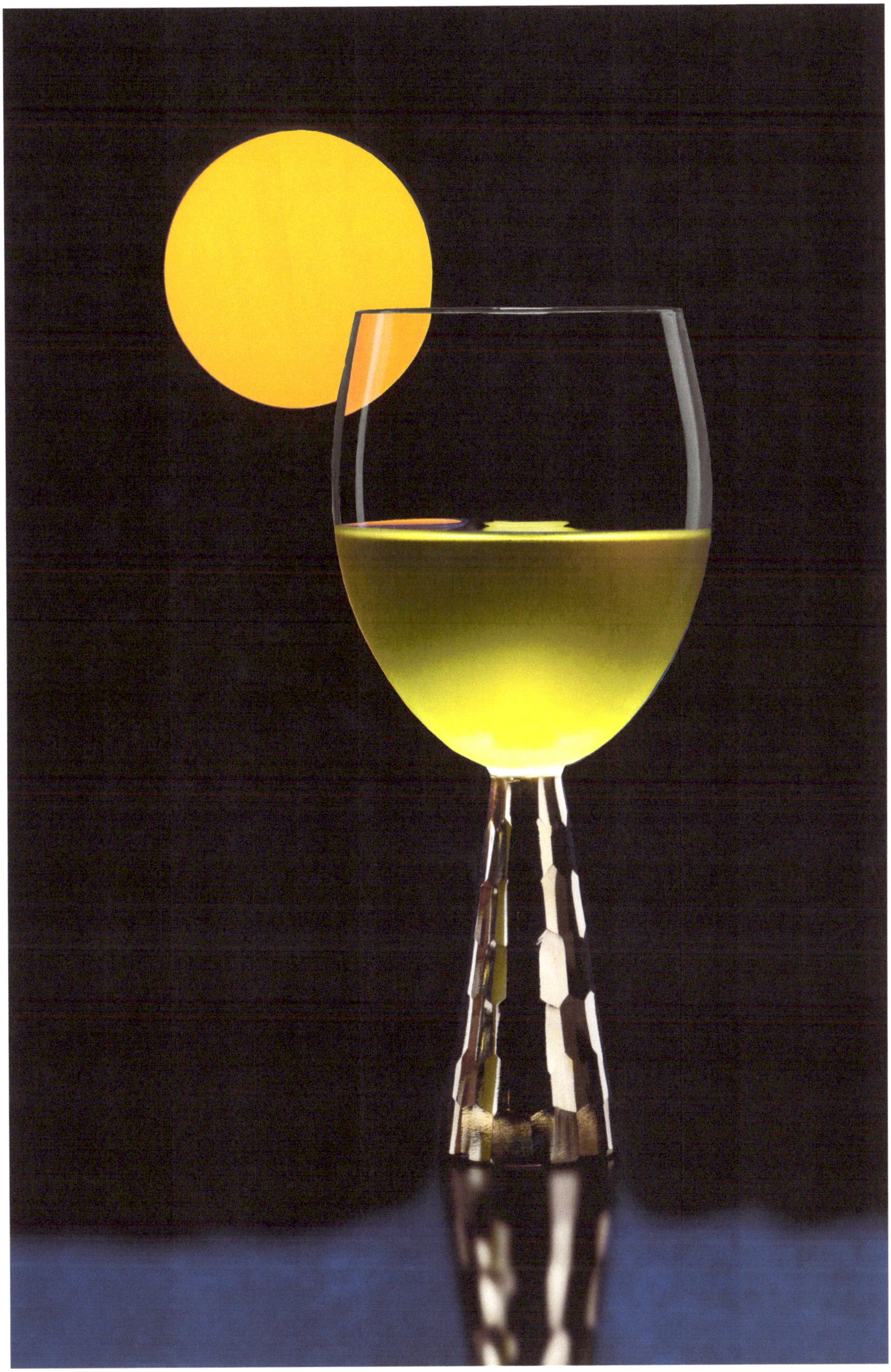

July 2011 291 New Sun

LightGathering

I'm part of a group of photographers from all over the United States, and beyond. The group was initially several of us that graduated from the Art Center College of Design. A couple of years after graduating we'd moved away from each other, but decided that we really needed to meet at least once a year in a place where we could take pictures. We would also show the work we'd done during the previous year. The name we decided on is LightGathering. This was in 1970 and we've been meeting ever since. Our group has grown from three to about fifty and we've been meeting for fifty years!

One of the advantages in addition to friendship and keeping up on technology is that the time between meetings is spent shooting new images, because we know we're going to need them to show at the next meeting.

Some of the images I have in this book are derived from those images.

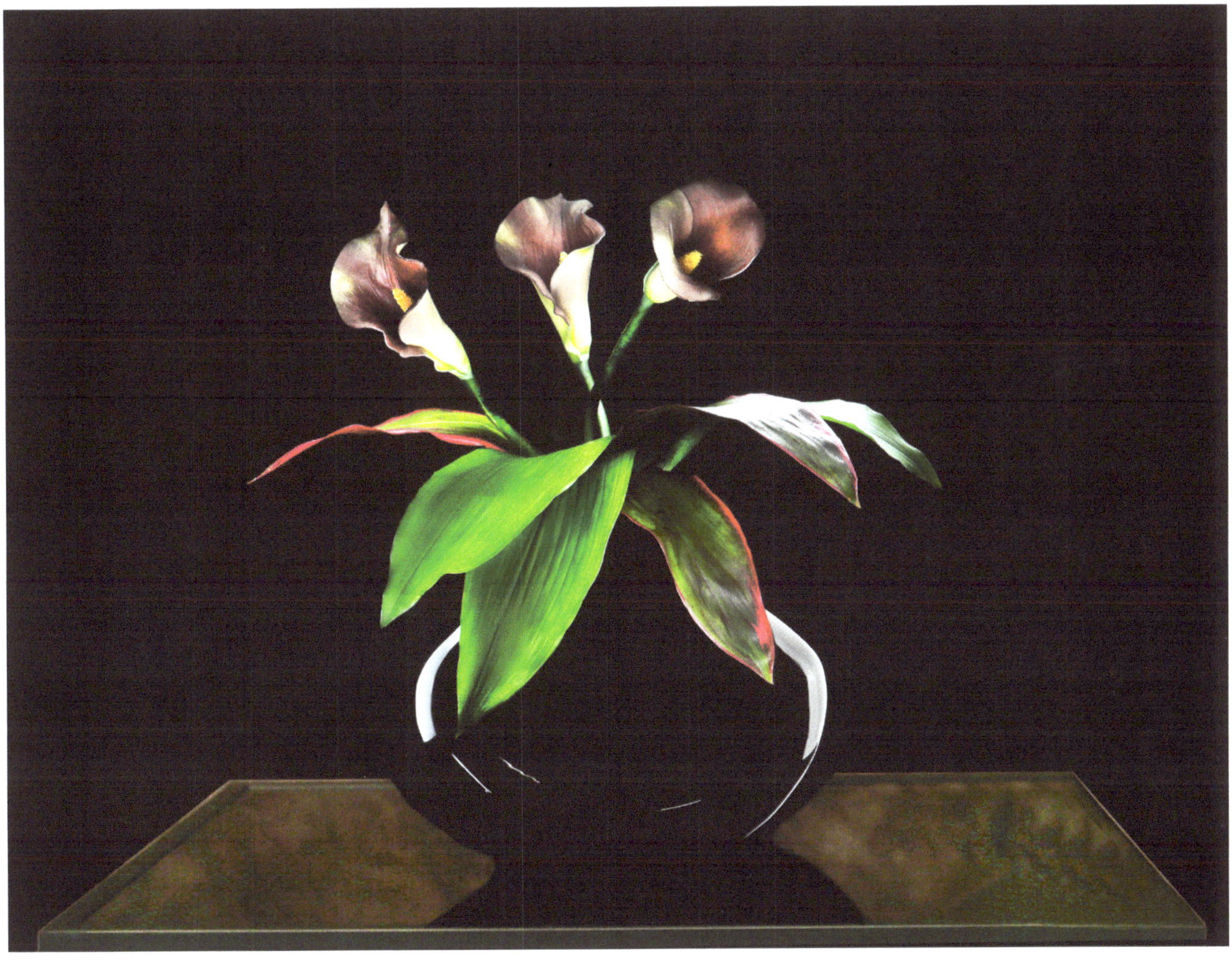

July 2017 362 Calla Lilies

There is a wonderful authentic medieval castle located on the outskirts of Calistoga. Dario Sattui's Castello di Amorosa, the Napa Wine Castle.

One of the jobs of a photographer is problem solving. The wine barrel room was one of these challenges.

It may well be one of the most impressive barrel rooms in the United States. It is 12,000 square feet, 14-foot high ceilings and 40 crossed vaulted bays with ribbing constructed of ancient Roman handmade bricks.

Needless to say, the barrel room is something that each visitor wants to see, so it's always crowded. I knew I wanted to show the room with a wine glass in the foreground. It was all I could do to get the room itself photographed without people. I waited until closing time and shot the empty room. The second challenge was to photograph the wine glass setup without being in the way.

The solution was to do the wine glass setup in my studio and strip it into the barrel room photo. The thing is, I wanted the beautiful chandelier lights and the brick archways from the barrel room reflected in the wine. As a side note, I chose a wine glass that repeated the curved brick arches in the stem.

So, the solution was to have a large 16" x 20" transparency made of the barrel room photo. I put the transparency behind the wine glass in my studio and illuminated it from behind with a strobe and soft-box. I now had the wine glass looking like it was photographed in the barrel room itself.

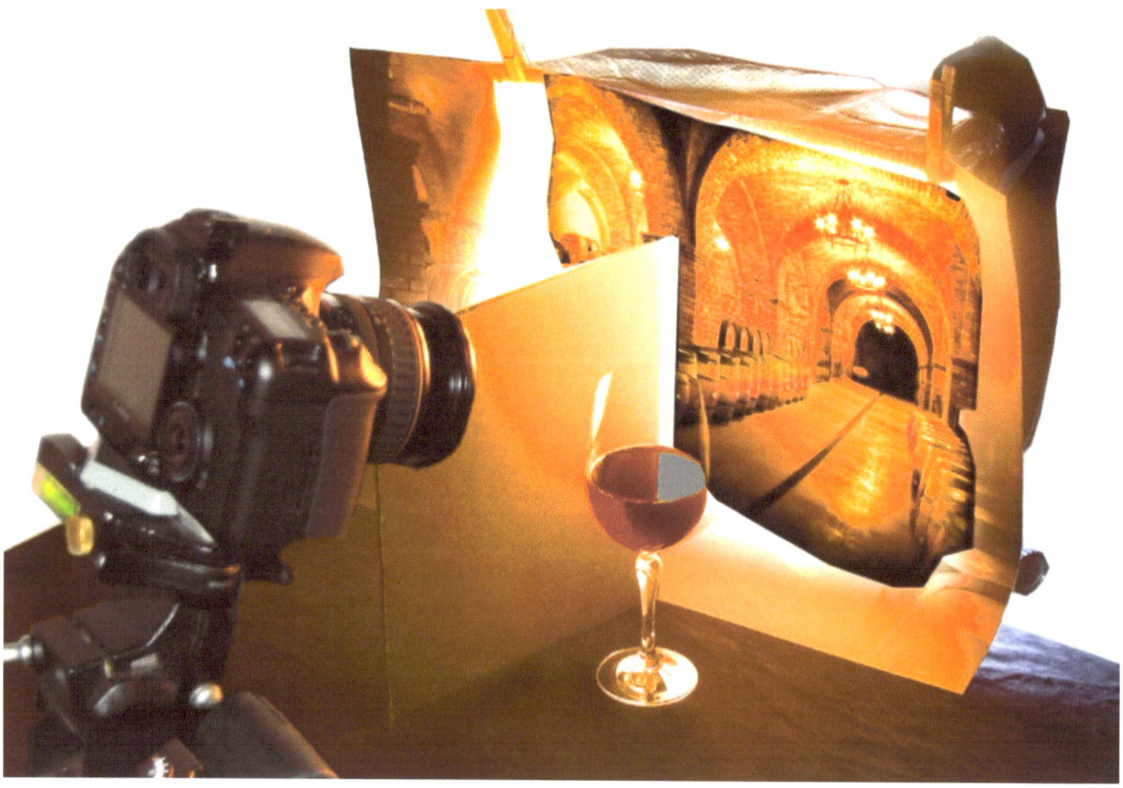

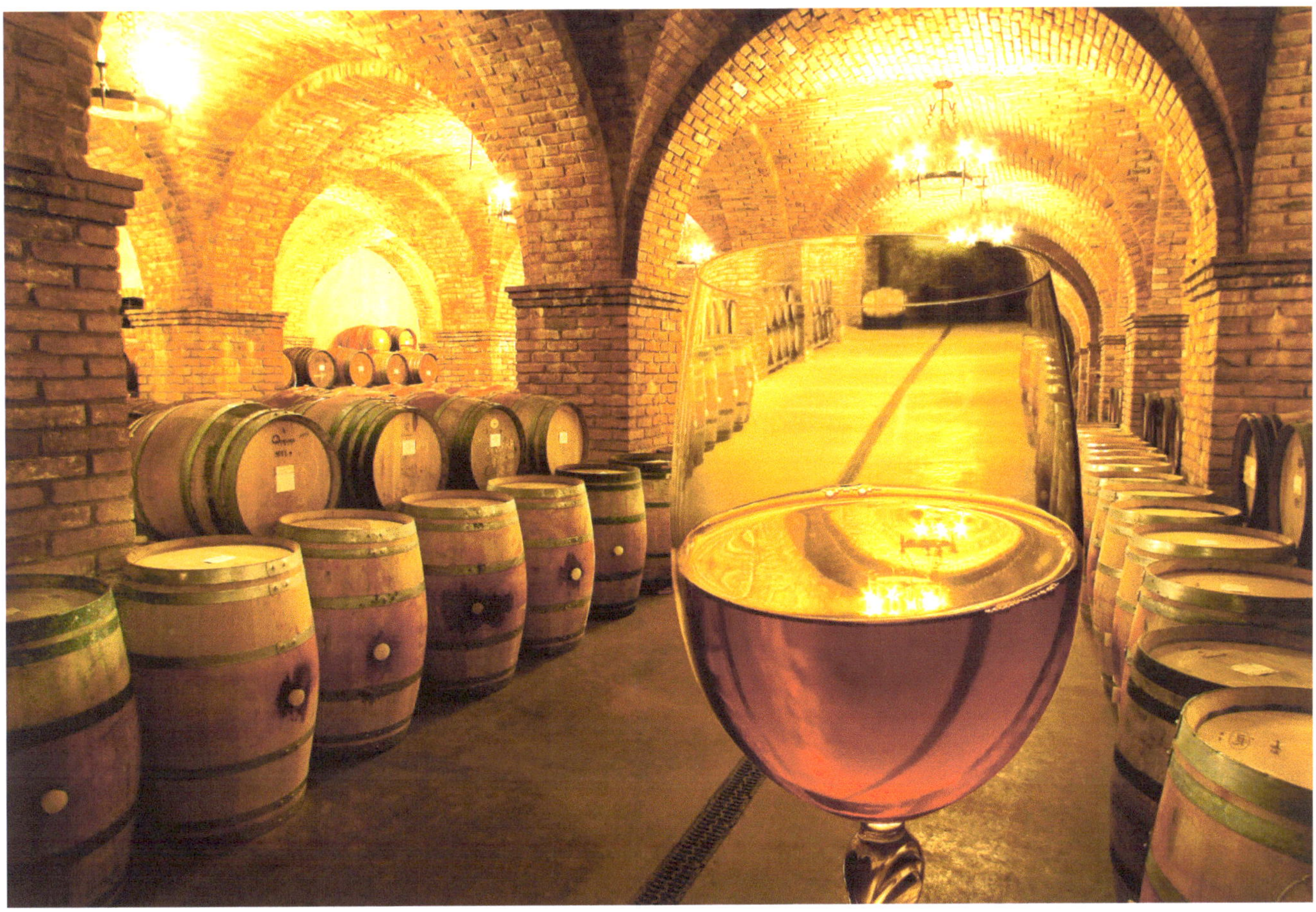

May 2007 288 Barrel Room Castello di Amorosa

The castle was a challenge; I wanted a complete and finished look to it. First of all, it was the wrong time of year, the newly planted vines were bare. I lived in Kenwood, over the mountain from Calistoga where the castle was located. Kenwood is in Sonoma Valley, Valley of the Moon. Well, over the years I had photographed lots of vineyards in my area. So, I put one of my vineyard photos in front of the castle in the fall of the year to add the warm colors against the stone walls.

Next, I filled the moat with water and added the sparkles from the moon's reflection. The moat was designed to have water, but it only had a little from recent rains.

There was bare earth to the left of the castle, so I filled it in with trees and shrubs and a little lawn. The castle looked too stark, so I decided to turn it into a night shot with lights coming from the windows. Then, of course, you need a full moon over the castle.

Needless to say, this took quite a bit of time. But I am pretty happy with the results.

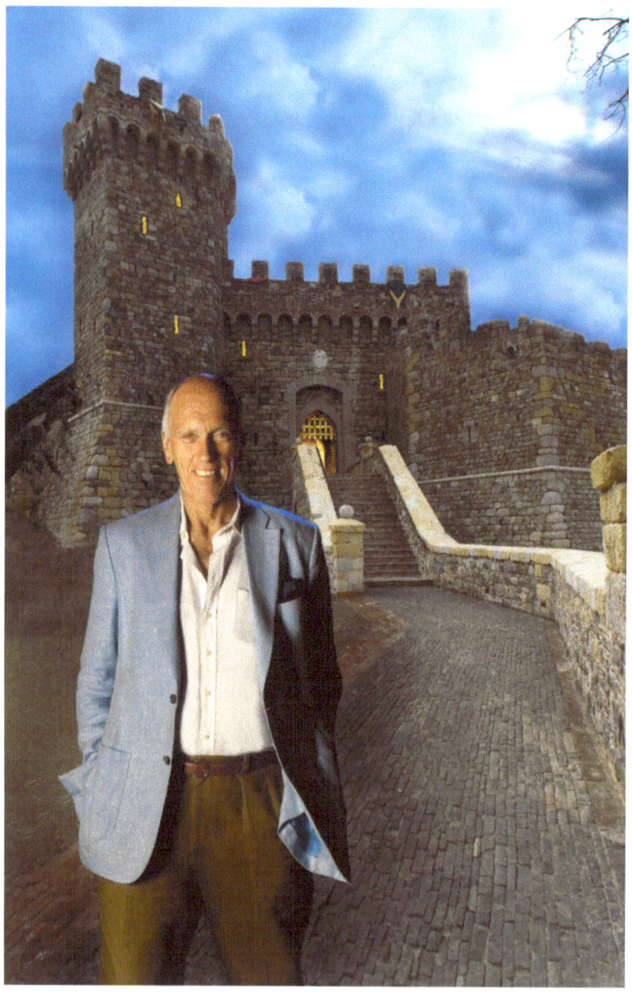

Dario Sattui in front of his castle

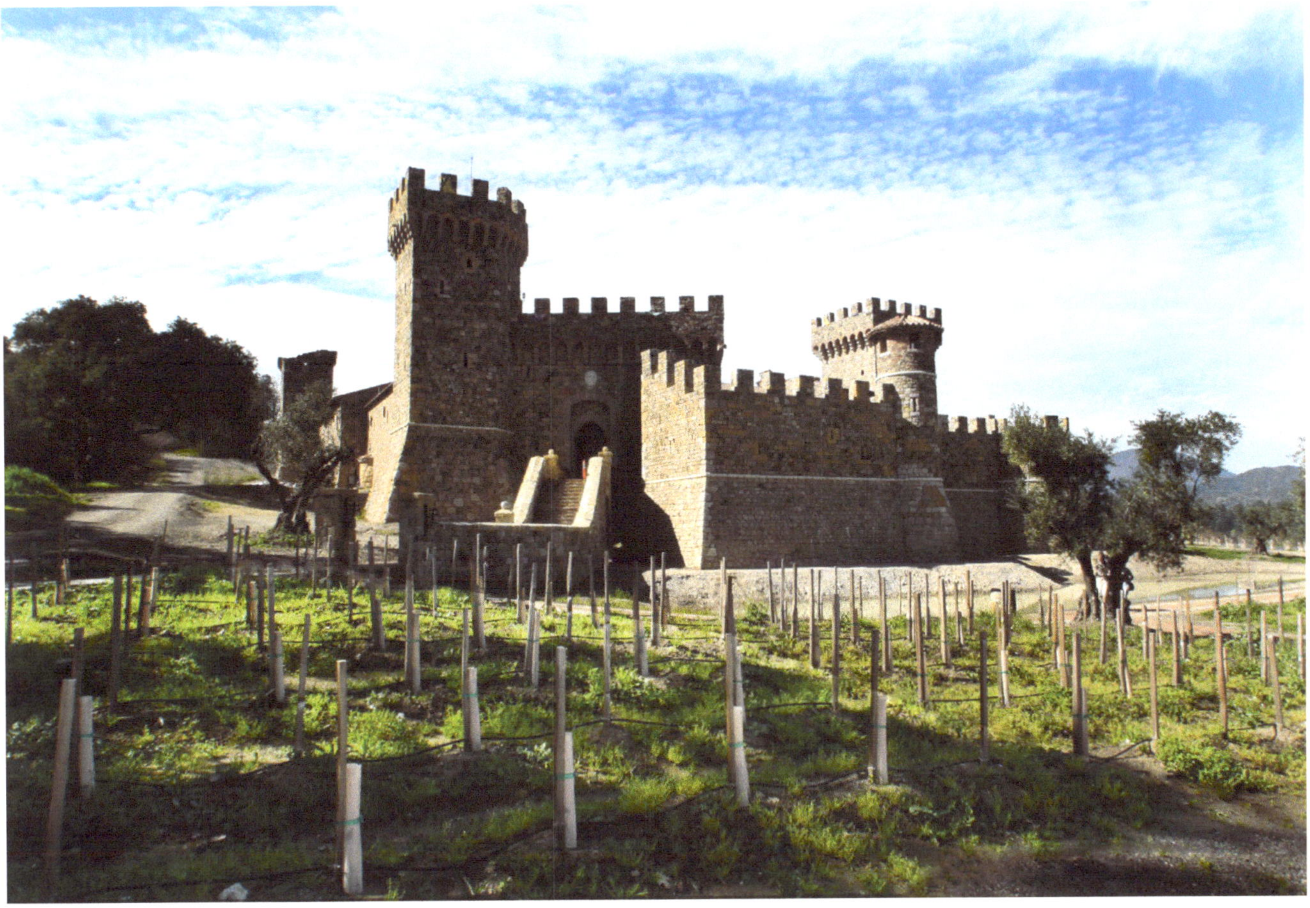

February 2008 The Castello di Amorosa as it looked before retouching

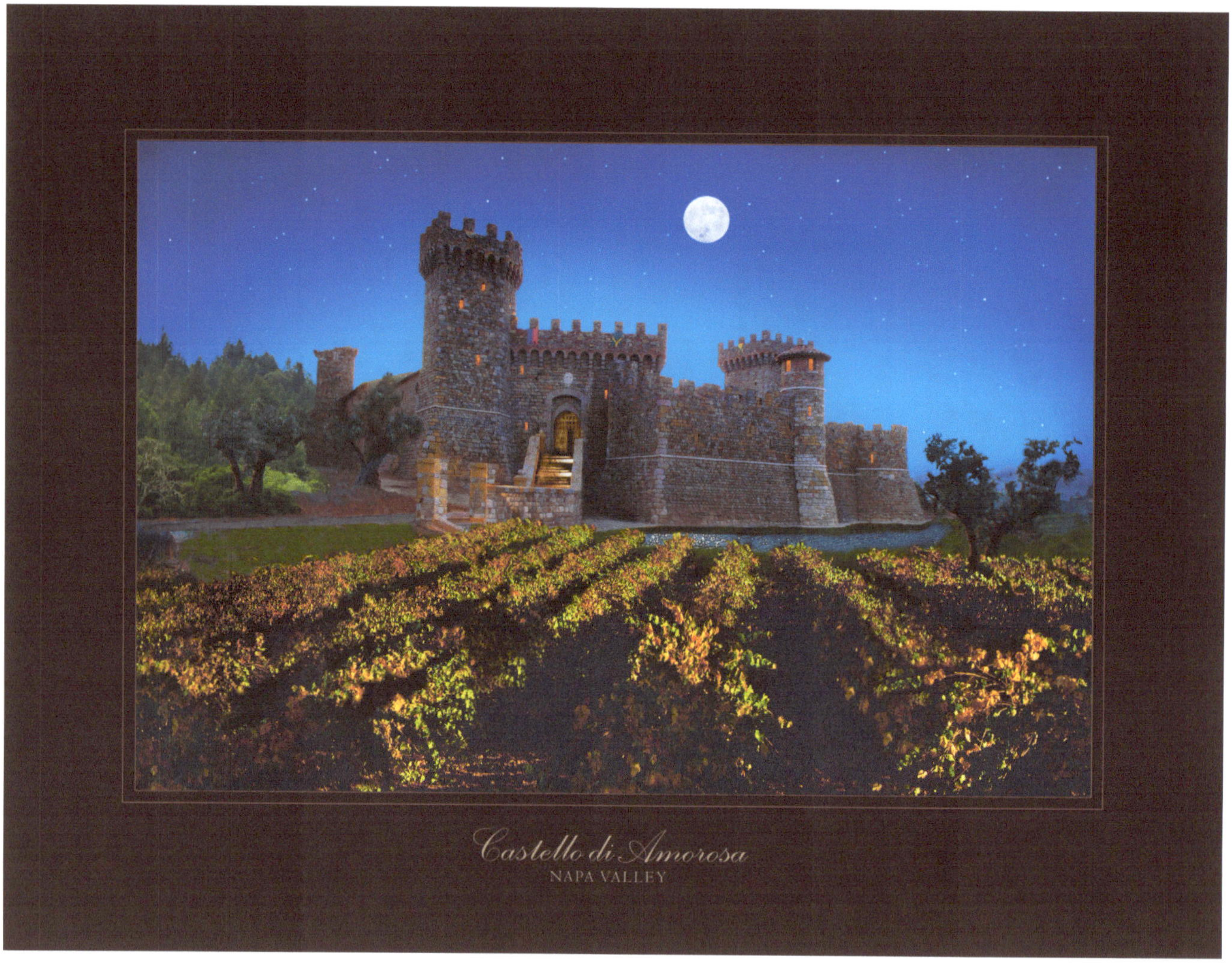

Castello di Amorosa as a poster after extensive retouching

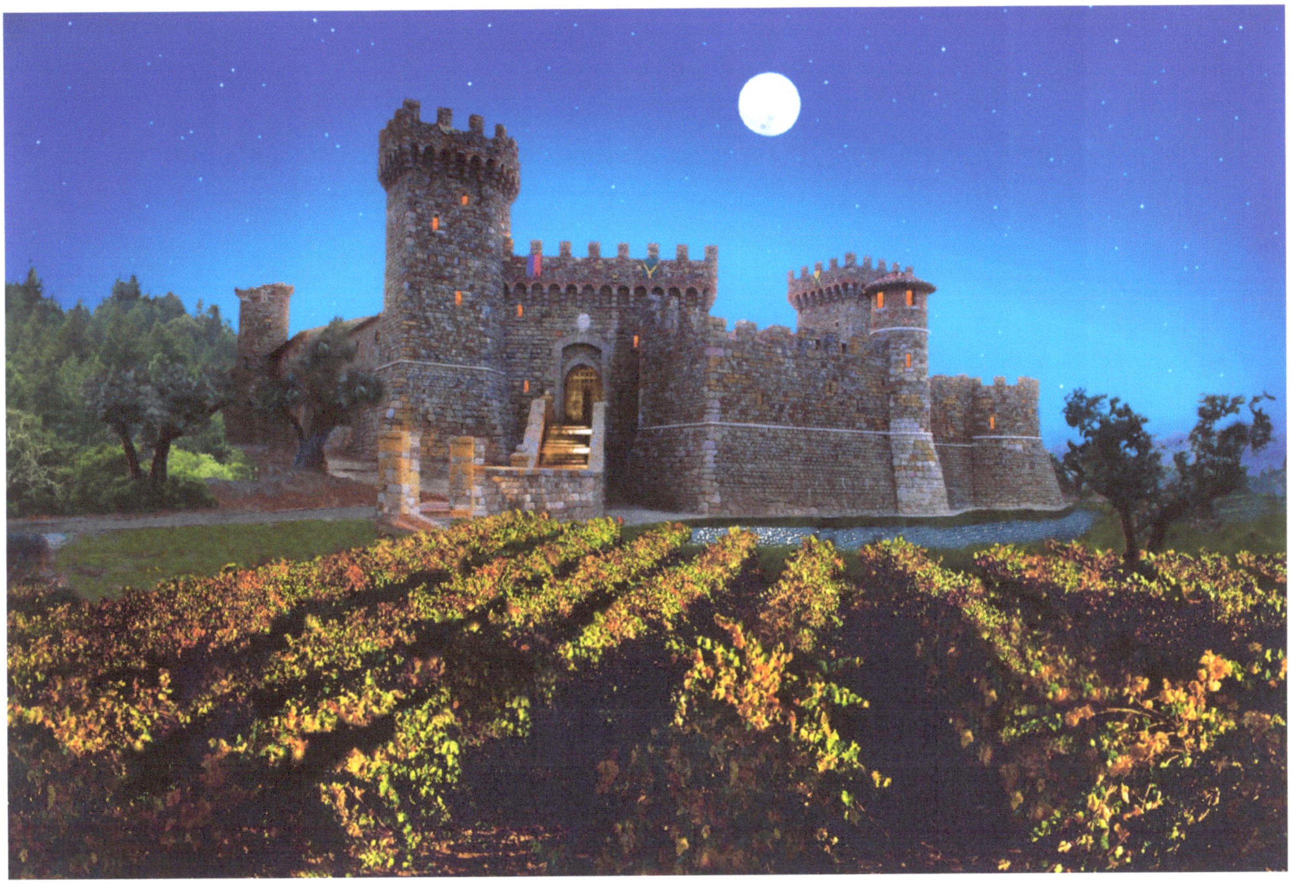

April 2008 370 Castello di Amorosa, Napa

Egret Ascending

Calling me at home a friend said, "You'd better get down here; the egrets are nesting in a tree on West Ninth Street in Santa Rosa."

So, I grabbed my photo gear and tripod and off I went.

The egret's nest in trees in the median of the road in Santa Rosa every year. The city puts up barricades along the road to protect the birds.

This was, as it turns out, very fortuitous. In just a couple of weeks I would take the photo called Laguna Morning and this egret would be just what I needed to complete the photograph.

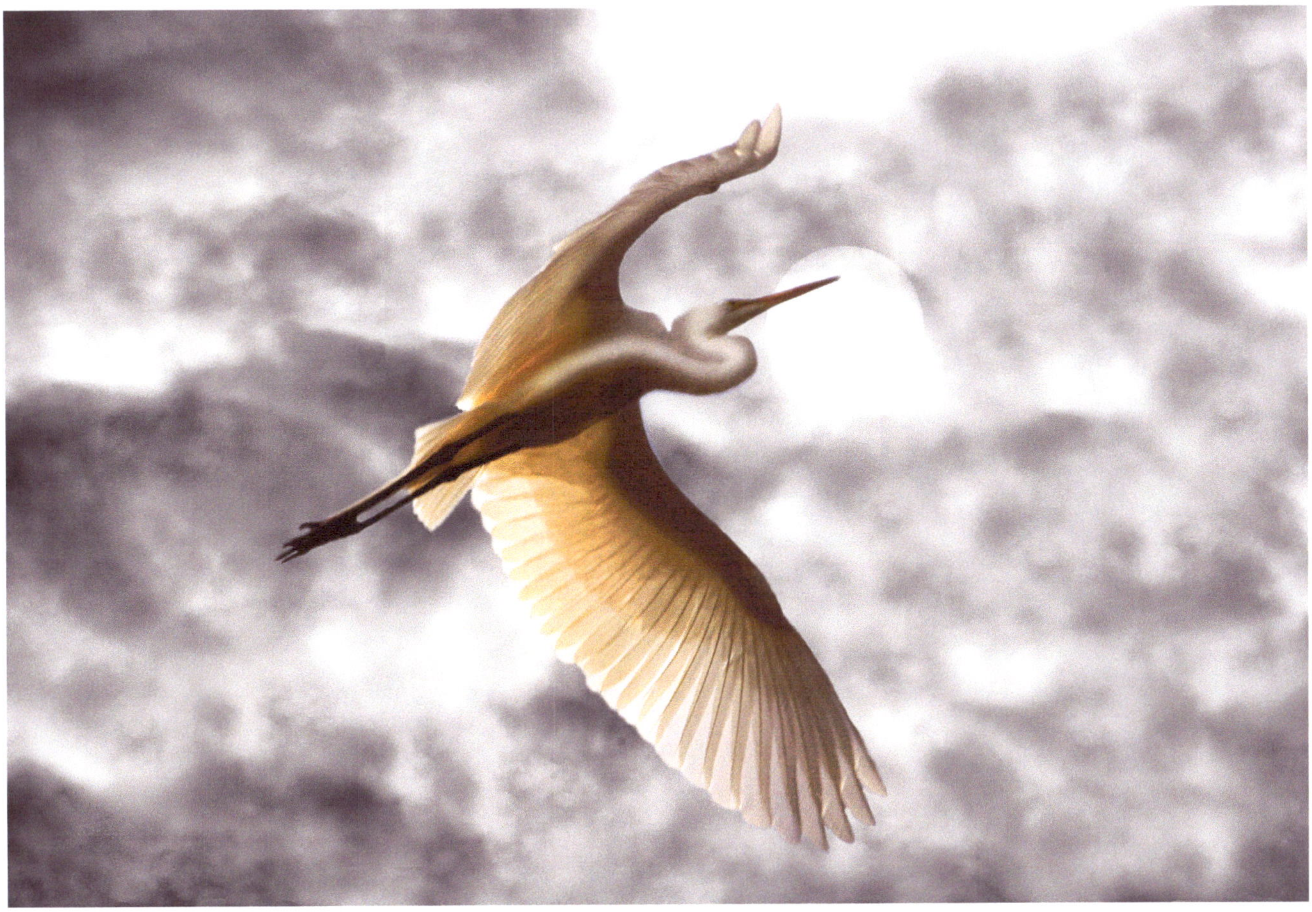

August 2006 234 Egret Ascending

Beach Party

This beach party was taken May 2017. I had been experimenting with long exposures at night. This particular night I hiked down a cliff and then out along the beach in Sonoma County.

As I was setting up my equipment a group of people started to gather, then they started a bonfire.

I was thinking they were going to ruin my shot, but the more I thought about it, the more I saw it as a blessing.

A park ranger showed up and told them it was illegal to have camp- fires on the beach. But he added they could let it burn itself out and to not add any more wood, which I thought was pretty fair. I really like the mood of the ocean and the colors and the beach party only adds to the shot.

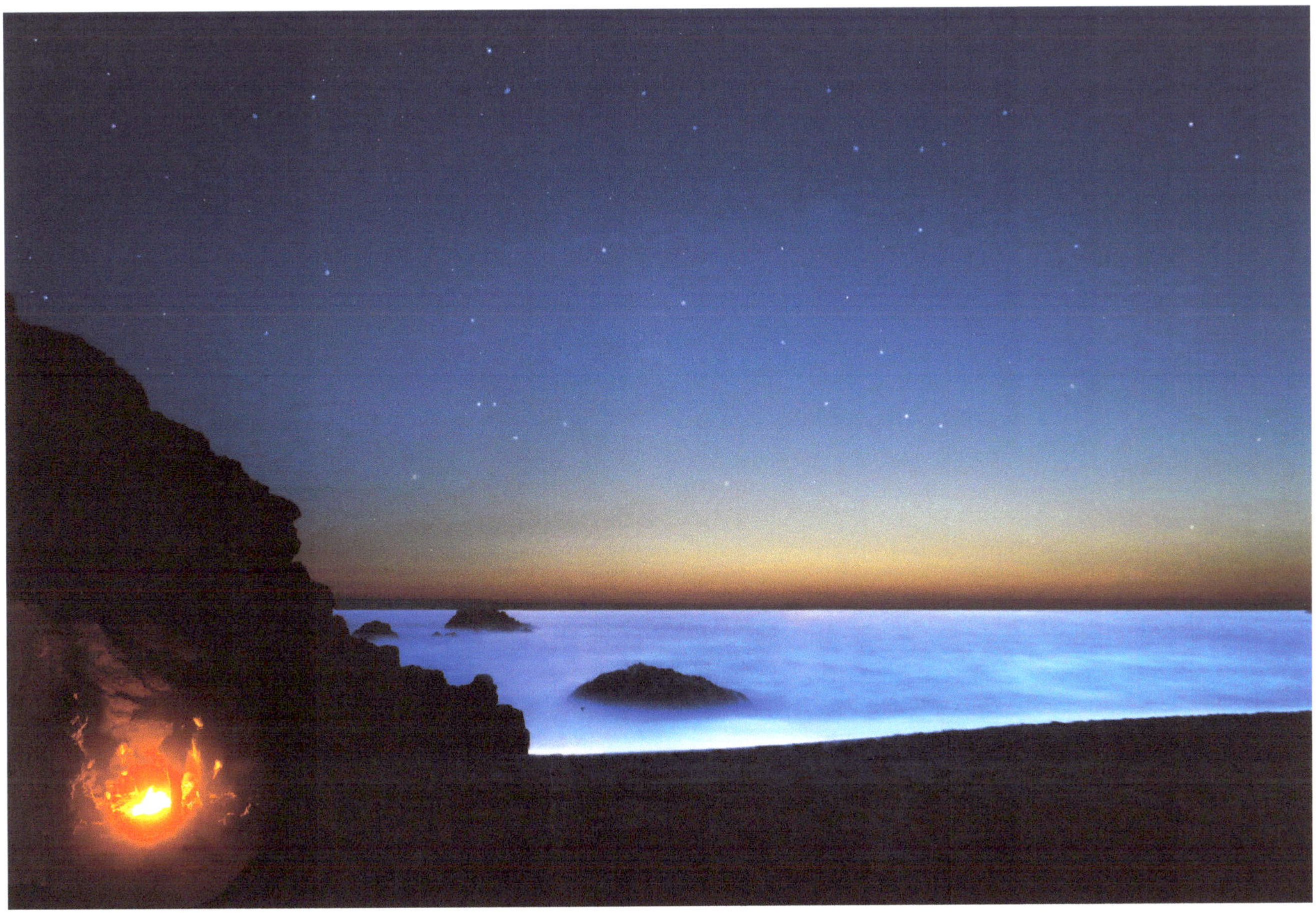

May 2017

371 Beach Party Sonoma Coast

Winery Poster

I've had some things occur in my career that absolutely mystify me.

I always have to create. I'll get an idea and then start working on it. This photo is one of them. In other words it wasn't specifically done for a client; it's what I call a portfolio shot.

After its completion, I did put it in my portfolio. I showed it to an AD agency and it got the art director excited. He said he was working on a project and needed another striking image to go in the series of posters he was designing for a winery. I'm not a negotiator so this was perhaps my first mistake. I met with the owner of the winery myself. He asked how much I would like for the image. I told him $1500 for the rights to print a poster and if he wanted to use the image in the future, say for a wine label, we could negotiate the price then. He wanted a complete buyout of the image for $1500, so he could own the image and use it for whatever he wanted. I said no, it doesn't work that way. Bear in mind, this guy is a multi-millionaire. I met with him several more times and I wasn't going to give in, nor was he.

The last time I met with him I told him he couldn't have the image for any price, it was off the table. Well, the next week I was photographing the old opera house in Petaluma. It just so happens that the property manager of the building showed up and said there was a photographer on the second floor and would I like to come up and meet him. I told her no but she insisted. Well, as we walked in, the manager introduced me. As soon as he heard my name he turned white as a ghost! I looked down to see what he was photographing and it was my image of the wine glass. He actually had a copy of the image and was duplicating it. I asked how could he be doing this, it's complete plagiarism, and then I said they must be paying him lots of money. He said he didn't know how much but that he'd do it for free just to get his name on the poster. How could I walk in at that precise moment? It had to be Karma.

Two weeks later my wife and I went on a wine-tasting; it became another bout with Karma. The wife of the man I was negotiating with was pouring his wine. I kept my mouth shut but my wife introduced me as the photographer who took the photo that her husband liked. She said, "My husband absolutely loves that image!" Life is stranger than fiction. They changed the image to look different than my image and to me it was a flop.

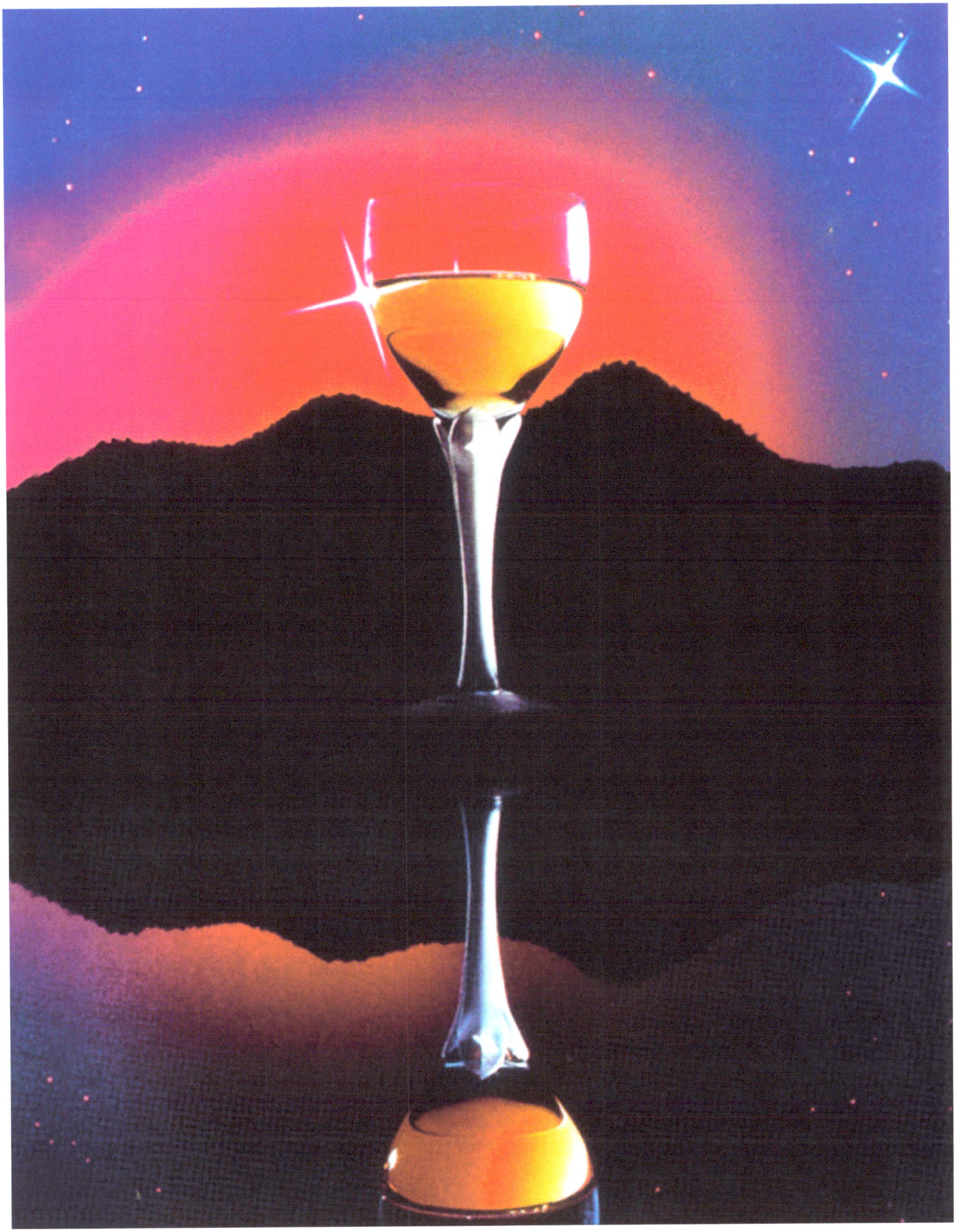

December 2006 372 Winery Poster

The First Light-Gathering

At this time I was in the middle of nowhere, but of course this was 1974. Now this rock face is adjacent to a golf course and a housing tract in Scottsdale, Arizona. This is in the early days of LightGathering. There were only a few of us gathering that year. And, of course, Will Chubb had to get some nudes from the art department at a local junior college. The other members didn't seem to mind though.

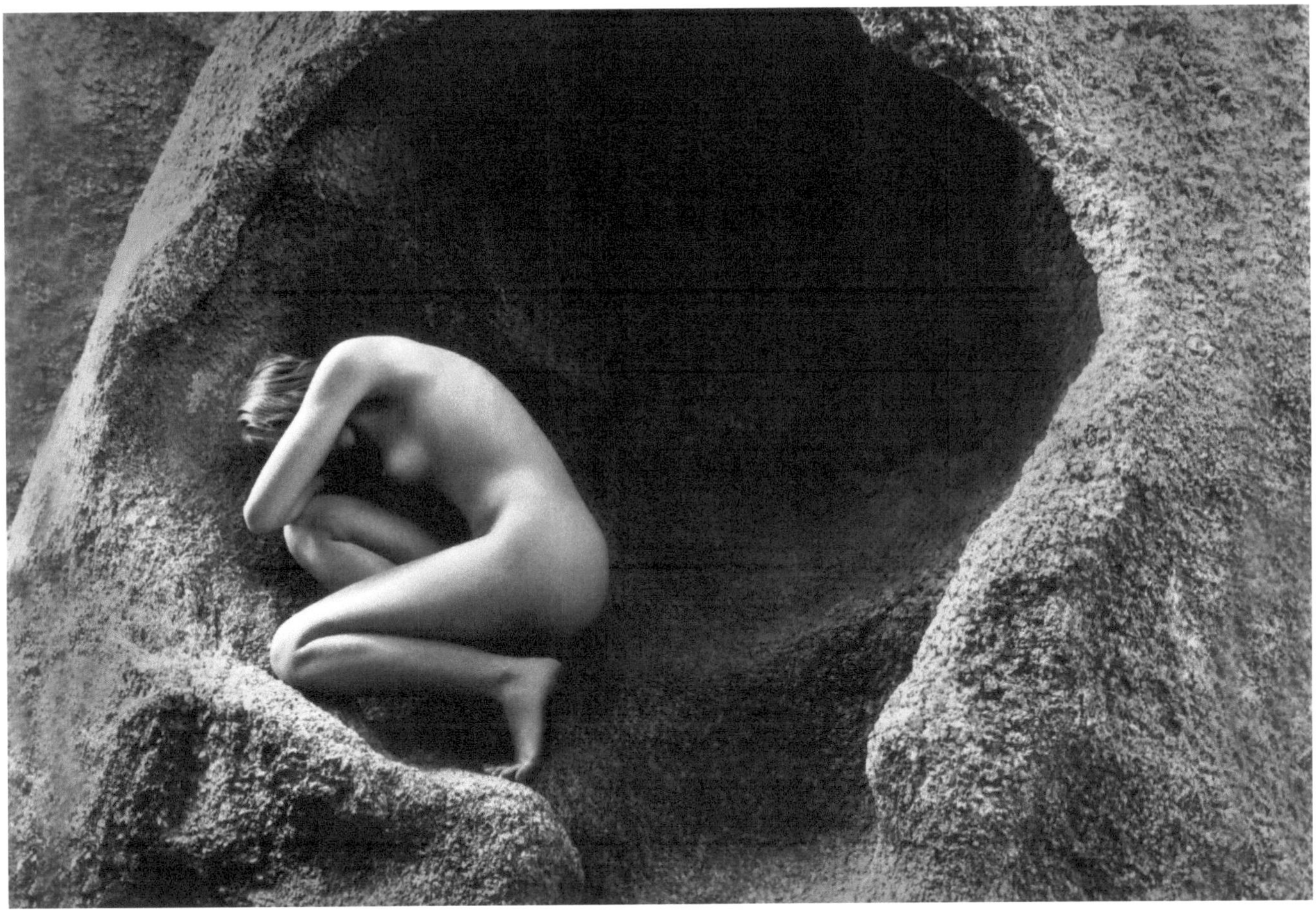

September 1974 130 Mother Earth

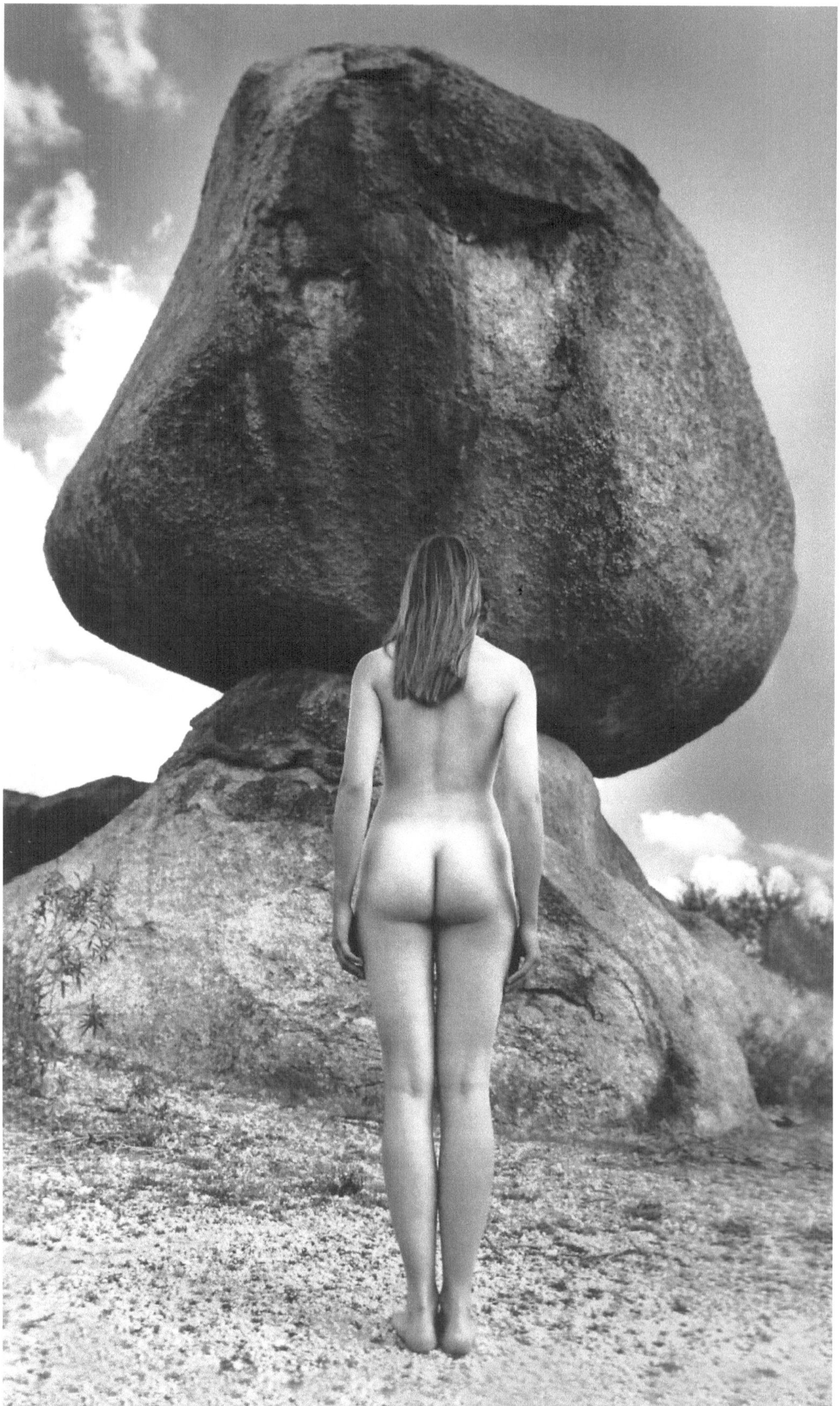

September 1974 **373 Reckoning**

Sacred Earth

This wasn't a Light-Gathering photo shoot. I got the model myself, after finding this dry lake bed. It's full of water now, but this was during a severe drought in Northern California in the mid-1970s.

I felt a bit of anxiety because there were already motorcycle tracks all over this beautiful lake-bed so I quickly found my model and went out there the very next day before new tracks could ruin the whole area.

This was back in the film days and I shot this with an RB67 2 ¼ by 2 ¾ camera, on a tripod of course. I pretty much always use a tripod.

I really liked the other world feeling. The ocean scene was one that I already had in my files. This was in my Jerry Uelsman days! Believe it or not, this is also before digital photography—all done in the darkroom and with one enlarger. Jerry Uelsman uses several enlargers. With one enlarger you have to move the negatives and refocus each time, as well as make the exposure on the sheet of enlarger paper. Then you put the paper back in the box, turn on the lights, reposition the new negative, and then turn the lights off and position the paper in the correct position to make the second exposure.

It is arduous, to say the least. But I really didn't mind so much because my mother-in-law was visiting and I could hide in the darkroom I had built in the garage. The only real problem was I built the 2x4 framework and covered it with black visqueen and it got boiling hot in there because it was mid-summer!

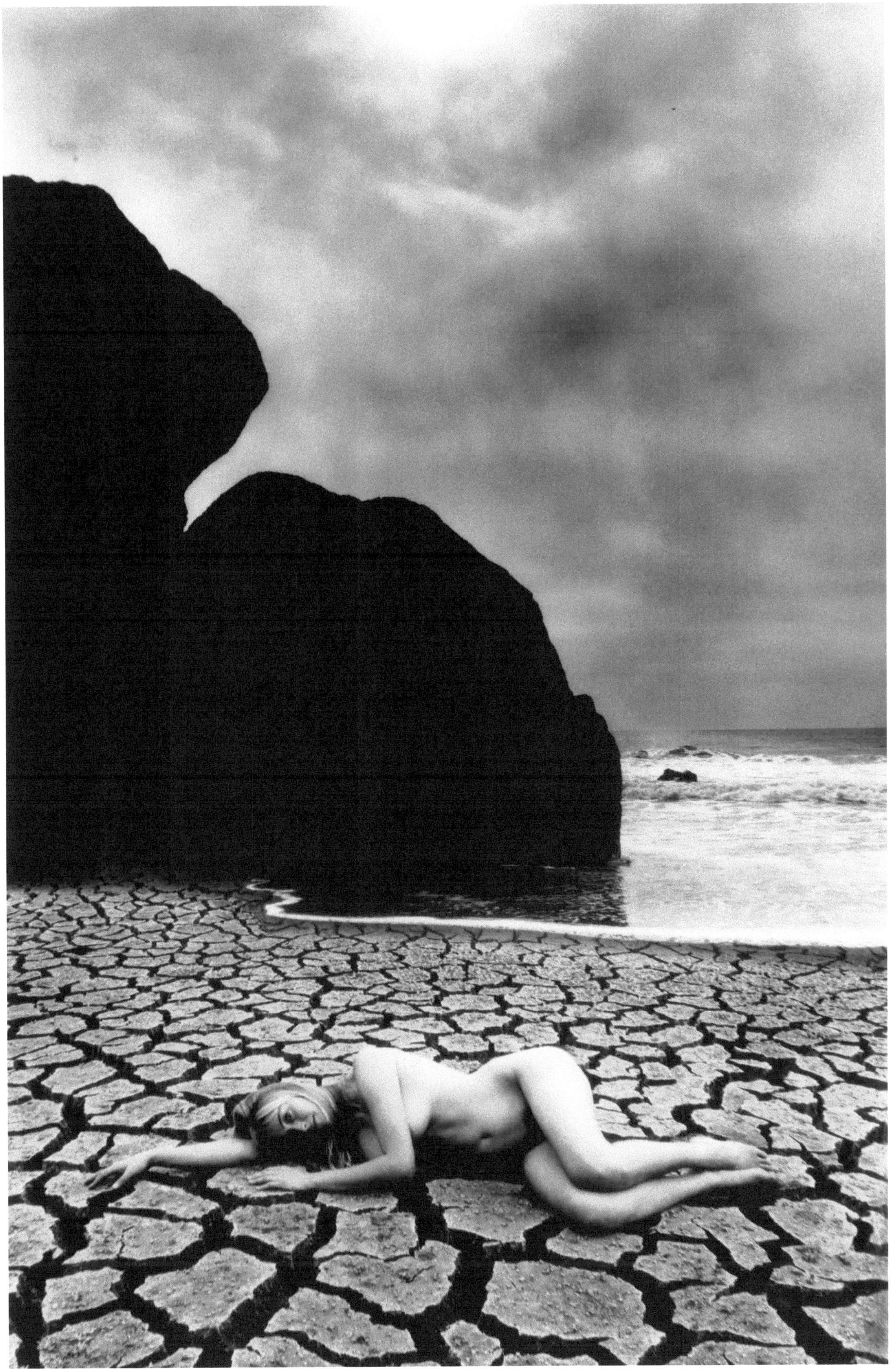

1977 139 Sacred Earth

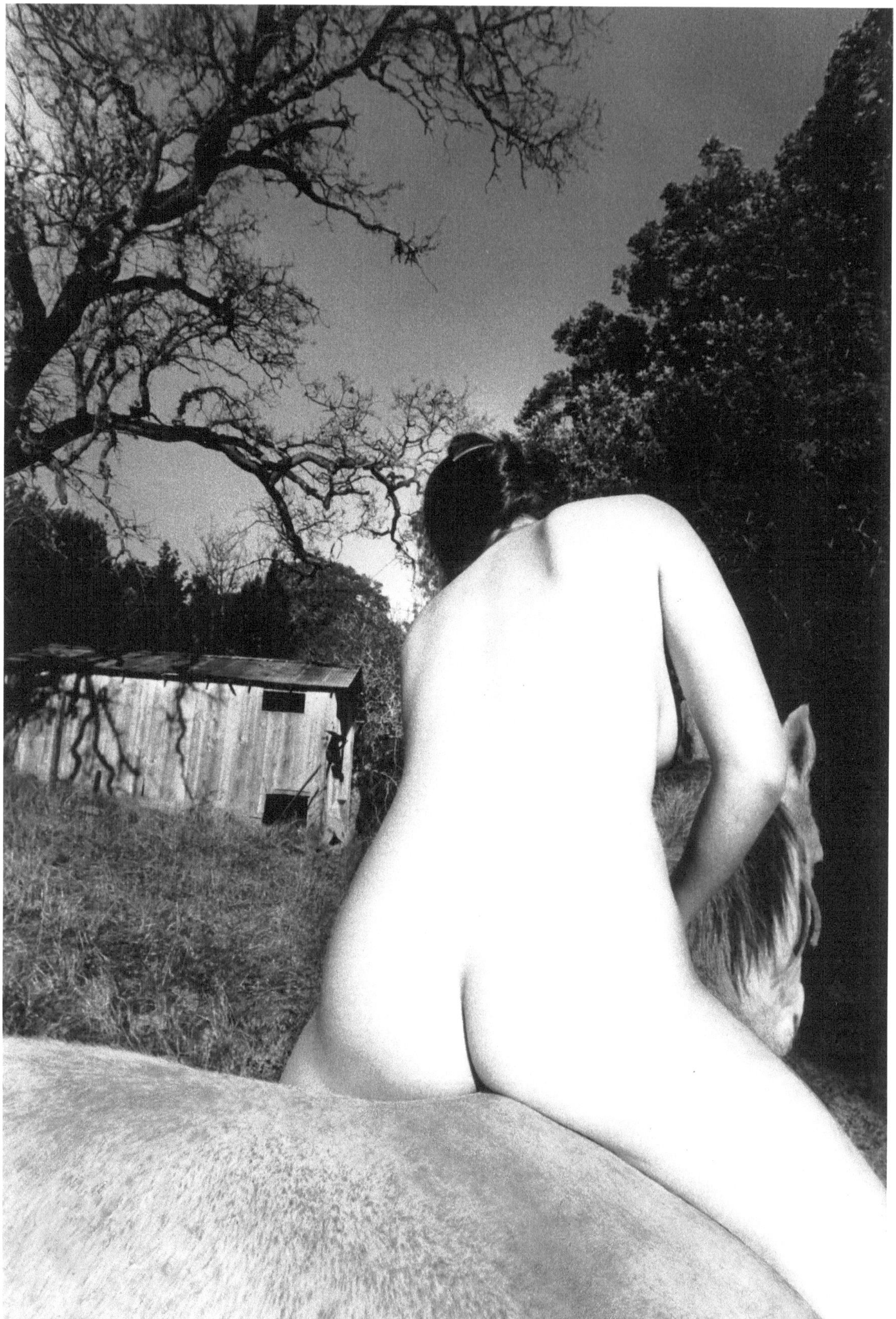

1978 225 Bareback

LightGathering 2004

Ten tears after the start of LightGathering which was in Scottsdale, Arizona, and after ten annual meetings we were back in the desert. This time it was Death Valley. We went to a variety of locations but this was one of the more interesting spots. I didn't think so at first, it seemed these stone structures didn't do anything for me and the light certainly wasn't right.

These were kilns built to burn wood to make charcoal used to smelt lead and silver from the local mines. They were built in 1877 and were only used for two or three years. There are ten kilns and they are twenty-five feet high and are in remarkably good shape.

I couldn't find a good angle from the outside. So, I peeked inside but it was completely black from burning wood. There was a ventilation hole on the upper wall, opposite the doorway. Not enough light to get a photograph I thought. But I thought I'd give it a try anyway.

I set up my tripod in the doorway and used my 14mm wide angle lens, making sure to give it plenty of exposure. Digital is so nice because you can see instantly what you've got. I was astounded at what I saw, it was like an extraordinary event was manifesting in front of me, a divine intervention, a miracle. There was a glow of light from the vent hole and it caused a blue haze to appear, and then there seemed to be stars in the blackness. The stars were from the little holes between the stone blocks. It proves a photographer should never give up but push ahead and keep exploring with your camera.

It was a week before we got home but I kept thinking about this miraculous image and how it needed something more to make it a complete statement. When we got home, I decided to double expose a baby below the blue haze. I photographed the baby against black and had his mom poised above him to get his attention. To me it's as if a new soul is descending from heaven.

Pretty amazing to get this from a bland stack of stones that I was ready to walk away from. I call this simply "Birth of a new age."

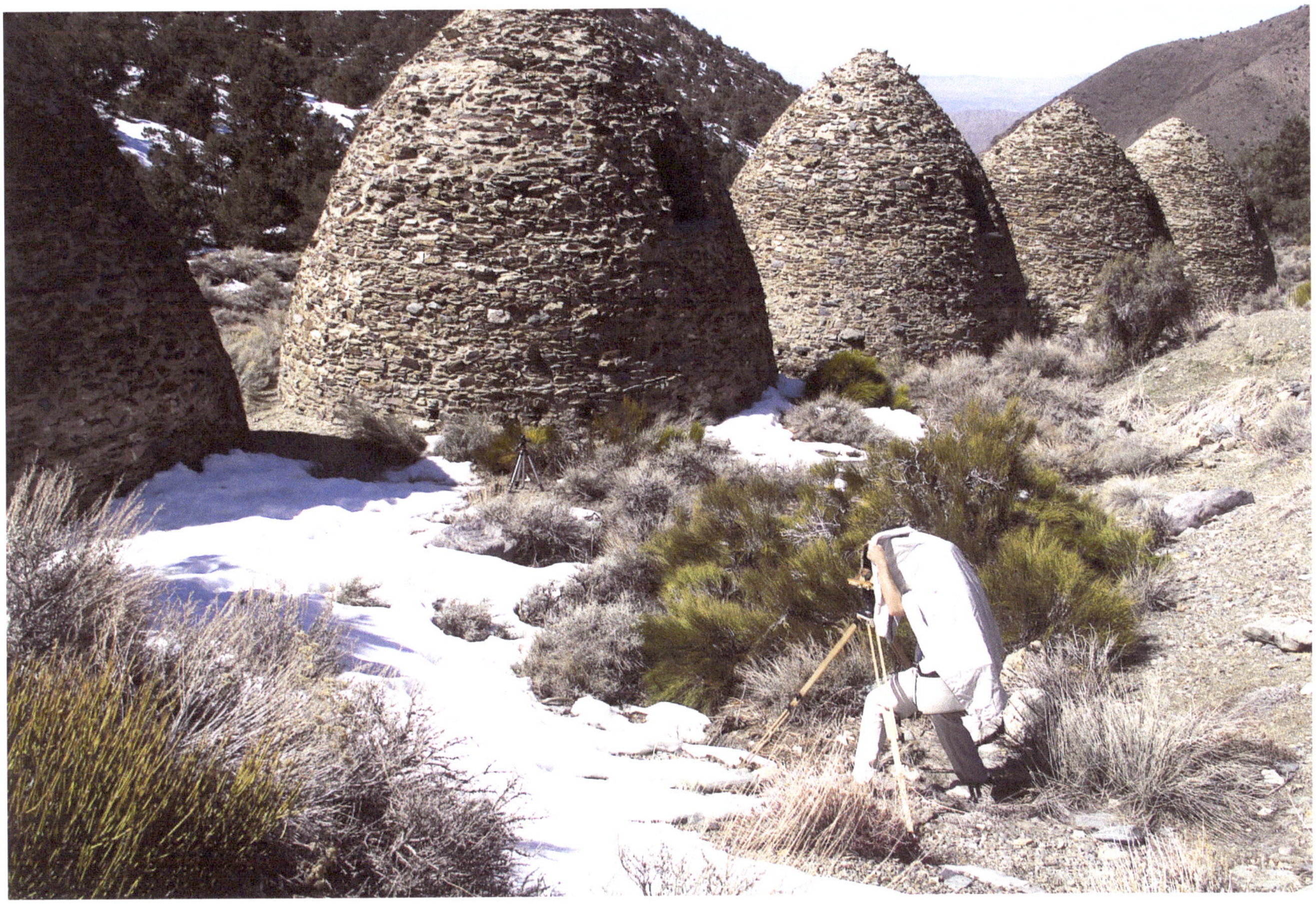

Beehive being photographed with a 4” x 5” camera

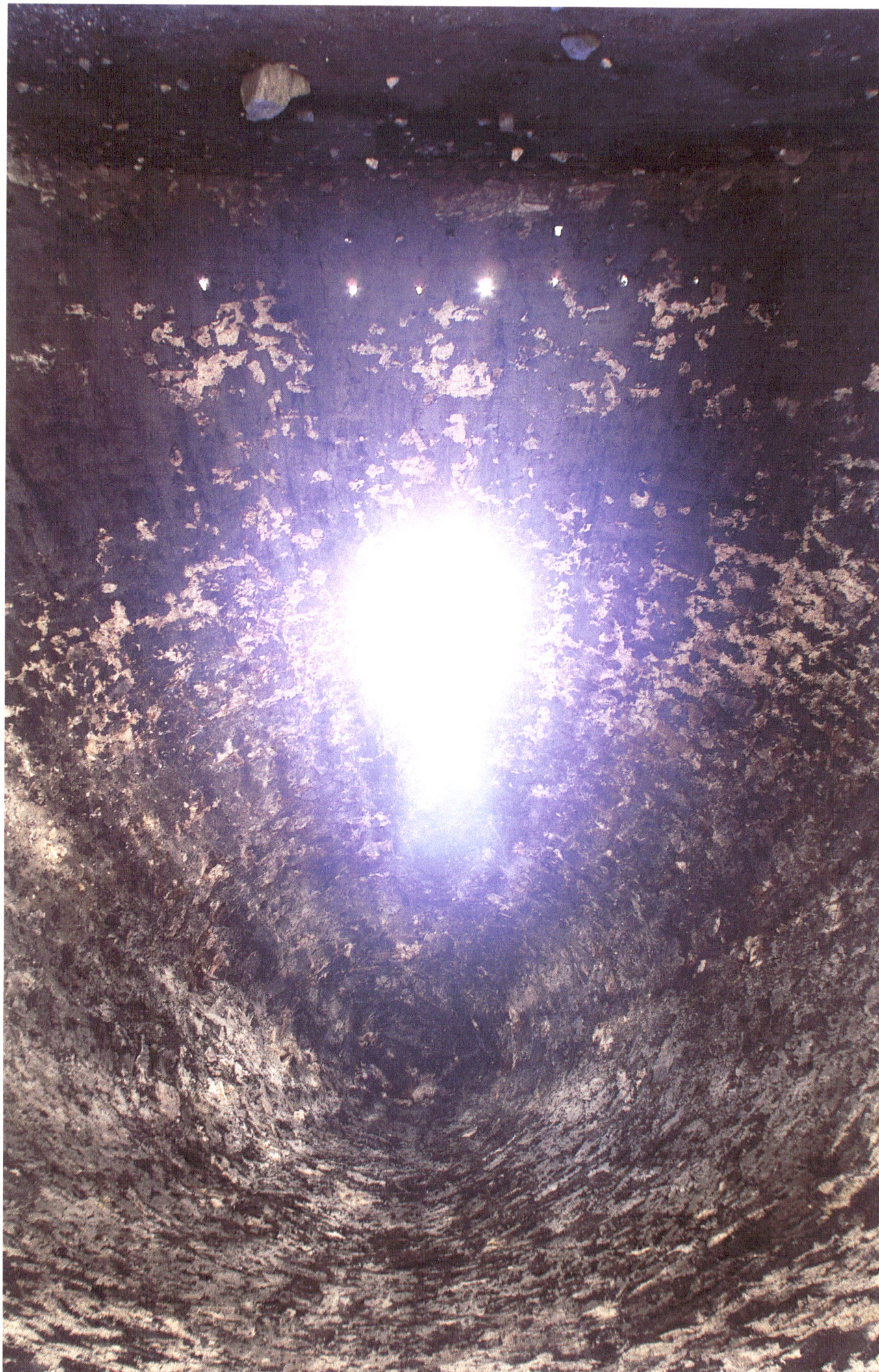

Inside the Beehive

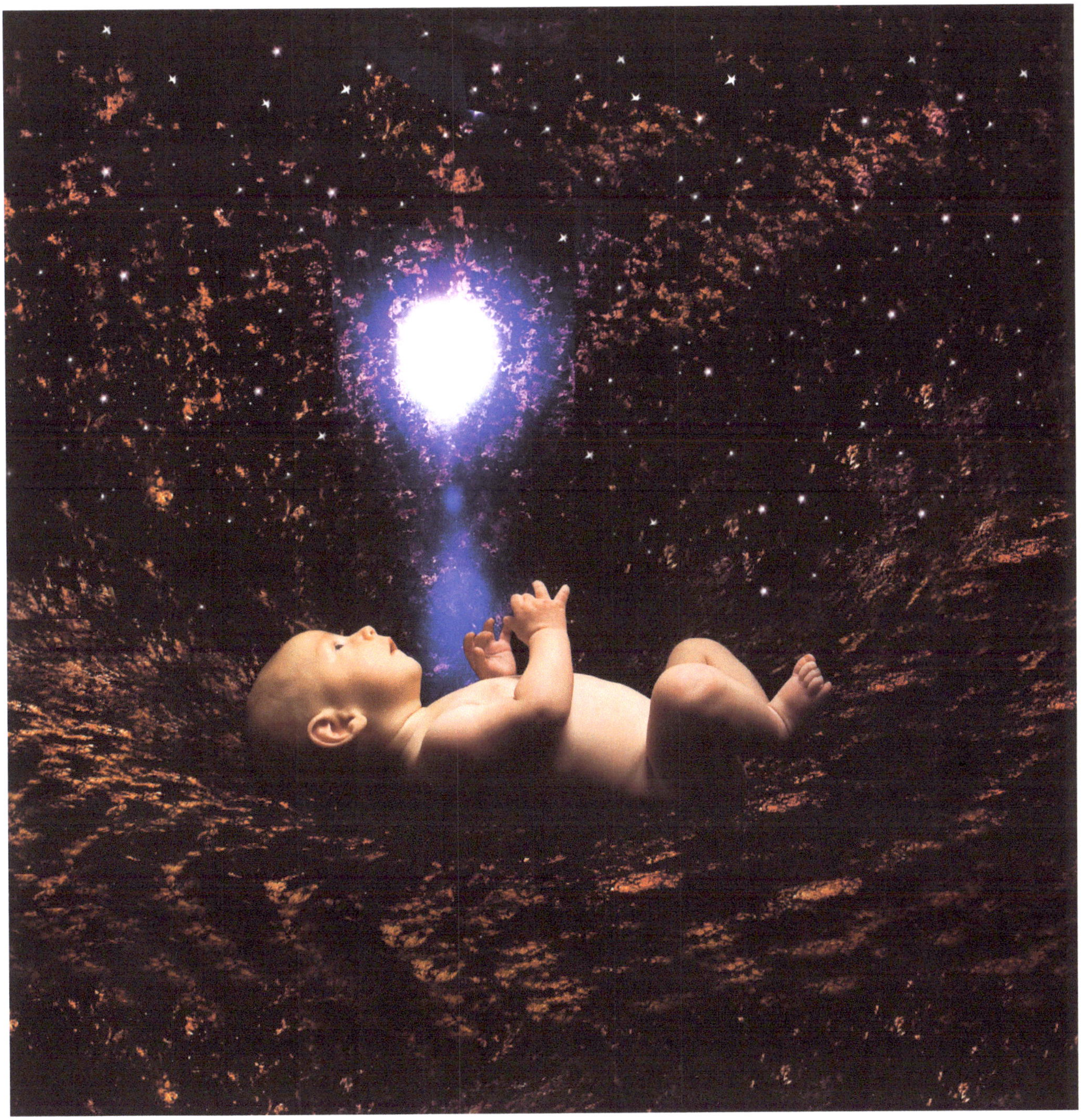

2004 NFS Birth of a New Age

Gloria Ferrer Winery Night Harvest

This day of photography started at 2:00 a.m. In recent years some wineries have been harvesting at night. Gloria Ferrer makes celebrated, award-winning sparkling wines and night harvests their hand-picked grapes to follow their heritage from Spain. Jose Ferrer ventured from Barcelona, Spain to Sonoma, California in the 1980s. He found the Mediterranean climate, rolling hills, and maritime influences, reminiscent of his native Catalonia. He produces wonderful sparkling Pinot Noir and Chardonnay wines.

Keeping grapes cold protects the delicate flavors. When the fruit is chilled, the grapes remain clean, crisp and fresh.

Warmth also changes the sugar composition of the grapes, promoting undesirable wild yeast fermentation.

Night picking is also better for the crews, to avoid work in the hot sun. They can work a lot faster and they're paid higher wages for working at night.

It's interesting because, unlike Chardonnay, Cabernet Sauvignon likes to be picked during the warm days, it brings out the rich flavors of the wine.

On this photo shoot it was magical doing photography at night with only the lights of the tractor to illuminate the way. I chose to do a romantic shot of a picker working without the lights and I got him silhouetted against the night sky with the stars shining.

It was also magical as the sun started to come up. The light was very different and very beautiful to shoot directly into the sun. I love the warm colors during the sunrise.

Another benefit was seeing the fog form across the landscape. The cool nights in Sonoma Valley, along with the hot days, brings another dimension to this region of the wine country.

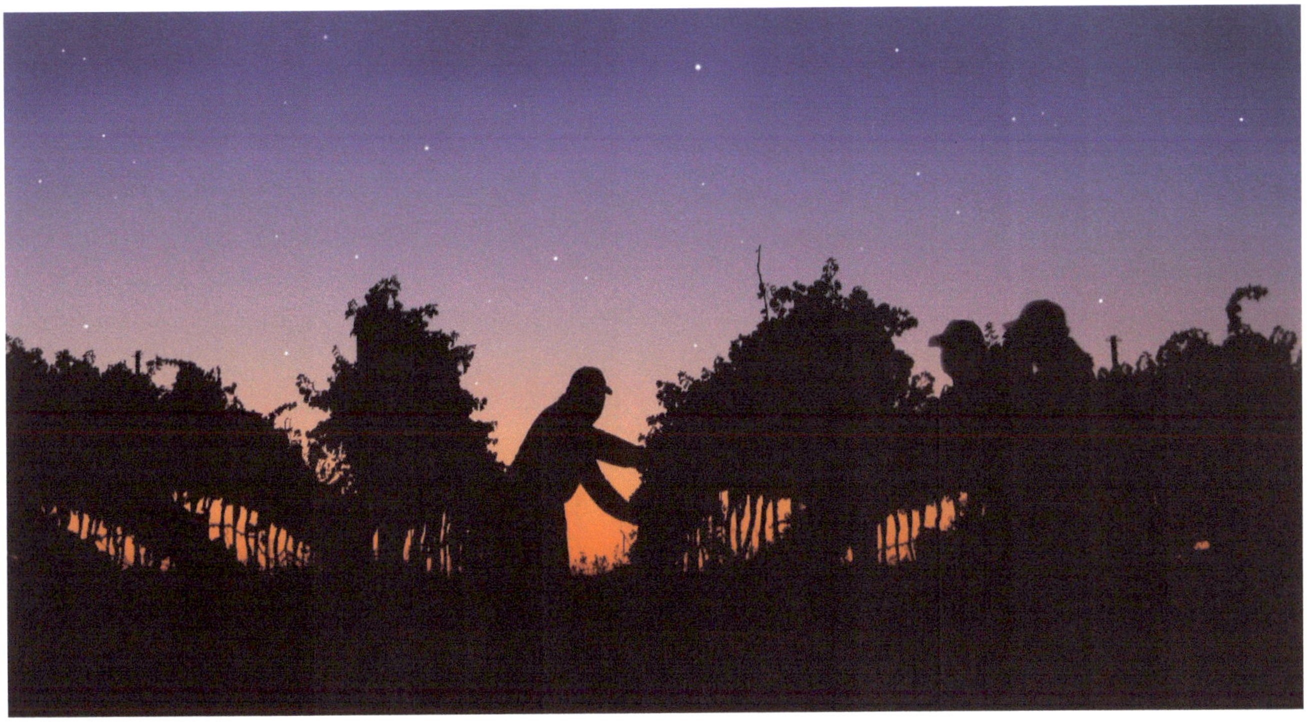

September 2009 364 Gloria Ferrer Winery Night Harvest

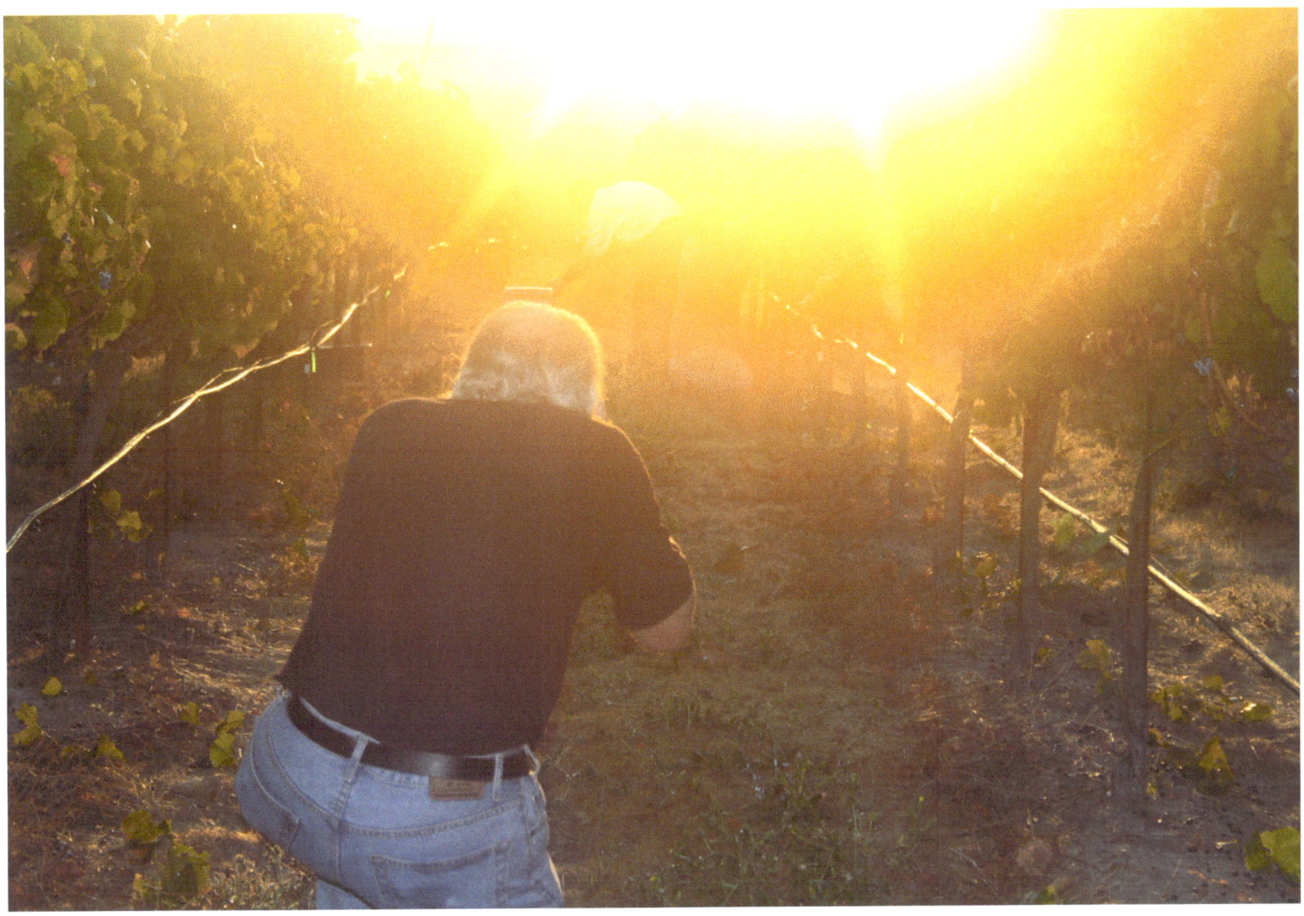

Will Chubb Photographing the Harvest Photo by Marie Gewirtz

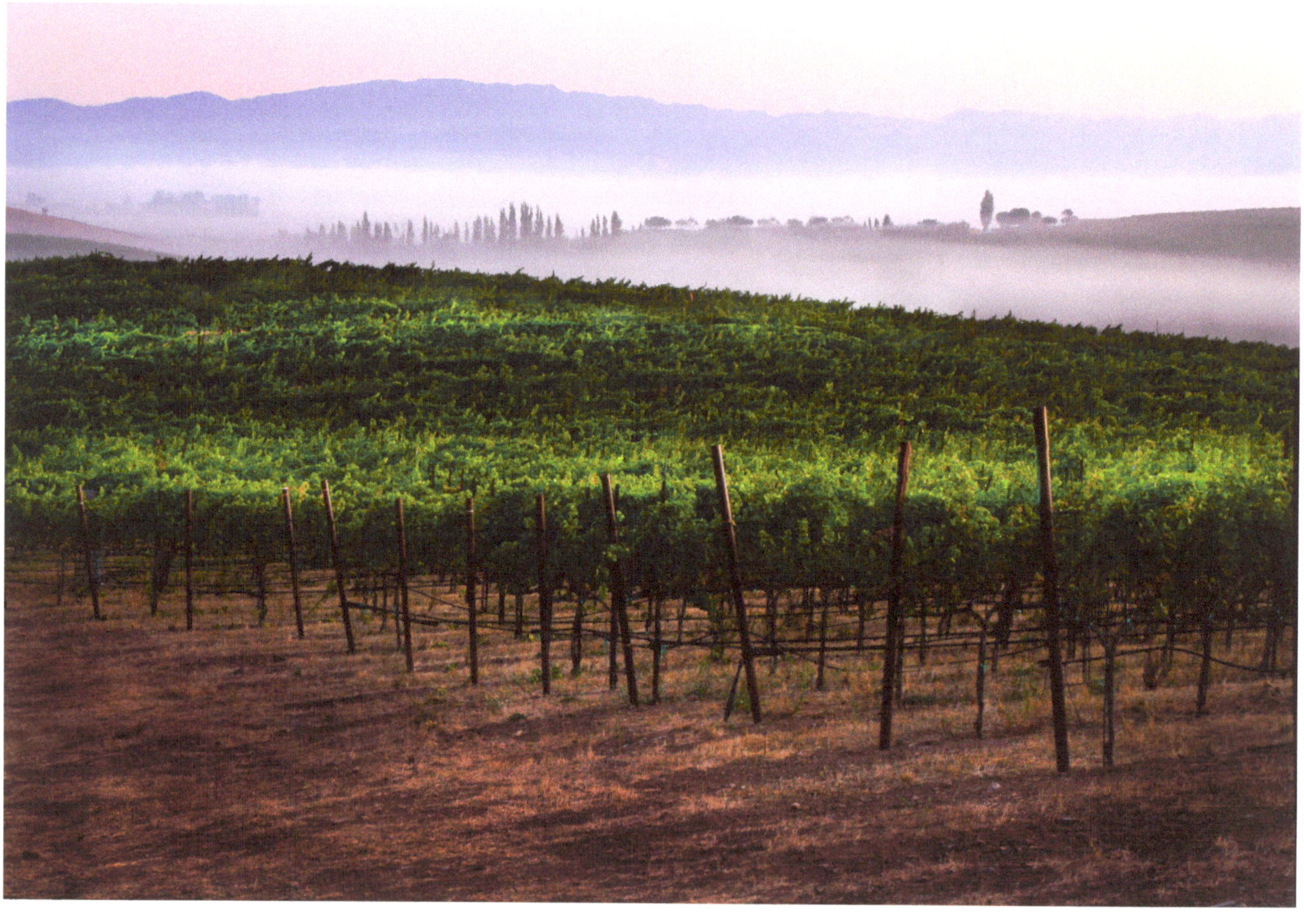

September 2009 361 Gloria Ferrer Vineyard

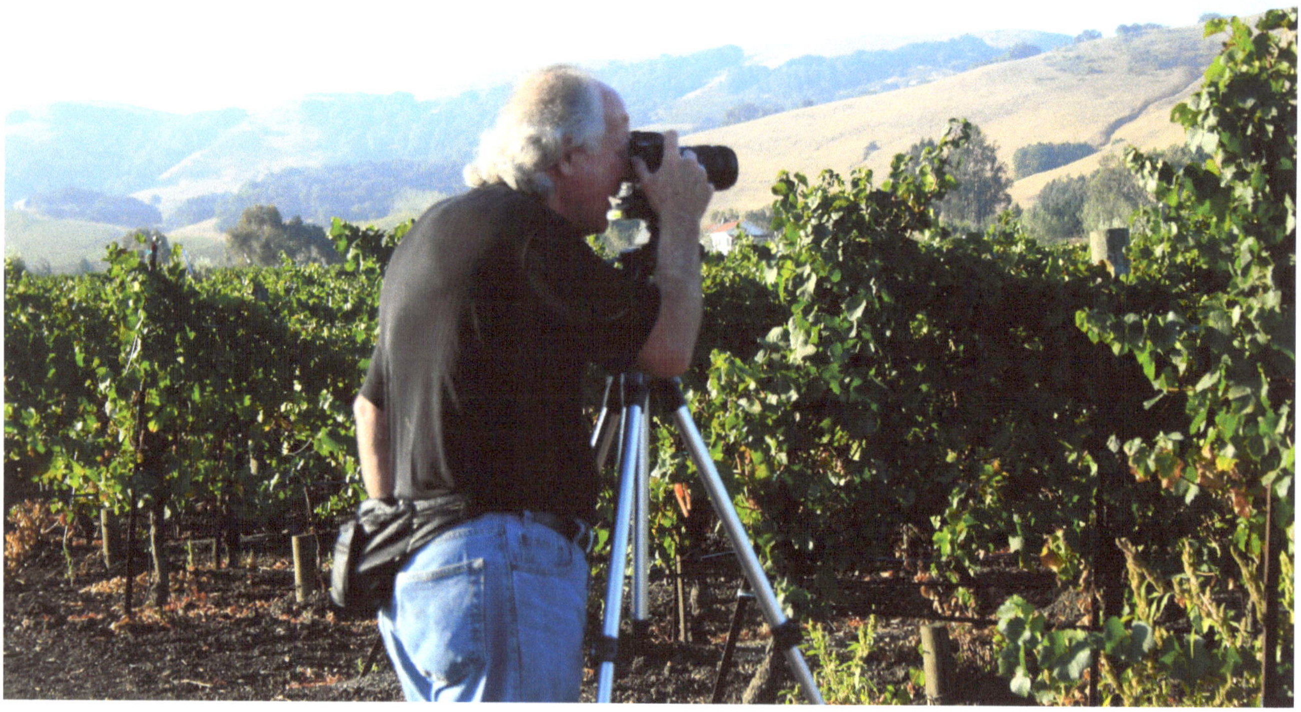

Will Chubb Photographing Photo by Marie Gewirtz

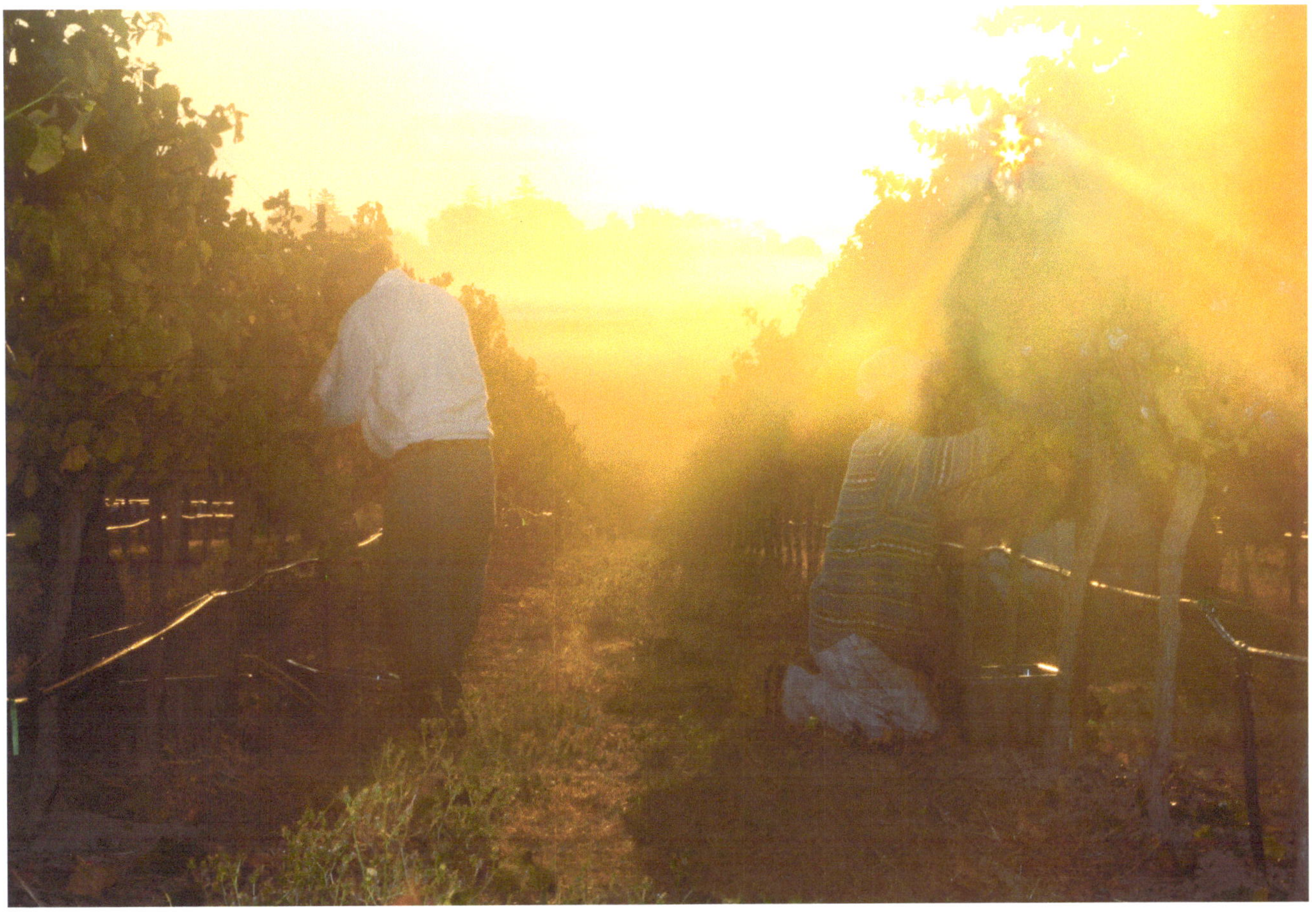

September 2009 363 Sunrise at Gloria Ferrer Night Harvest

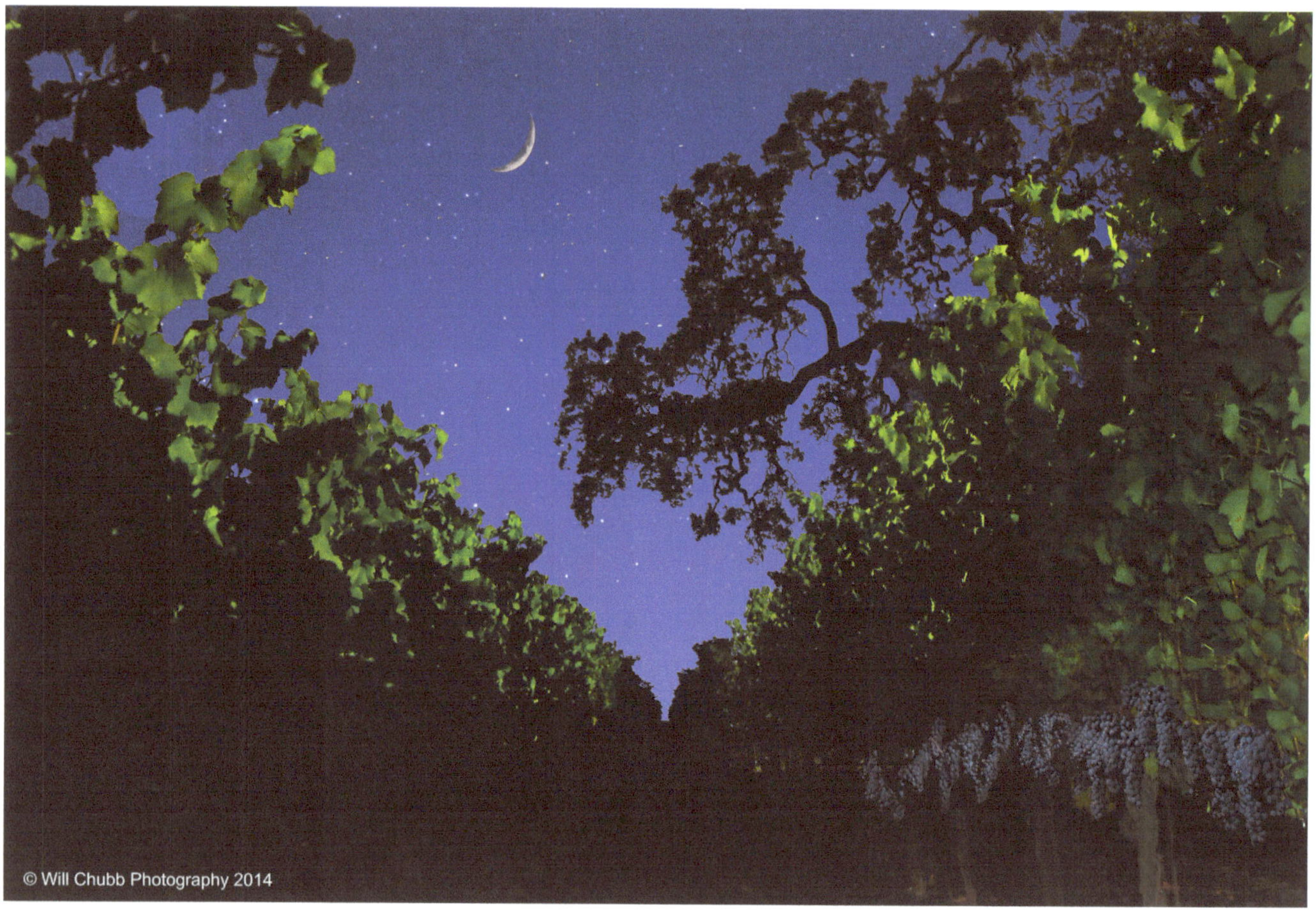

August 2014 **369 Vineyard at Night**

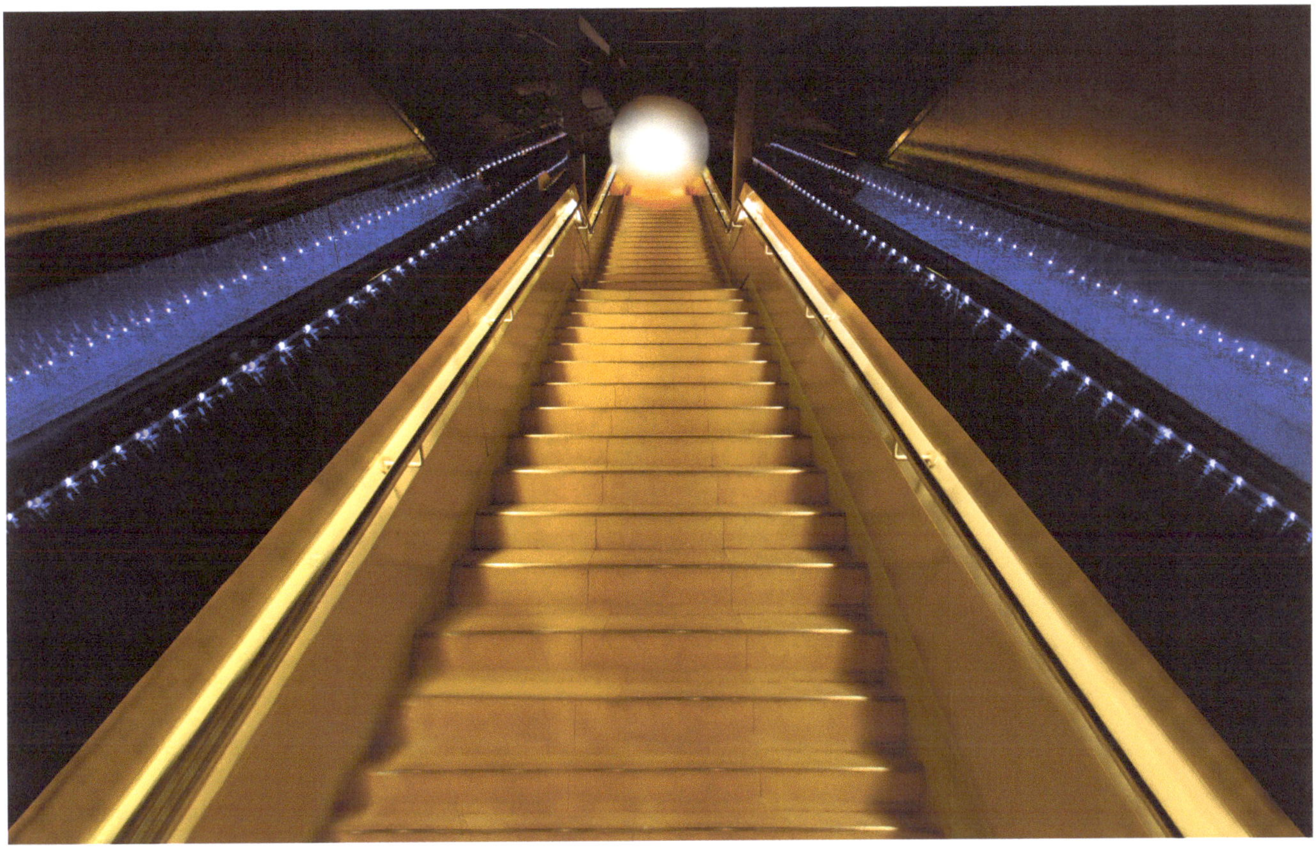

April 2012 327 Stairway to Heaven

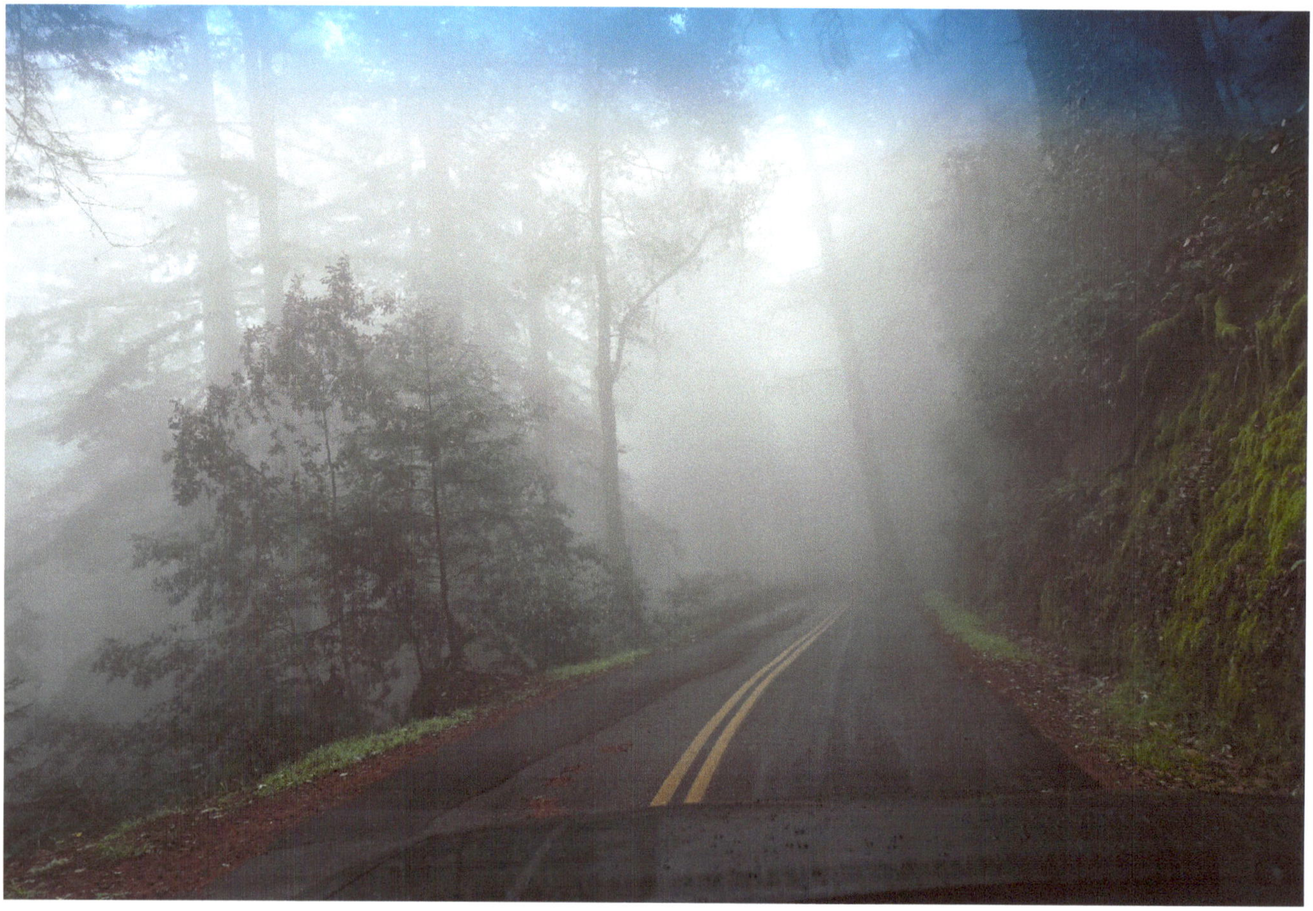

February 2018 274 Mt Tamalpais, Marin County, CA

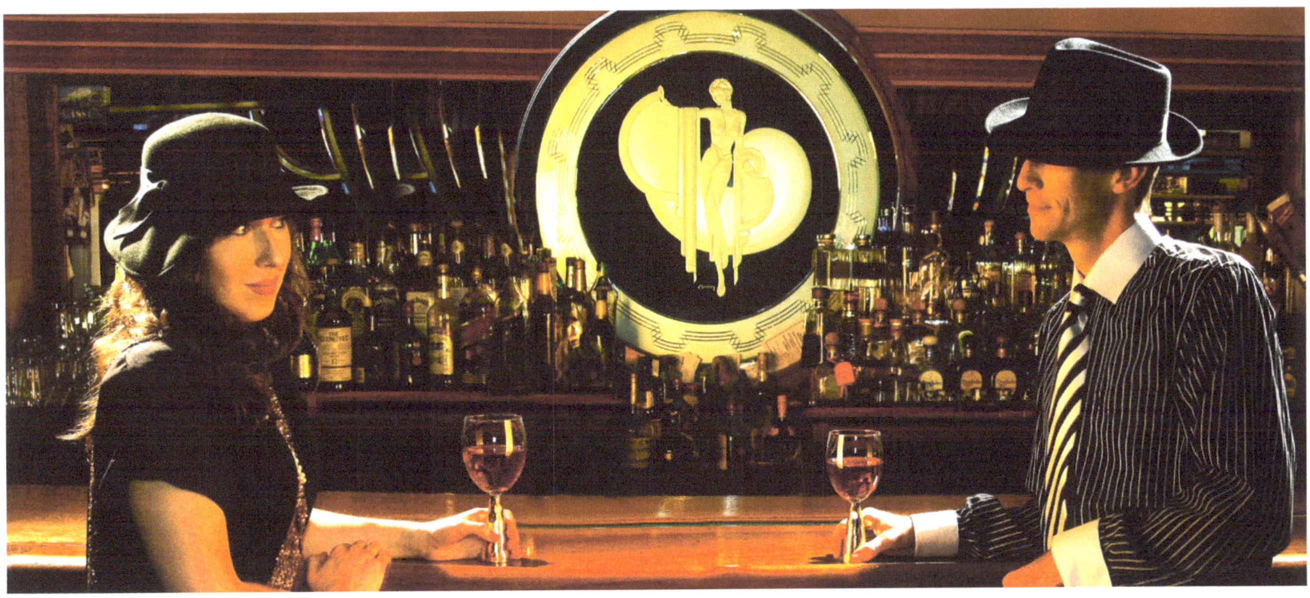

August 2011

275 the Look

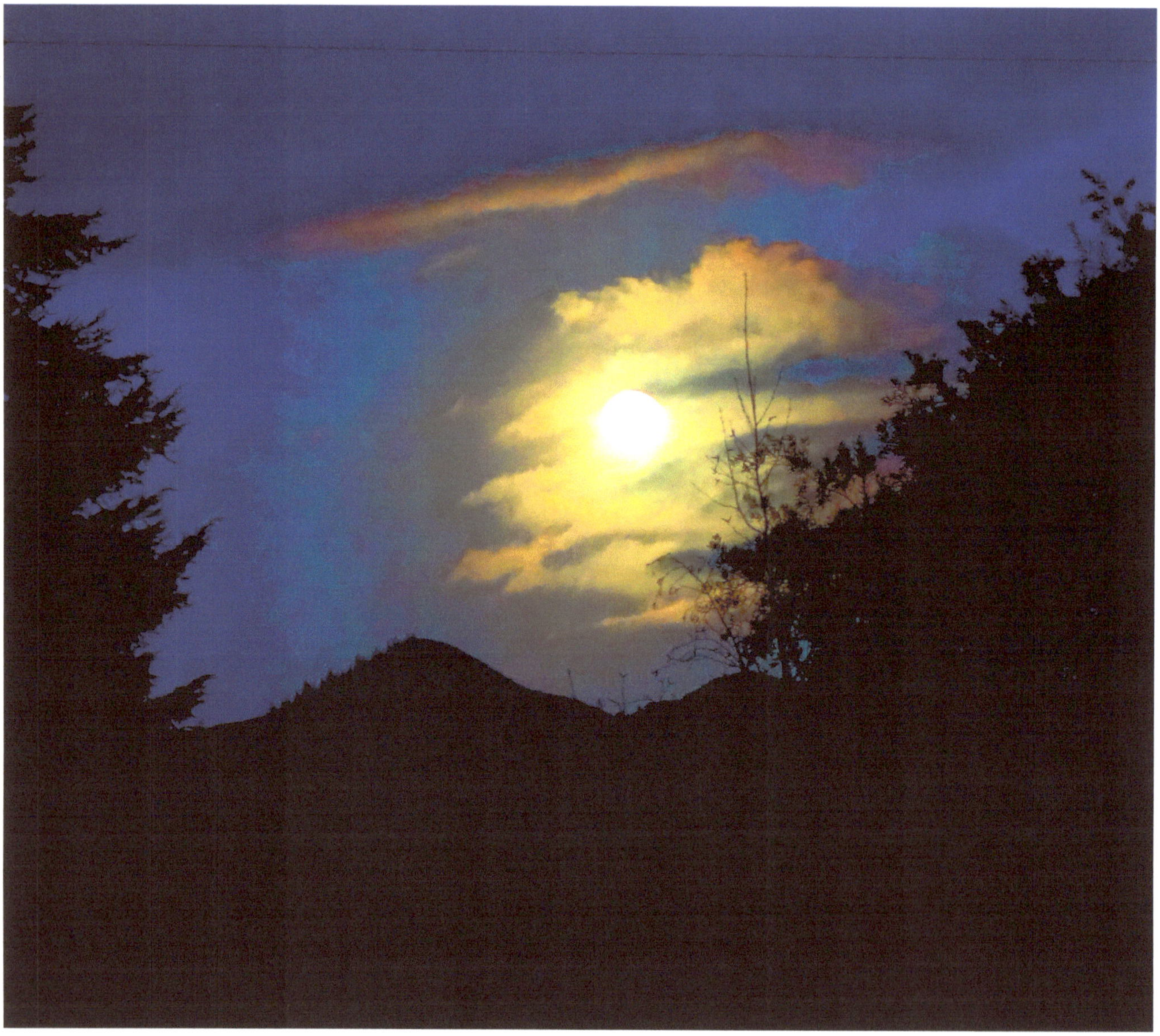

February 2019 **276 Moonrise Spring Lake Park, Santa Rosa, CA**

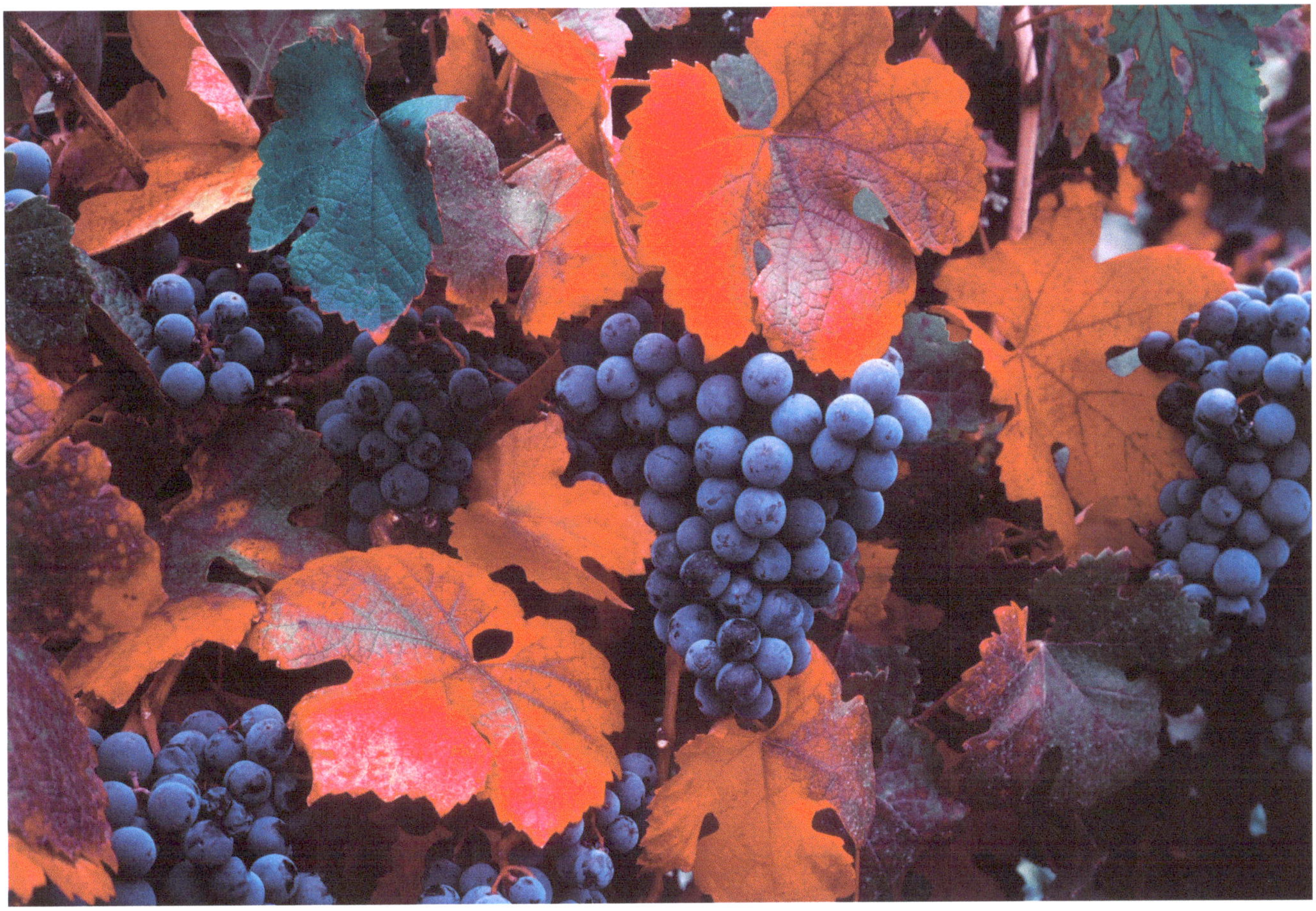

October 1977

120 Fall Colors

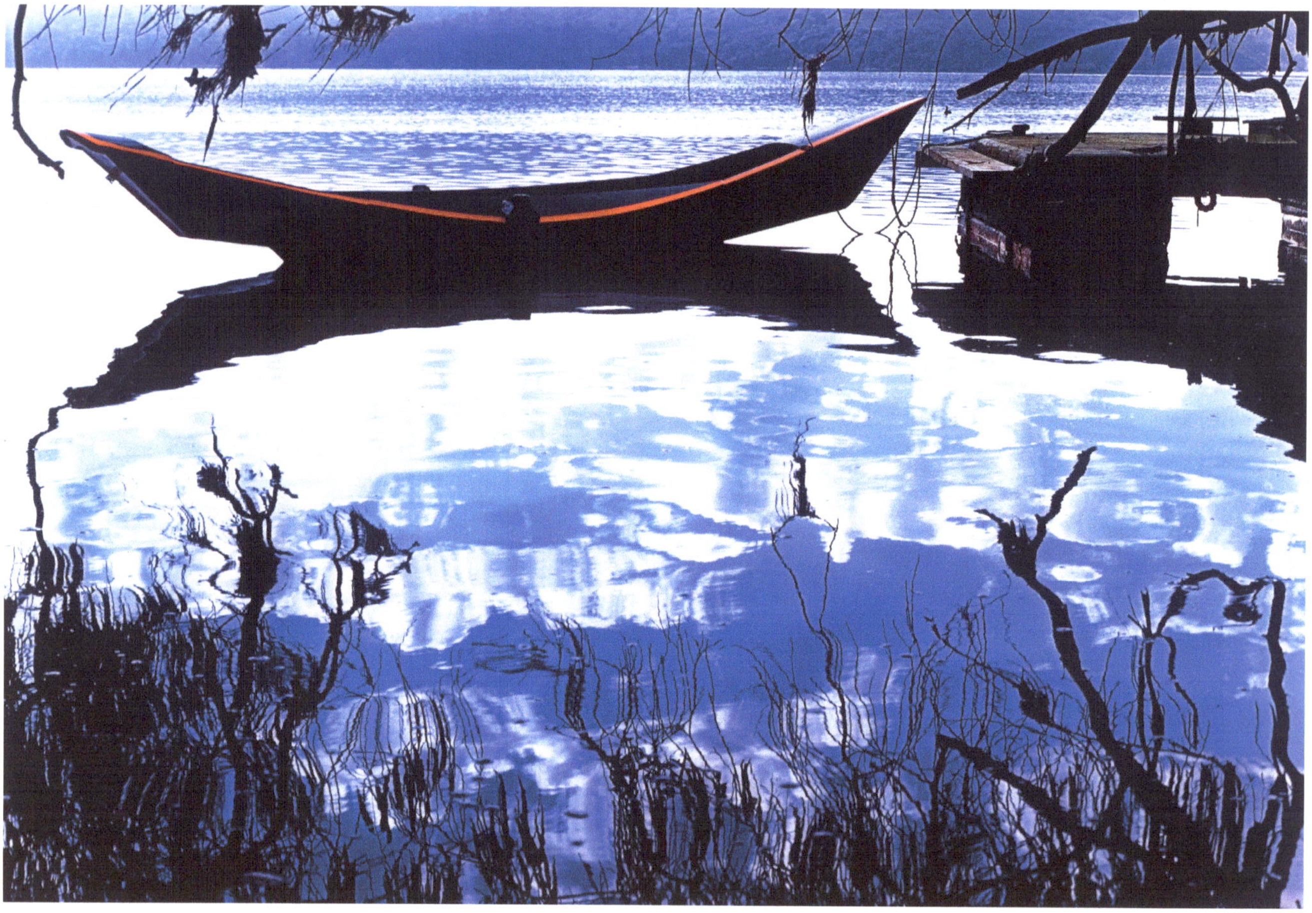

1981 Tomales Bay, Marin County **115 Blue Boat**

1988 Sonoma Coast, CA 141 Sailing into Sunset

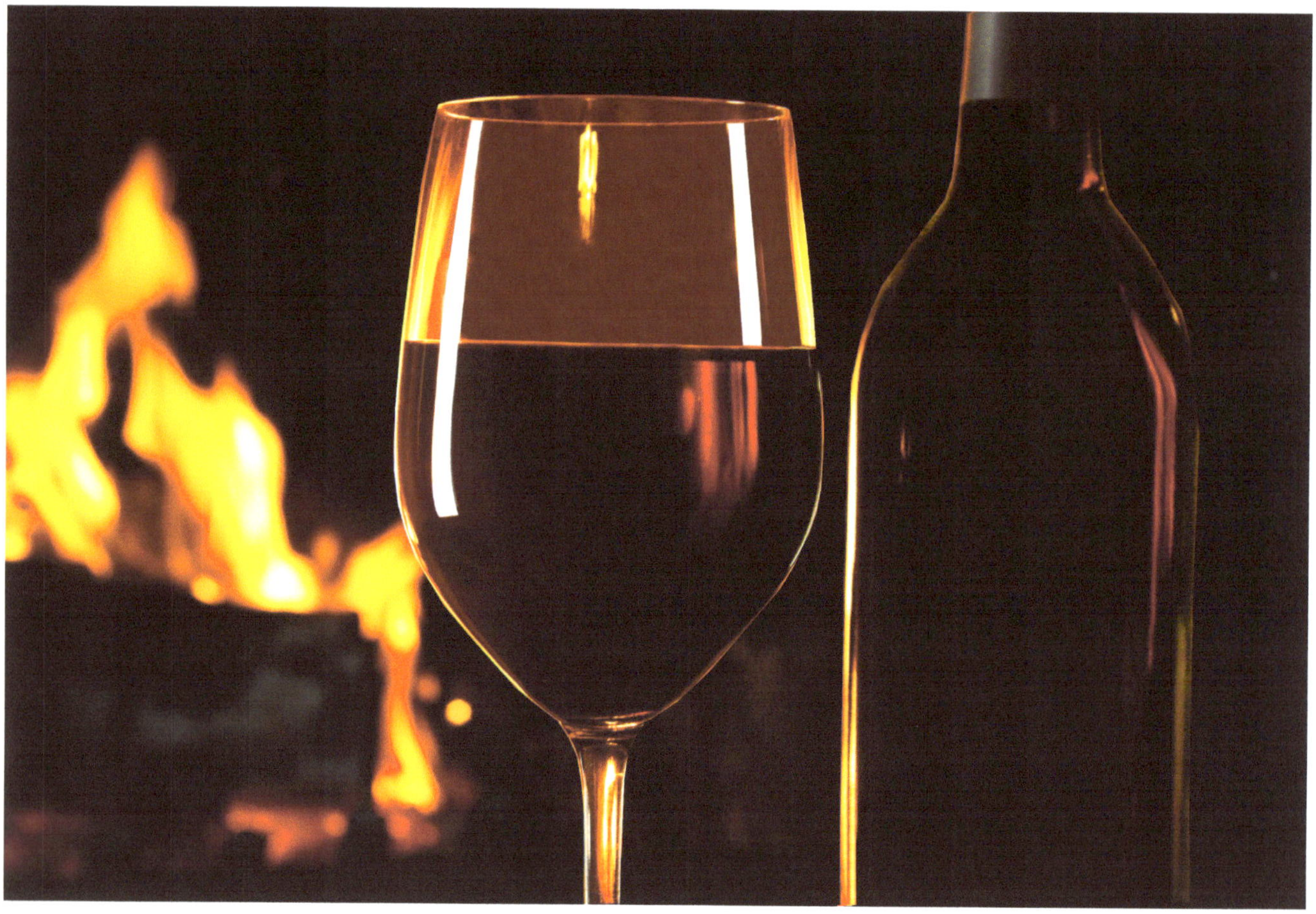

December 2009

332 Wine by the Fire

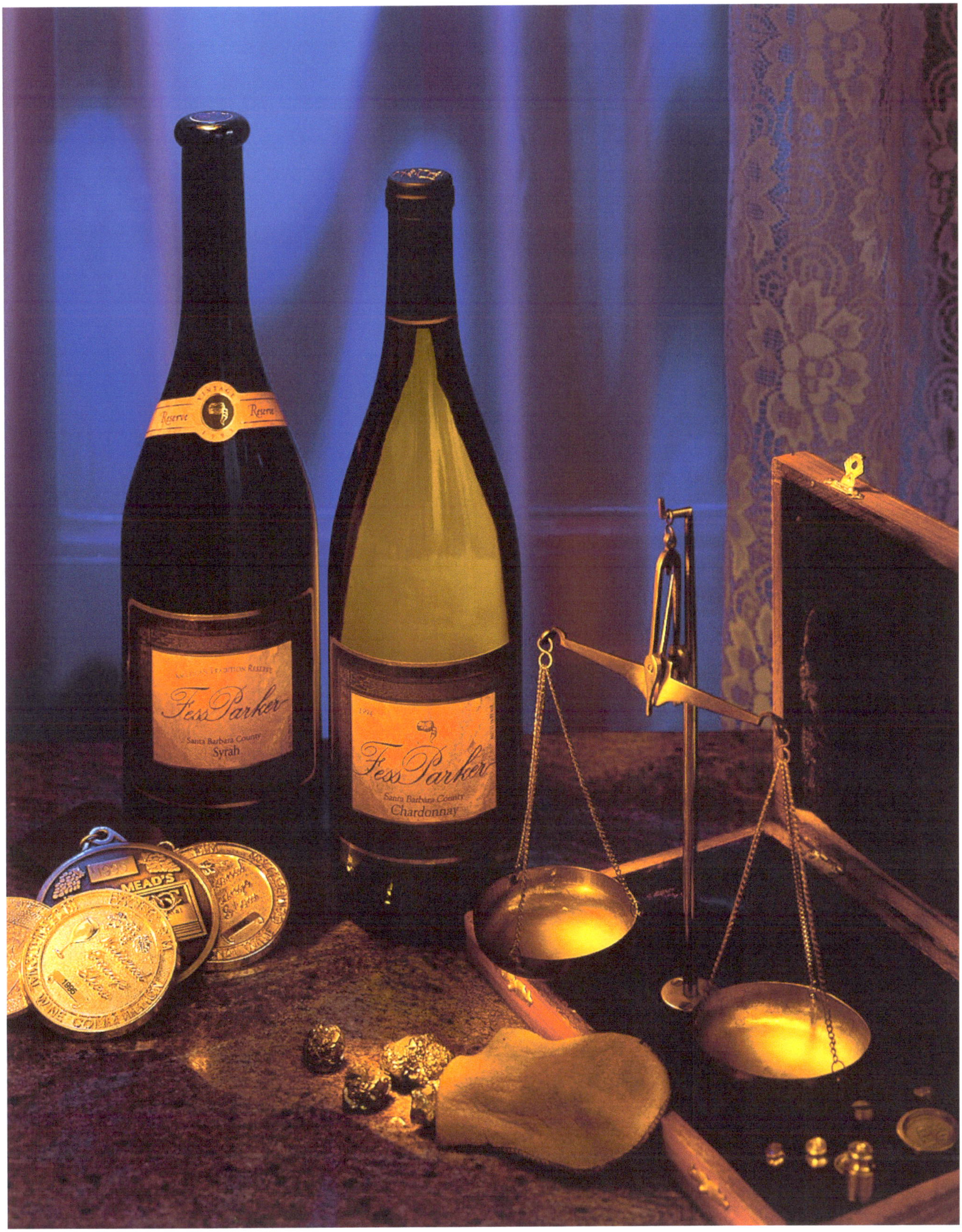

1991 277 Fess Parker Wines

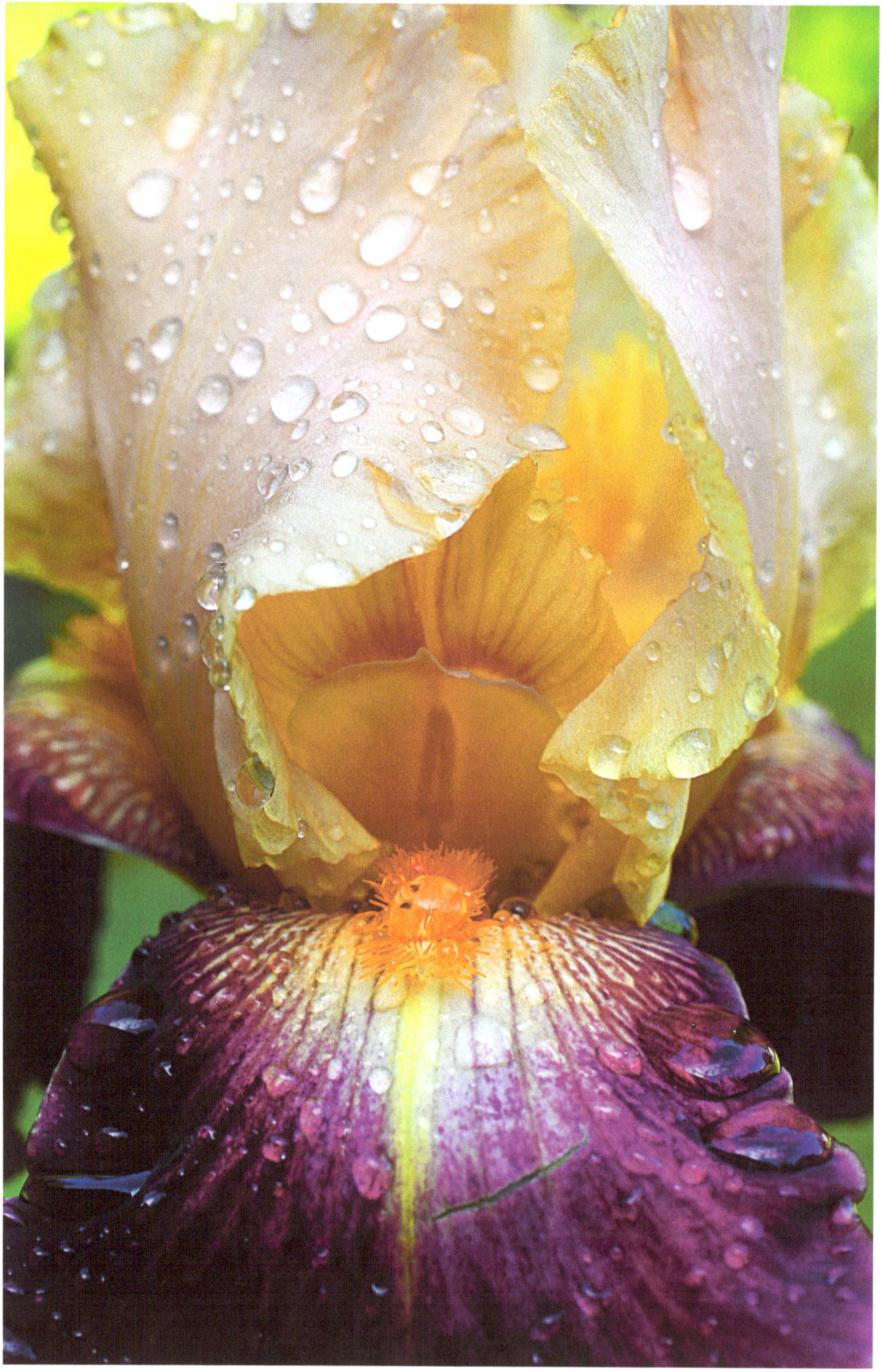

1988 286 Exotic Flower

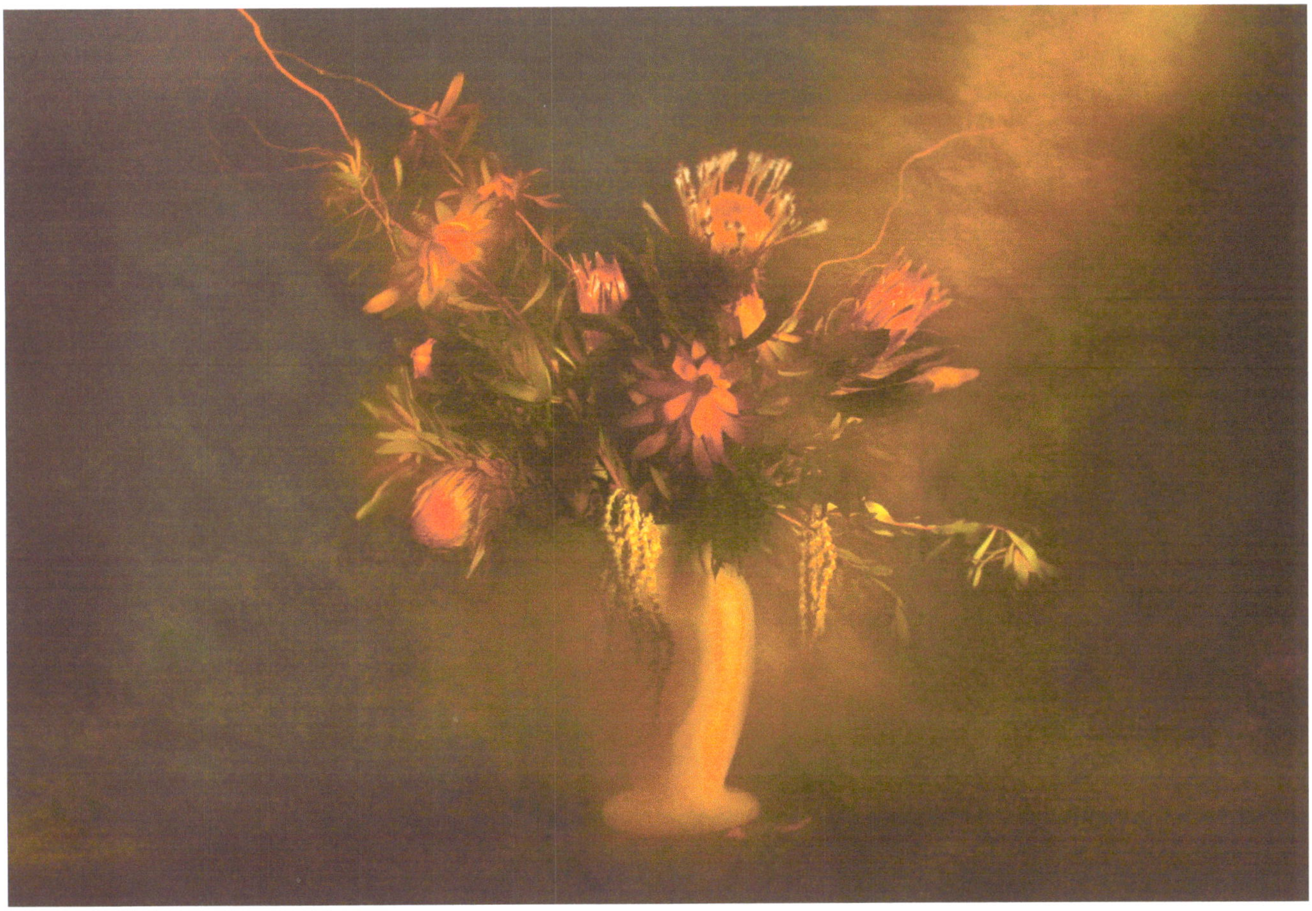

1987 183 Bouquet in the Light

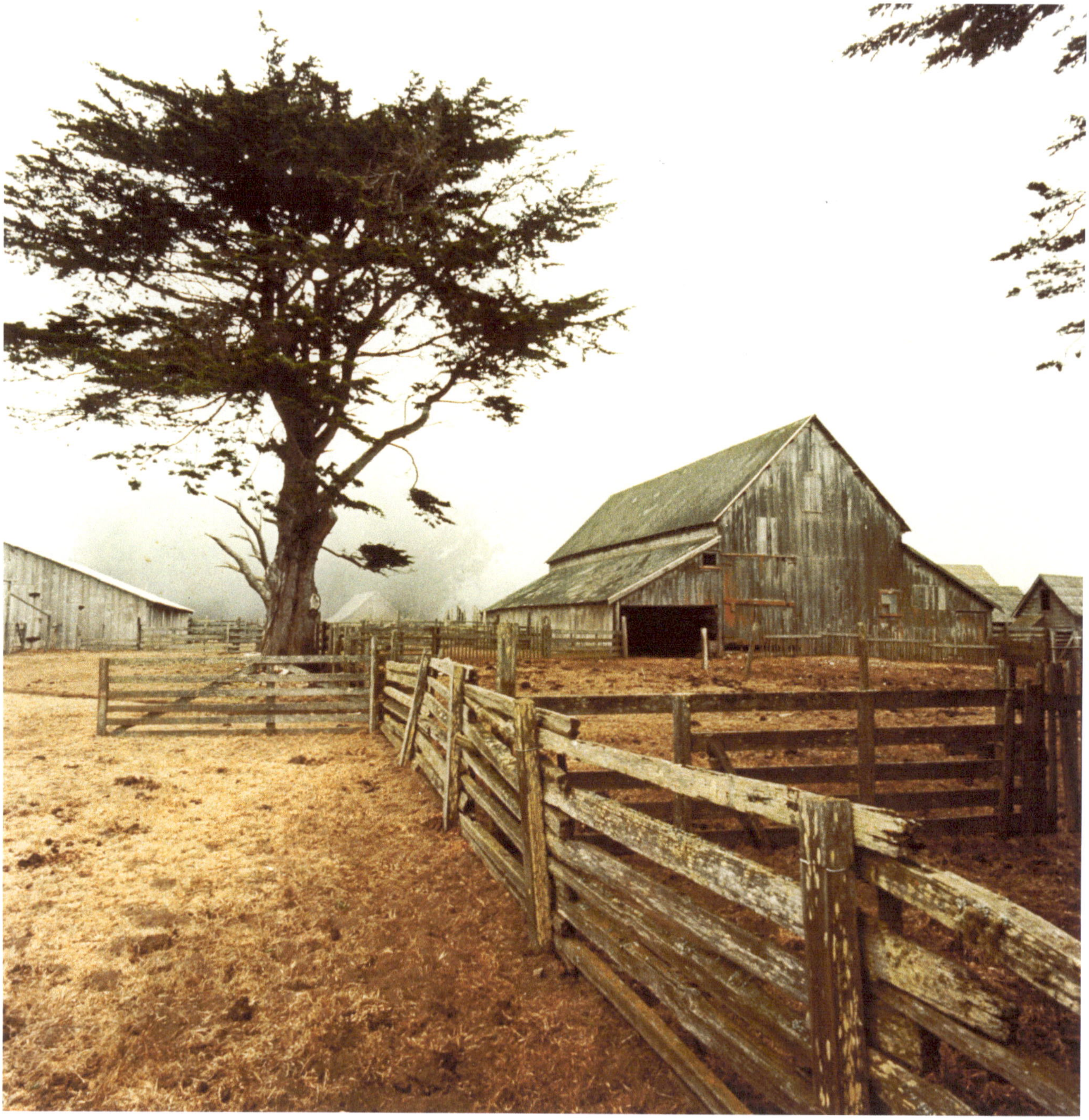

1977 222 Old Mendocino Barn

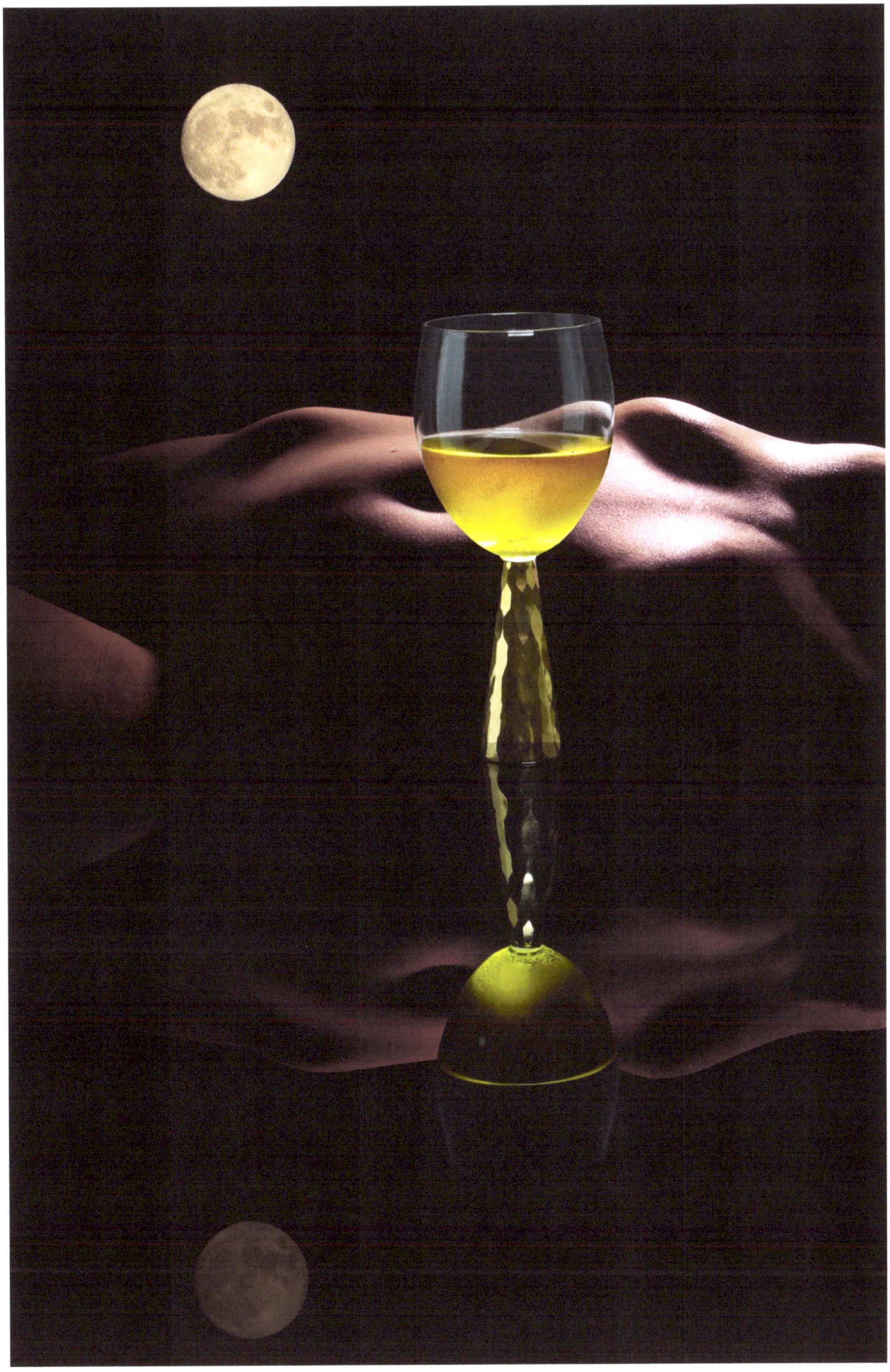

August 2011 **301 Wine & Nude with Moon**

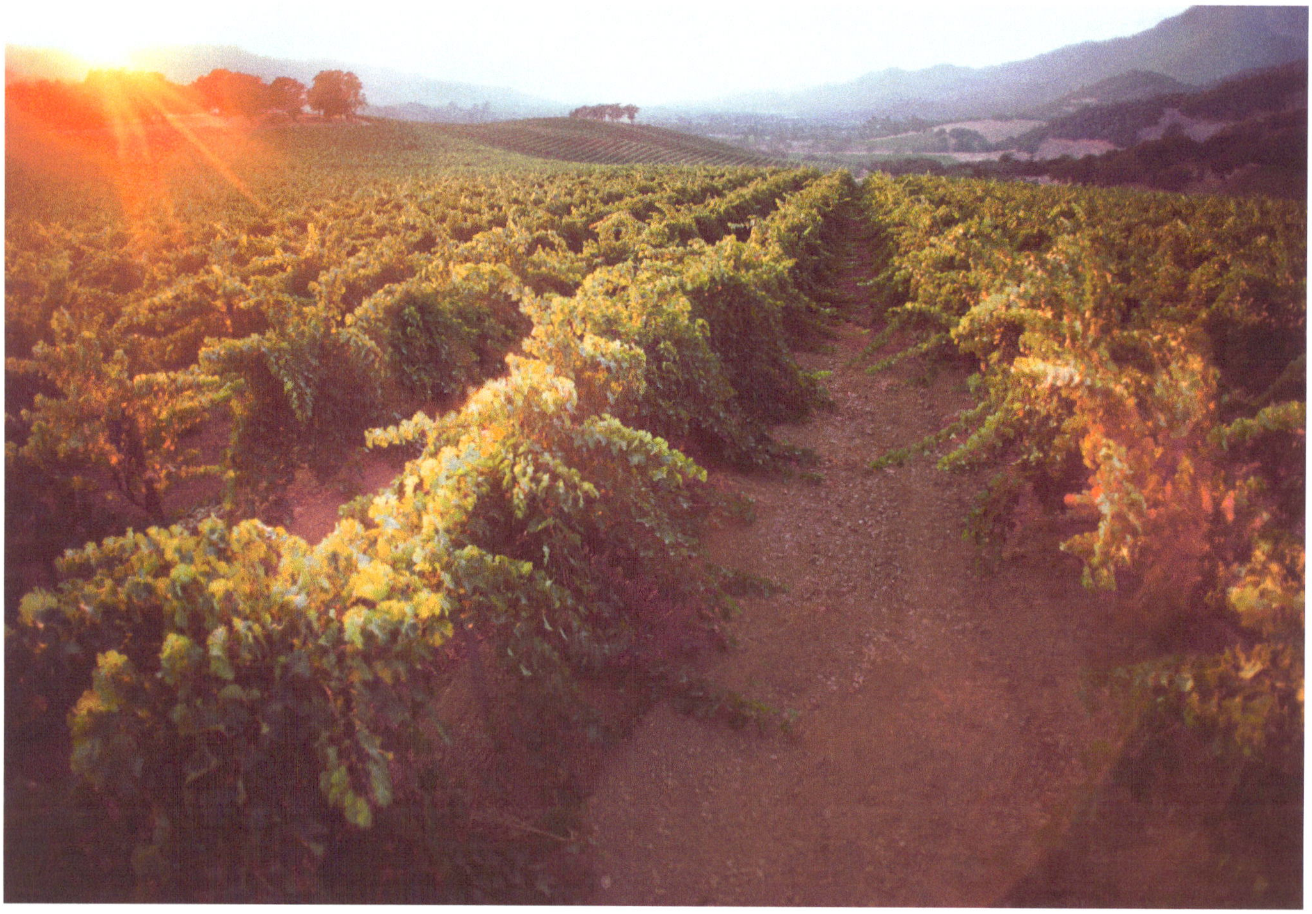

August 1978 122 Kunde Vineyard at sunrise, Kenwood, CA

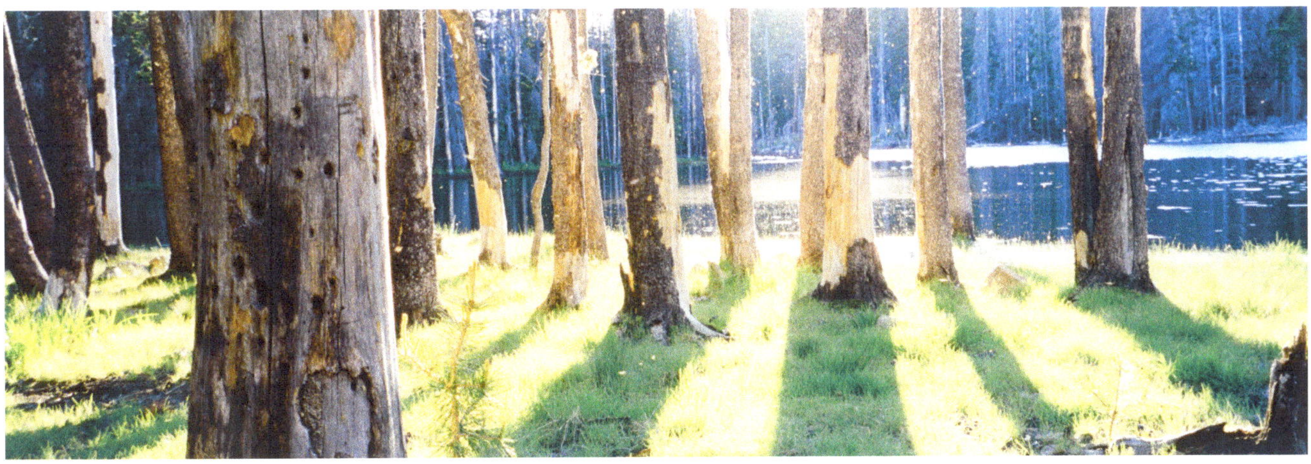

September 1999 **278 Thousand Lakes Wilderness**

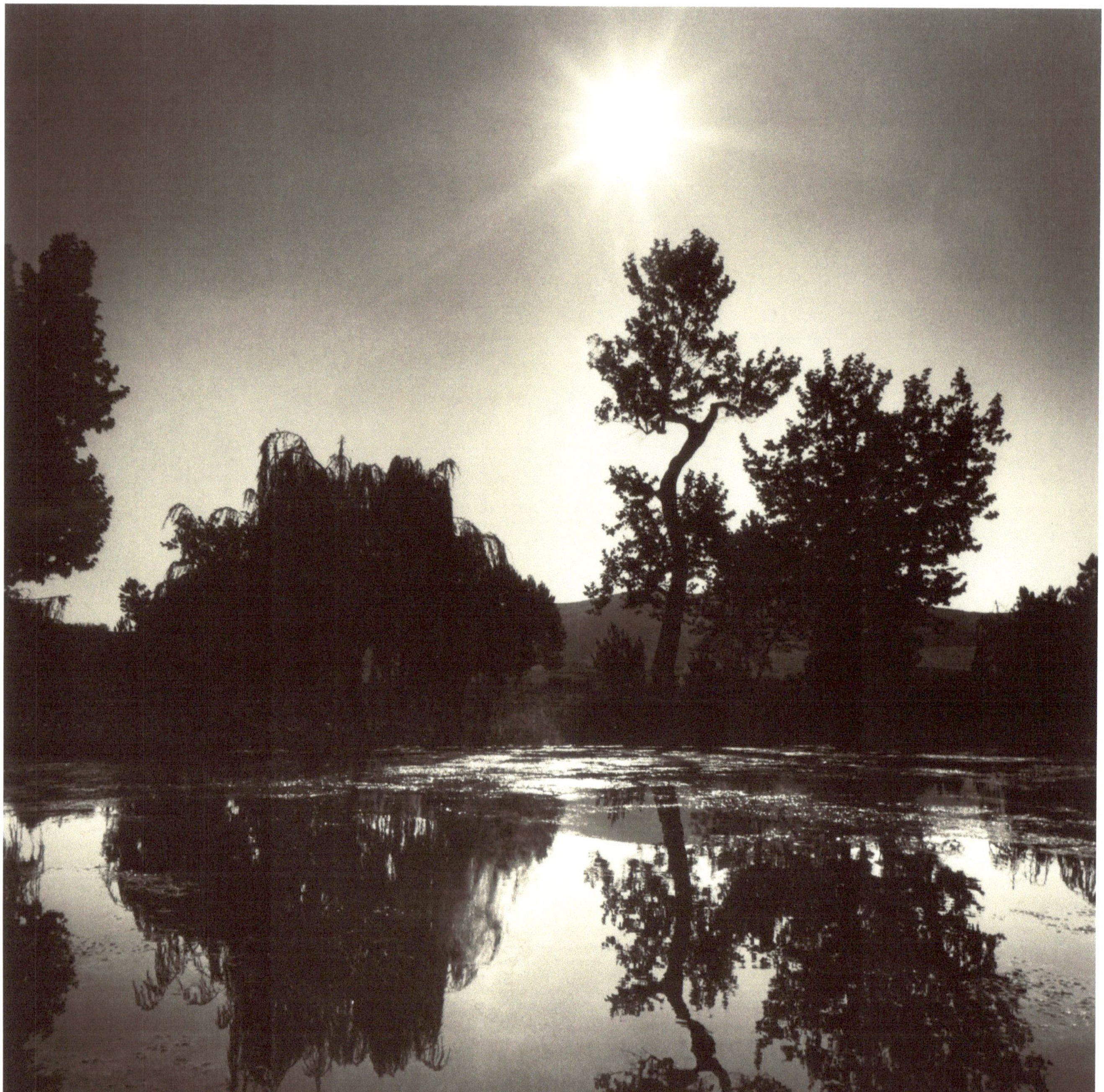

1969 279 Lagoon

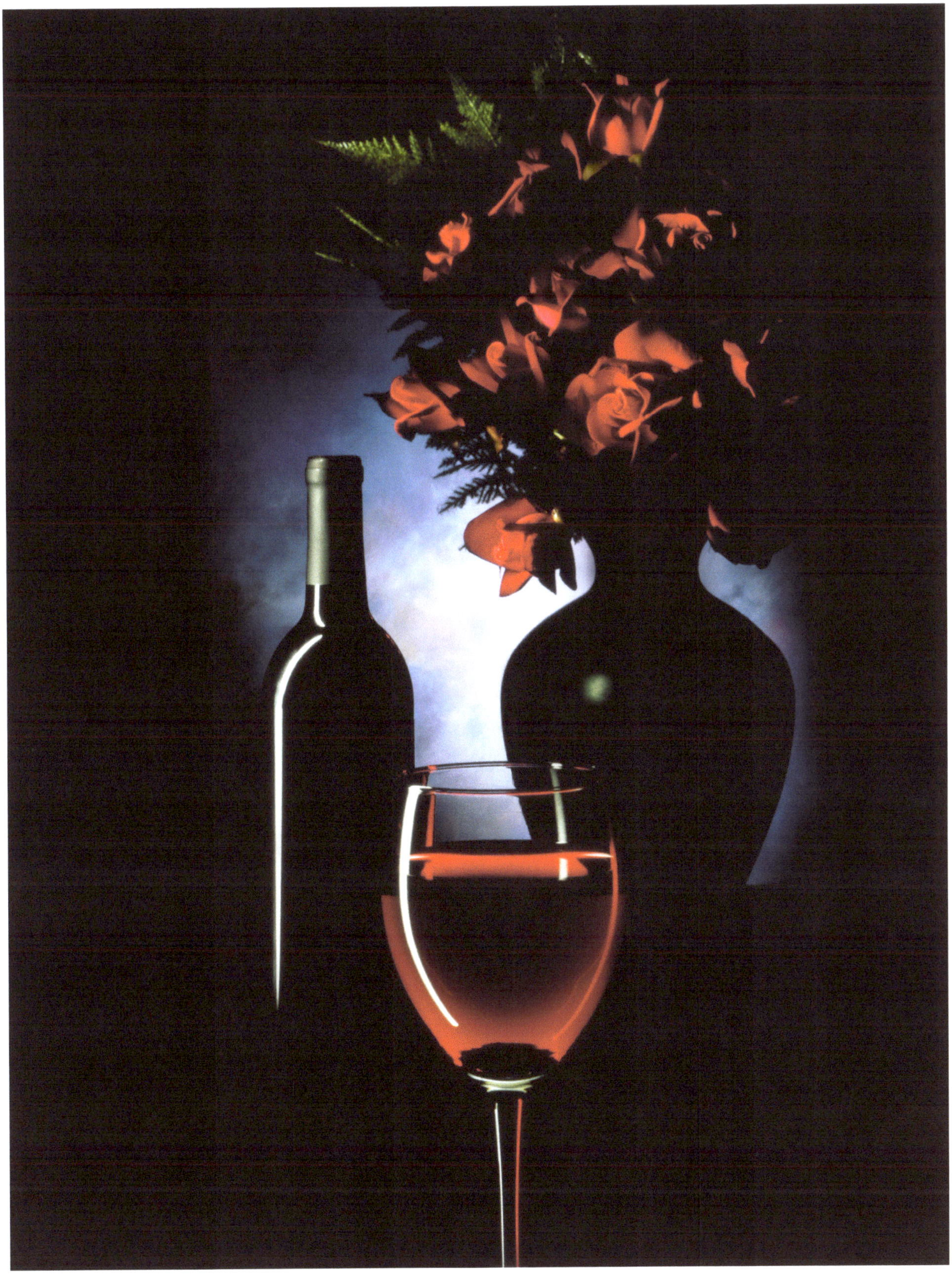

1987 175 Geyser Peak Winery Poster

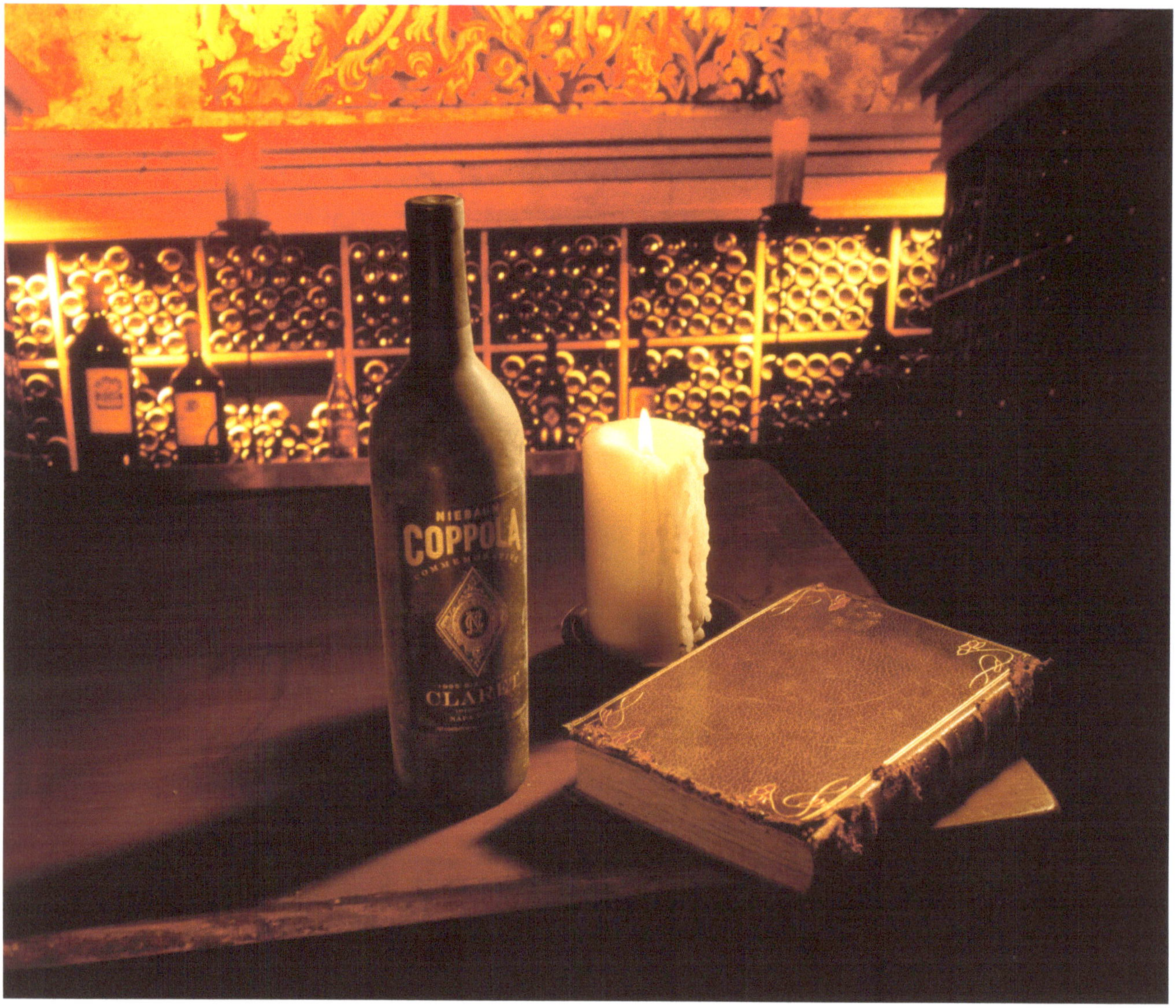

September 2005 179 Francis Ford Coppola's Wine Cellar

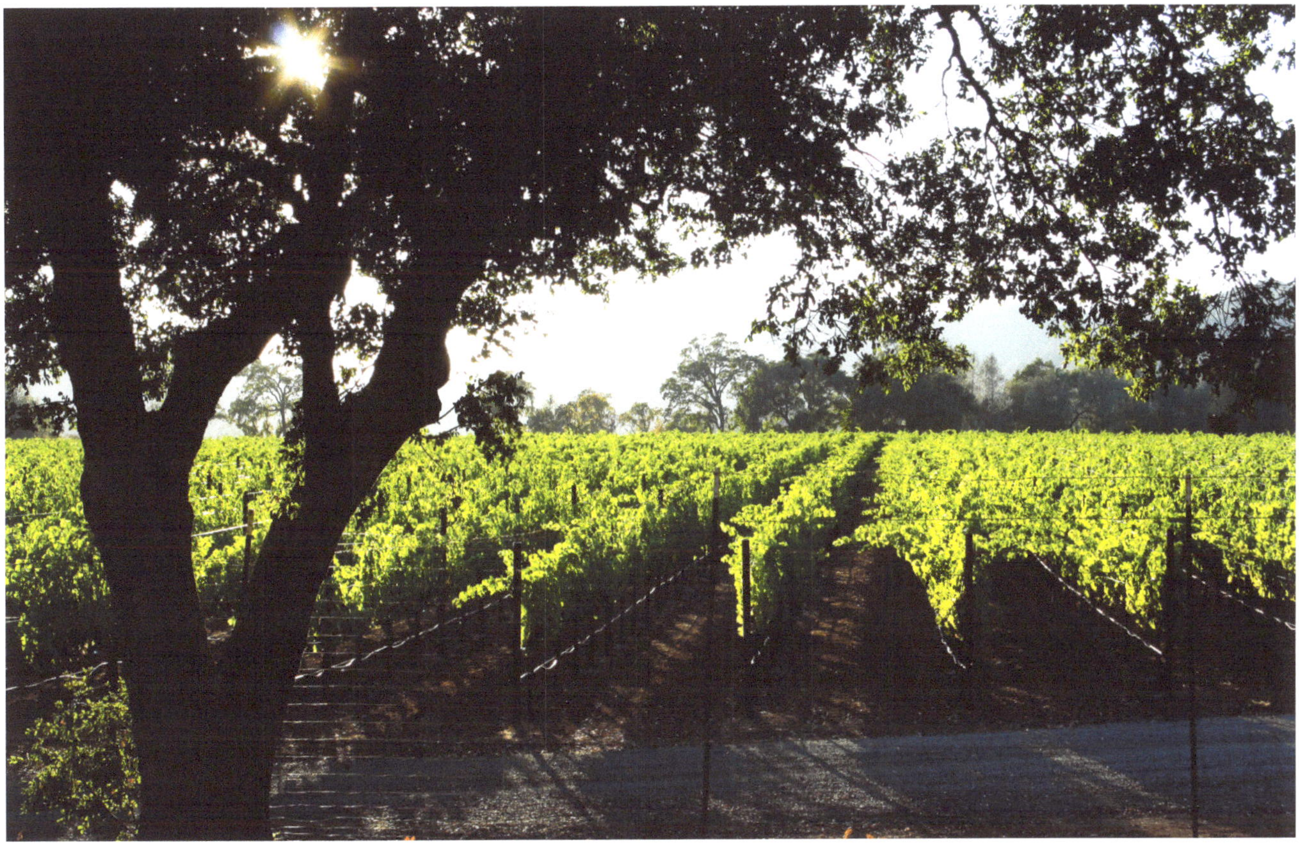

July 2009 303 Vines & Sun, Napa

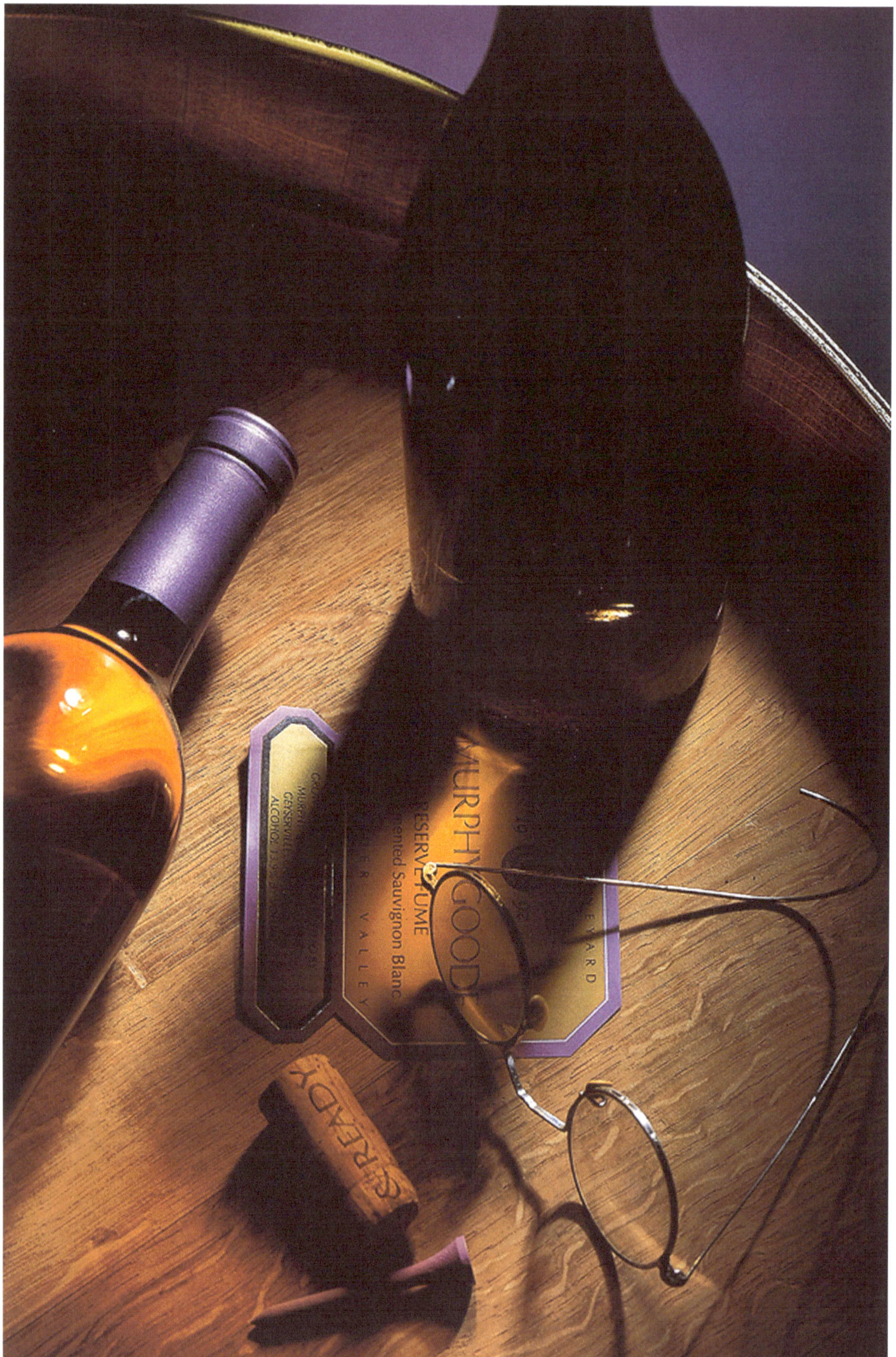

March 2009 **280 Murphy-Goode Winery Poster**

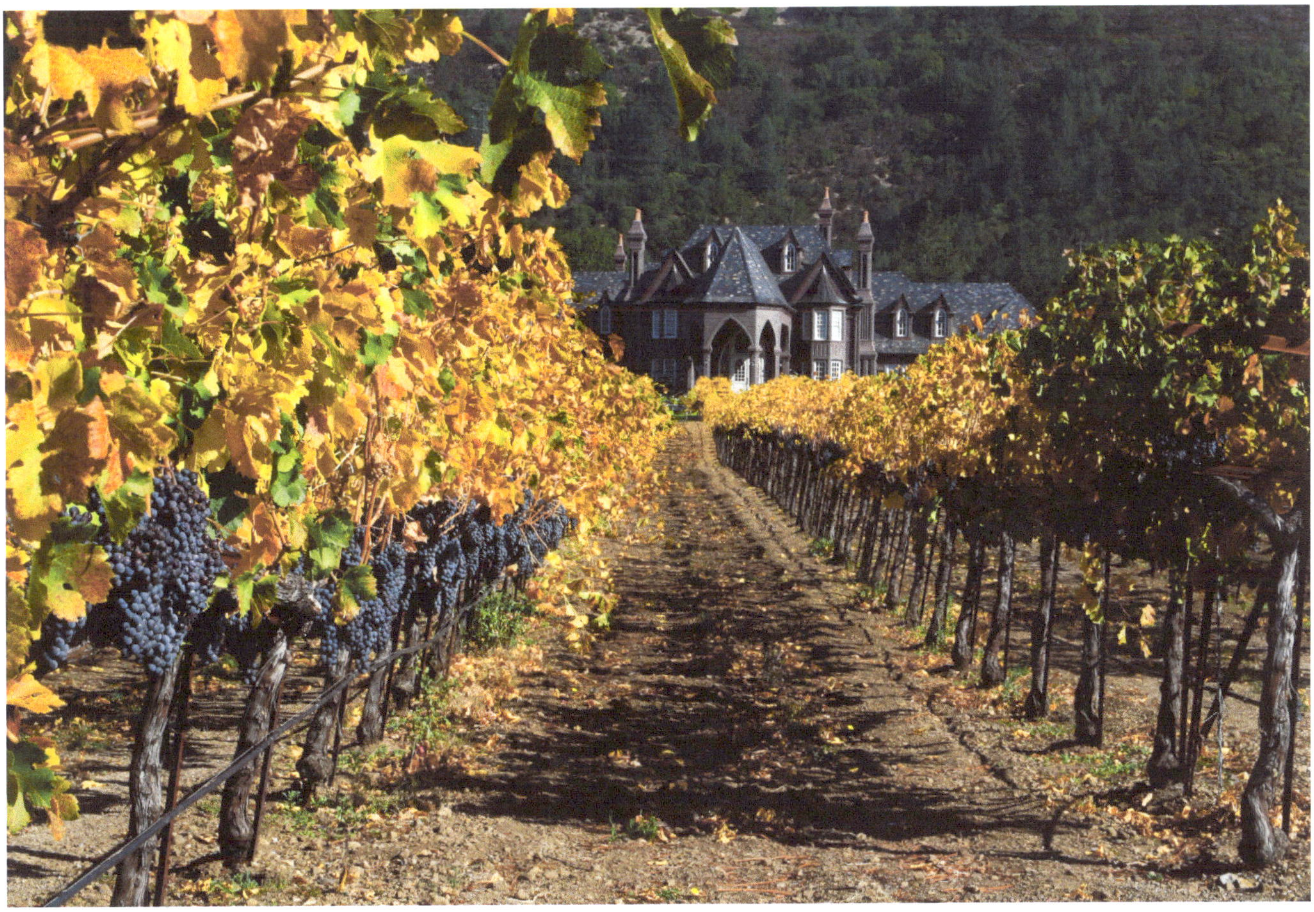

September 2011 282 Ledson Winery Highway 12, Kenwood, CA

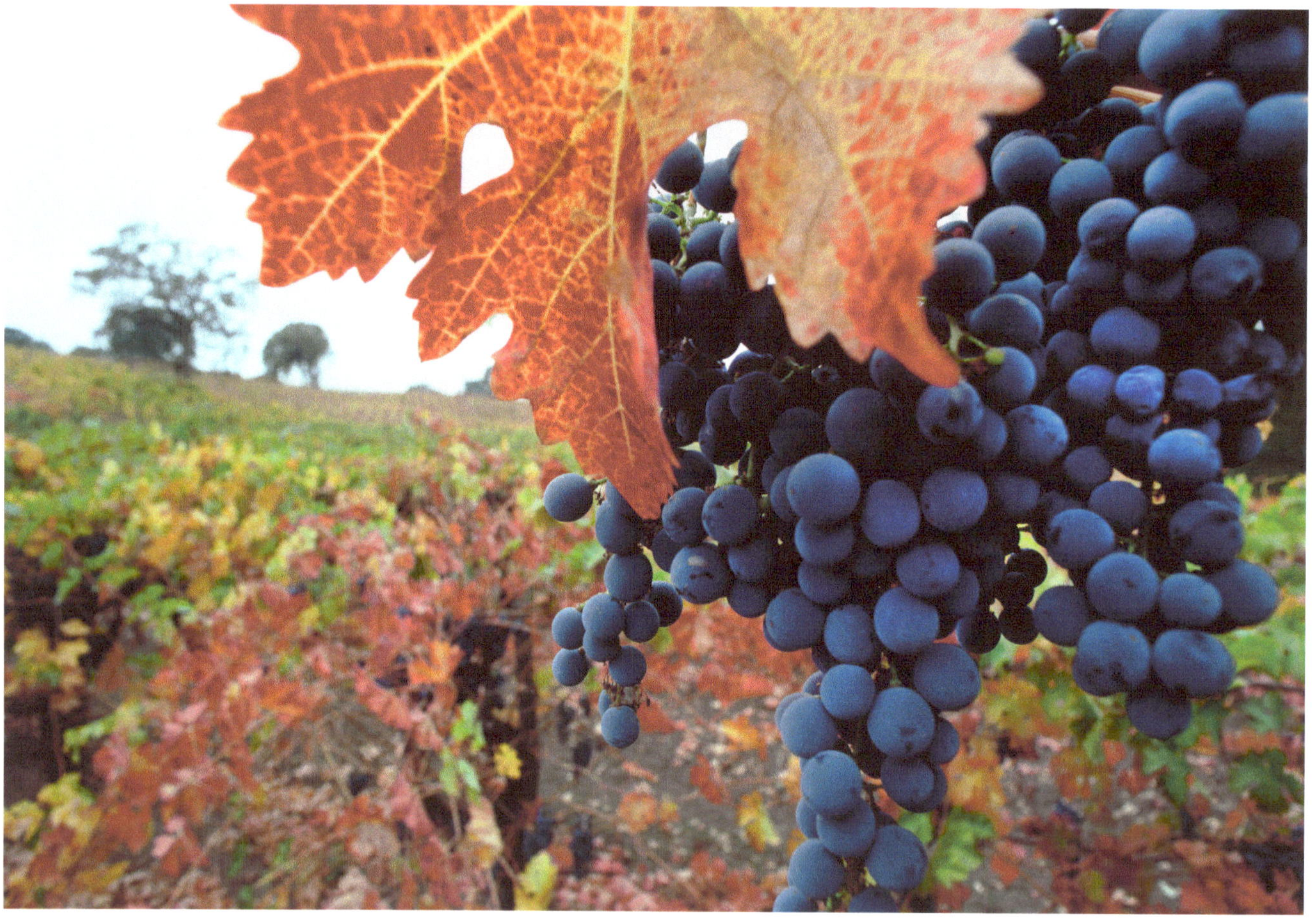

October 2001 110 Harvest Time, B.R. Cohn's Winery

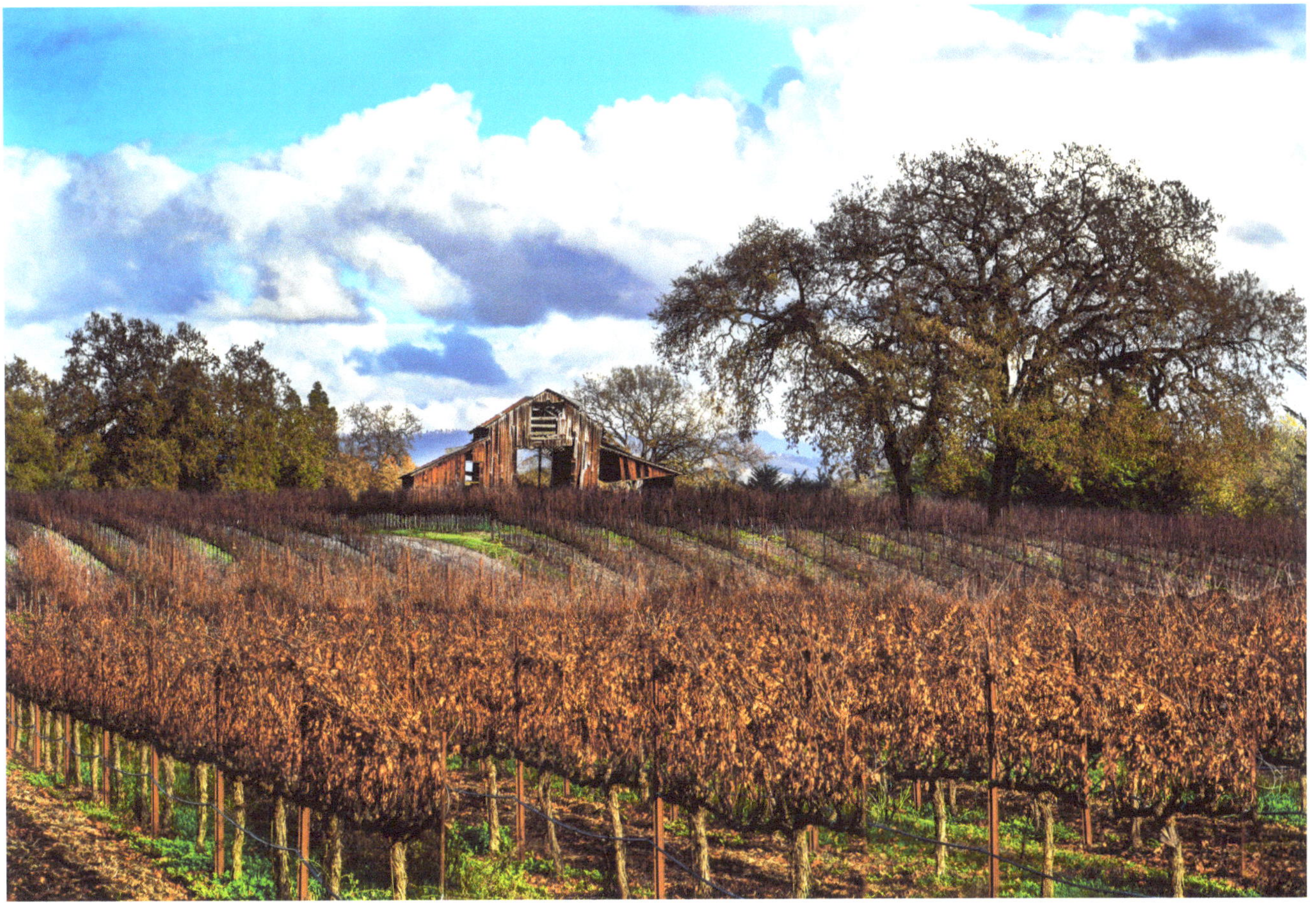

October 2018 281 Old Barn Slusser Road, Sonoma County, CA

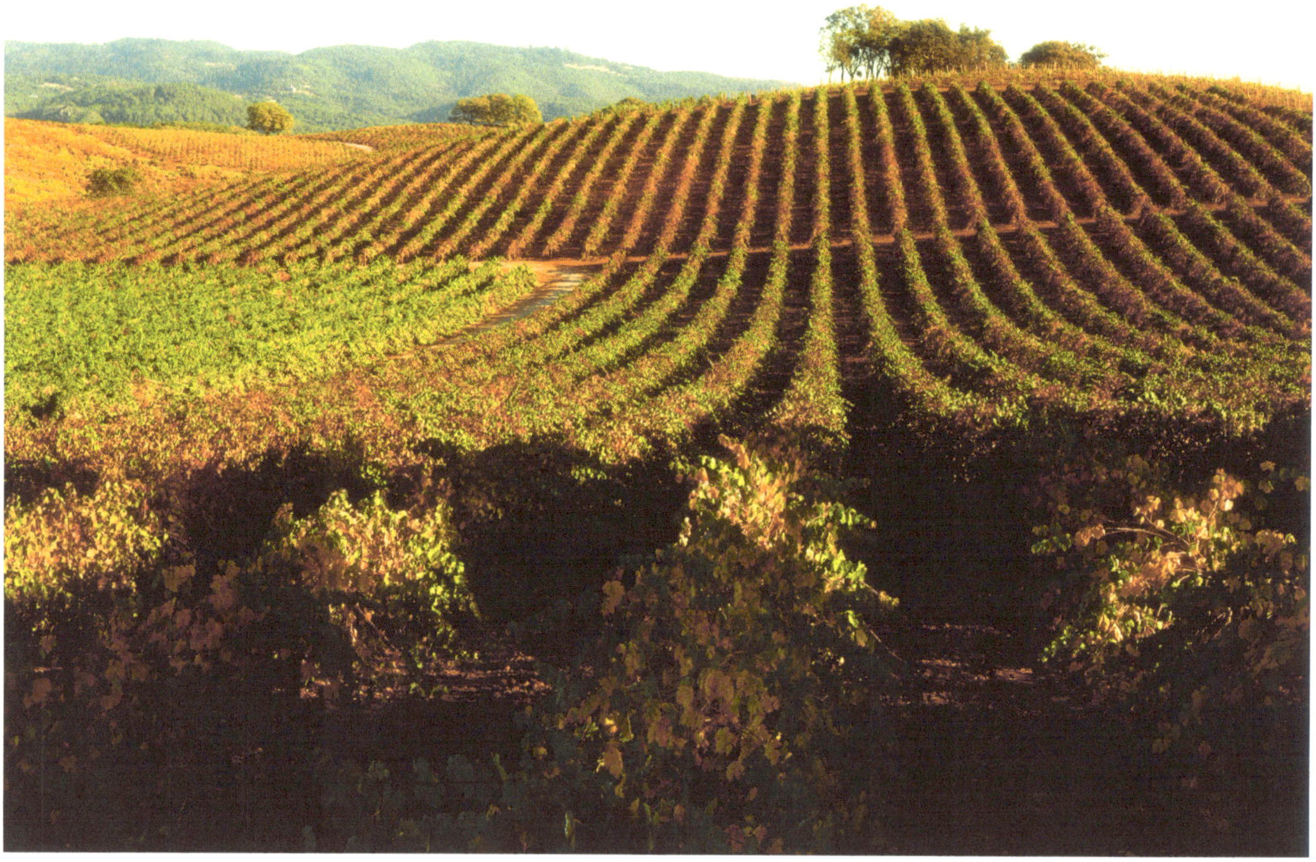

October 1997 134 Kunde Vineyards, Kenwood, CA

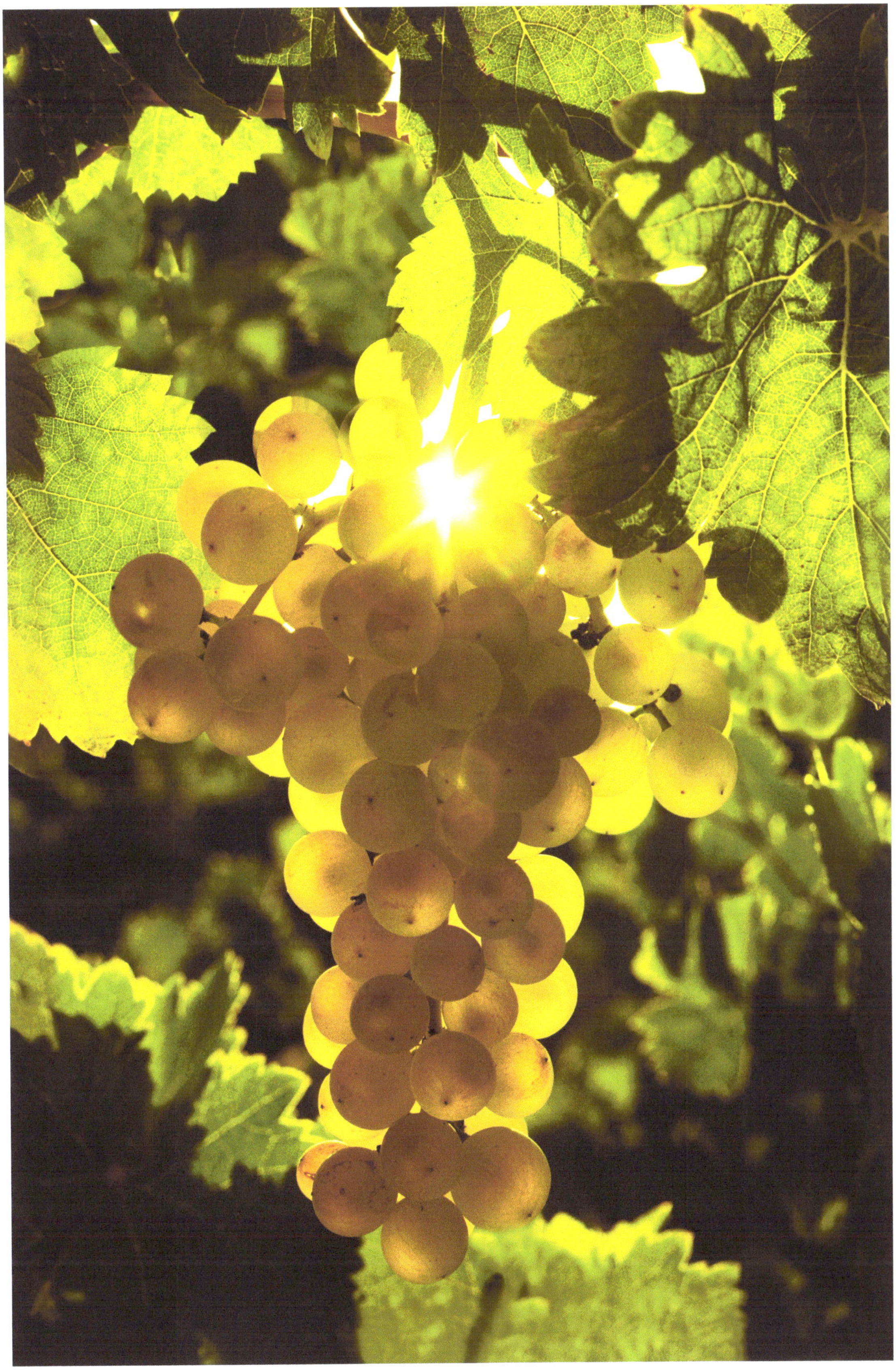

October 1997 121 Delicato Winery Poster

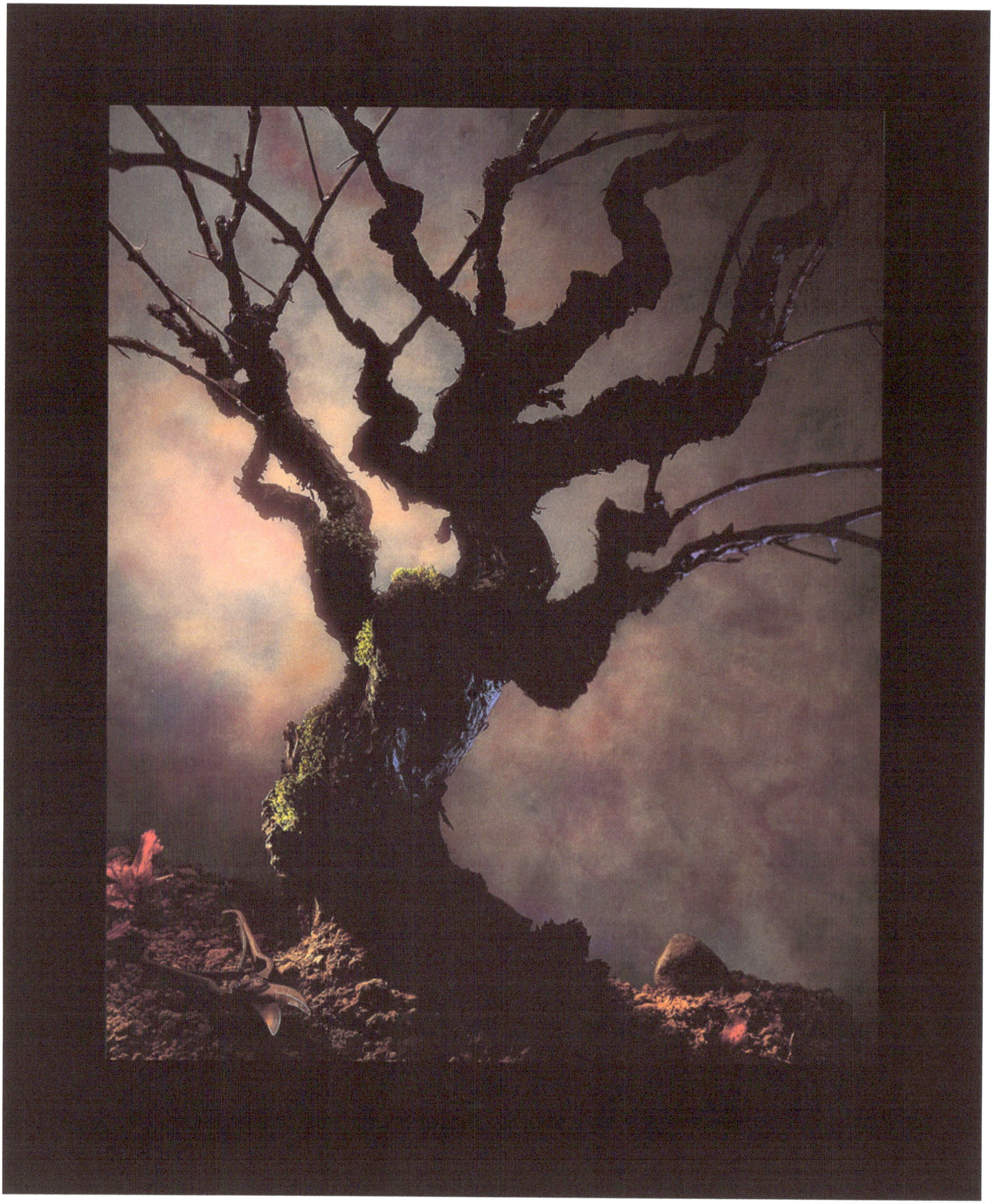

March 2009 282 Seghesio Winery Poster, Healdsburg, CA

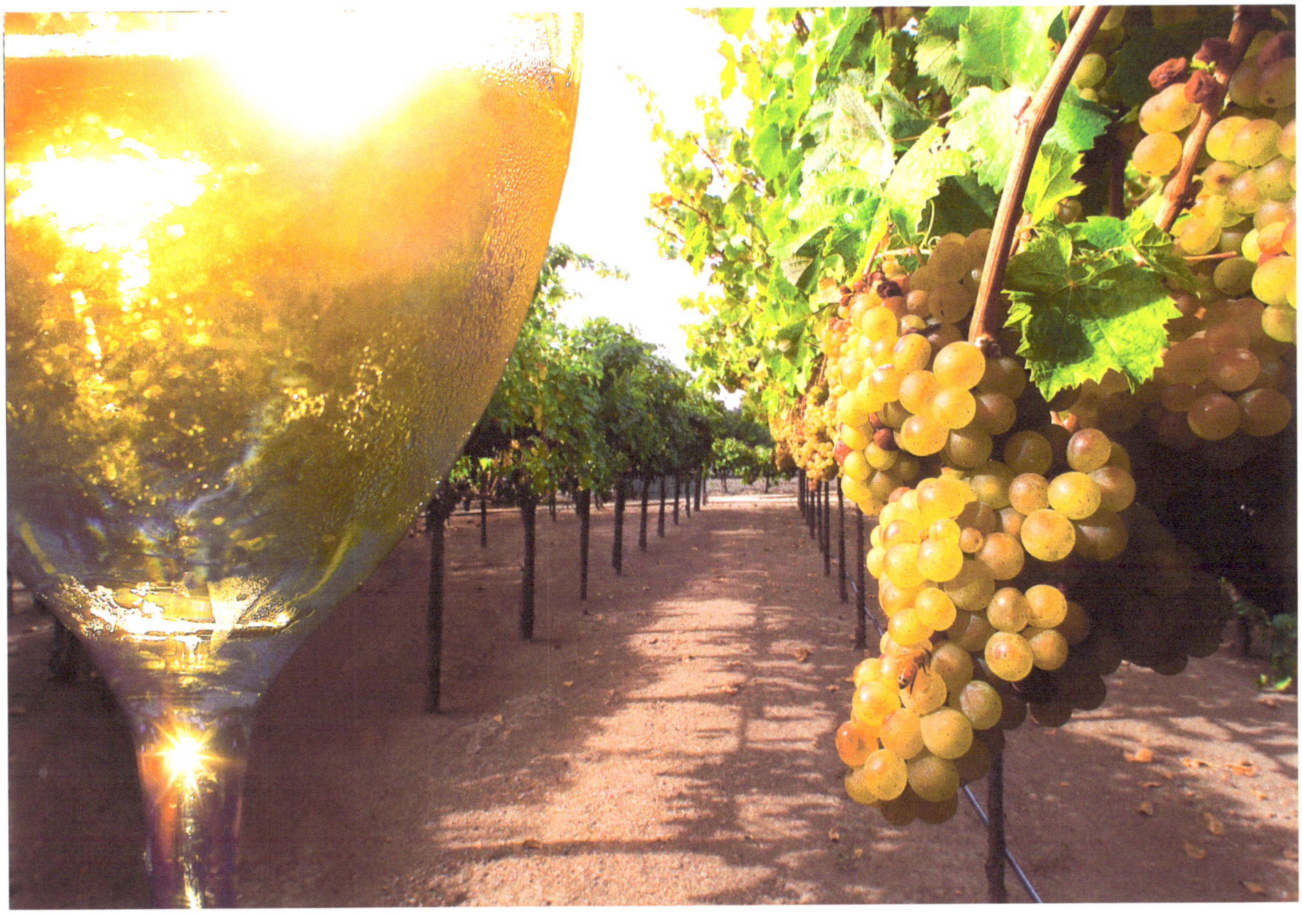

September 2005 176 Wine in the Vineyard, Kendall-Jackson Winery

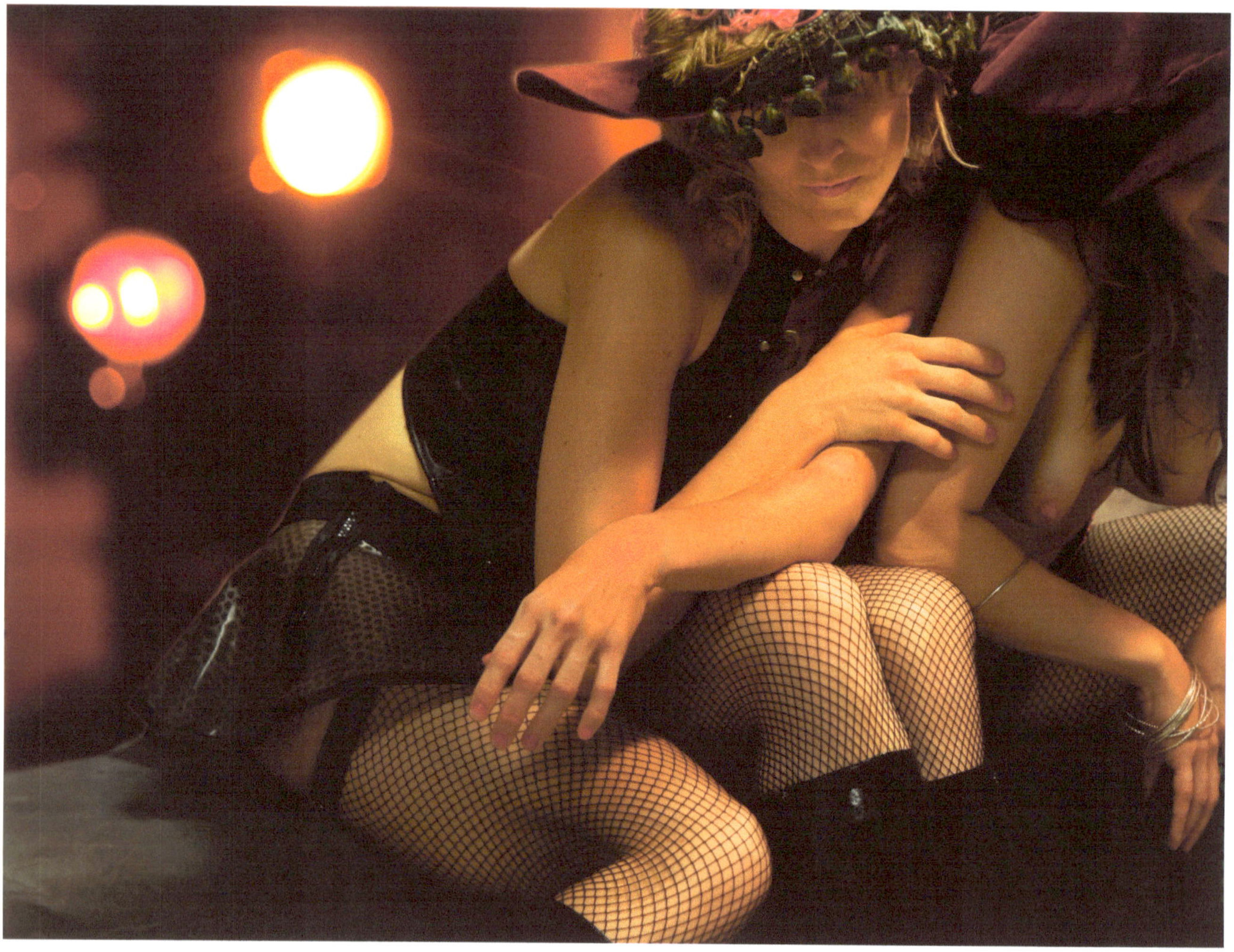

November 2011 197 Impressions of Tarkay

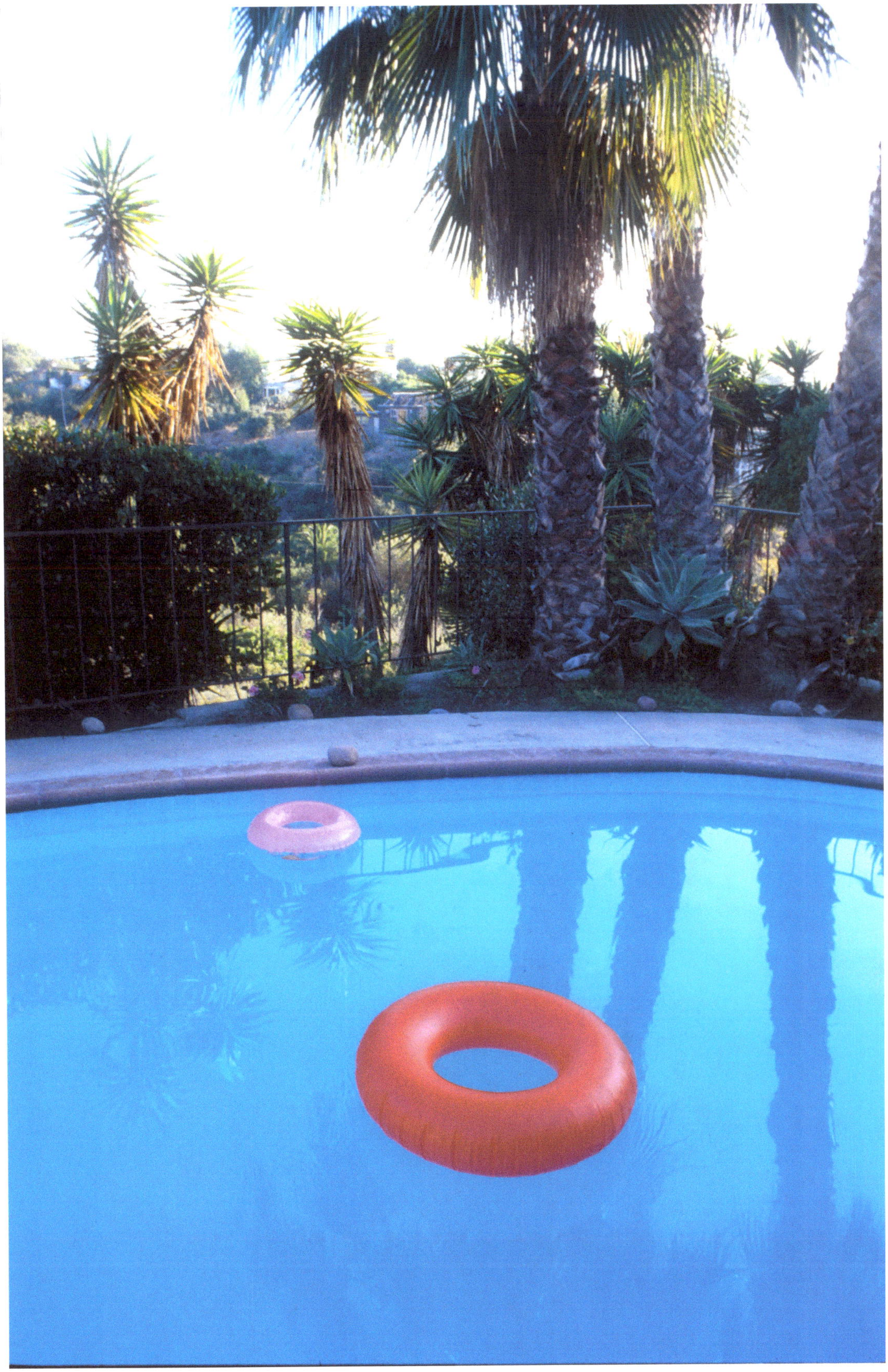

June 1967 232 California Summer

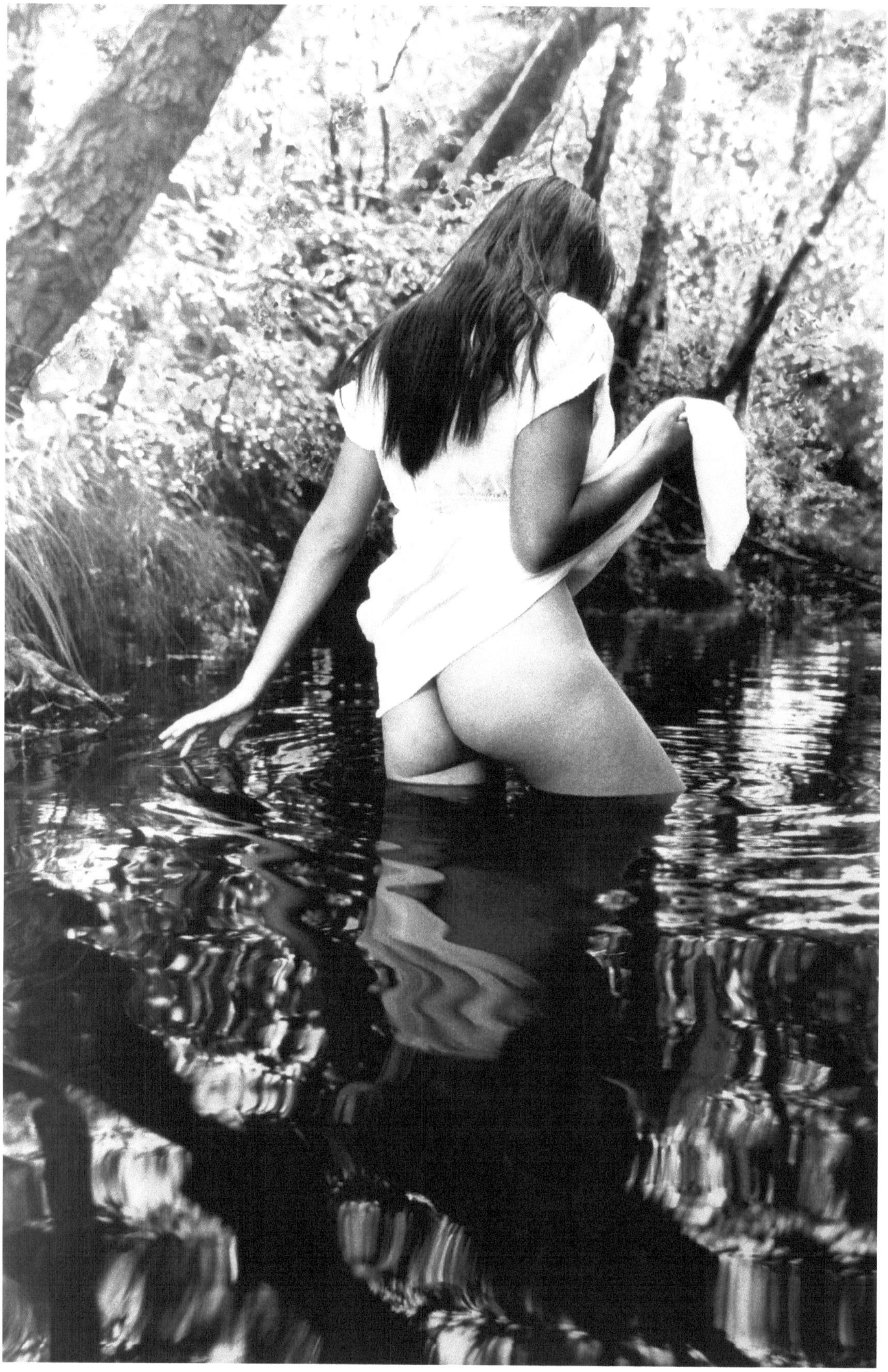

1979 220 Summer Fun

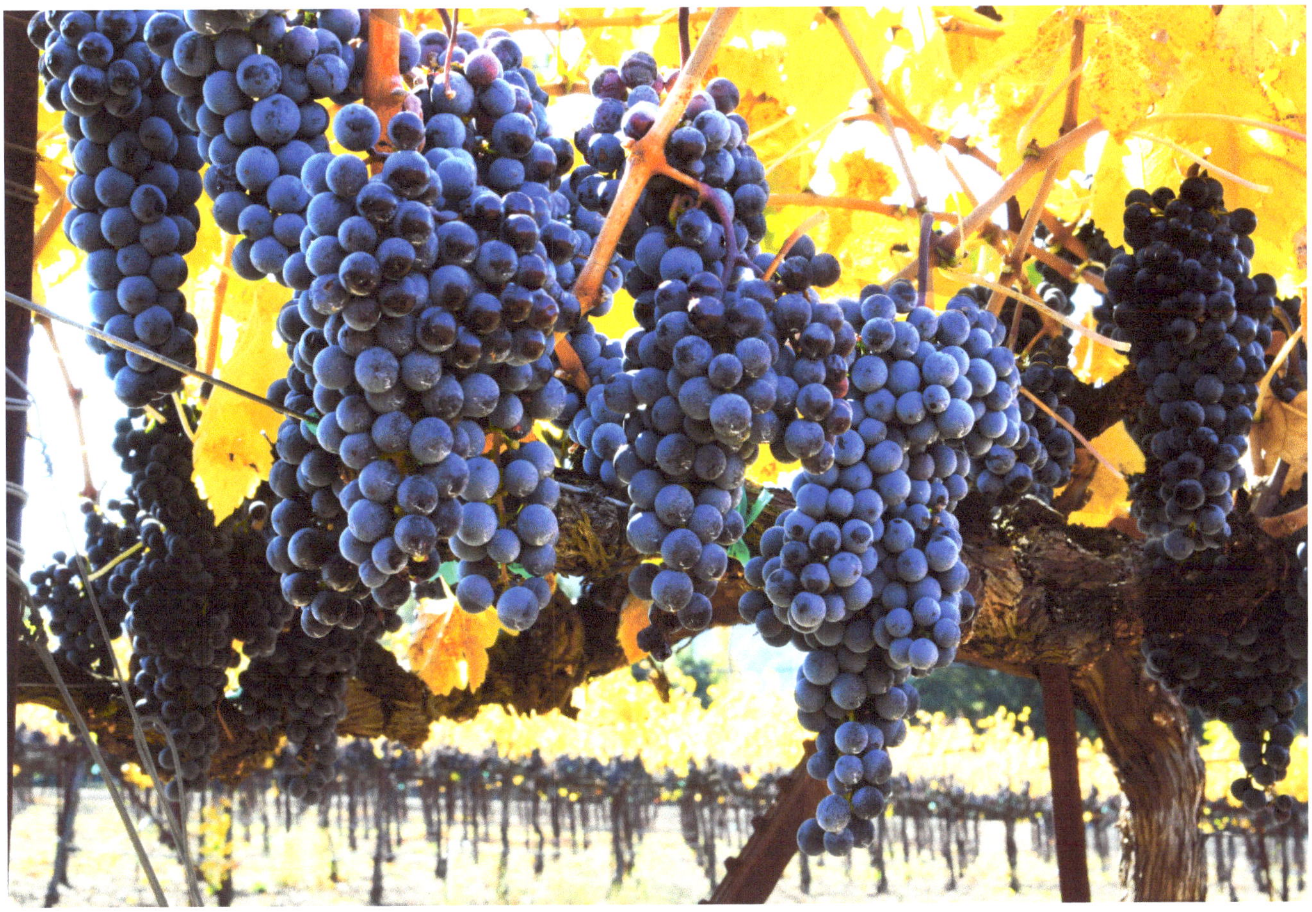

August 1997

284 Kenwood Winery

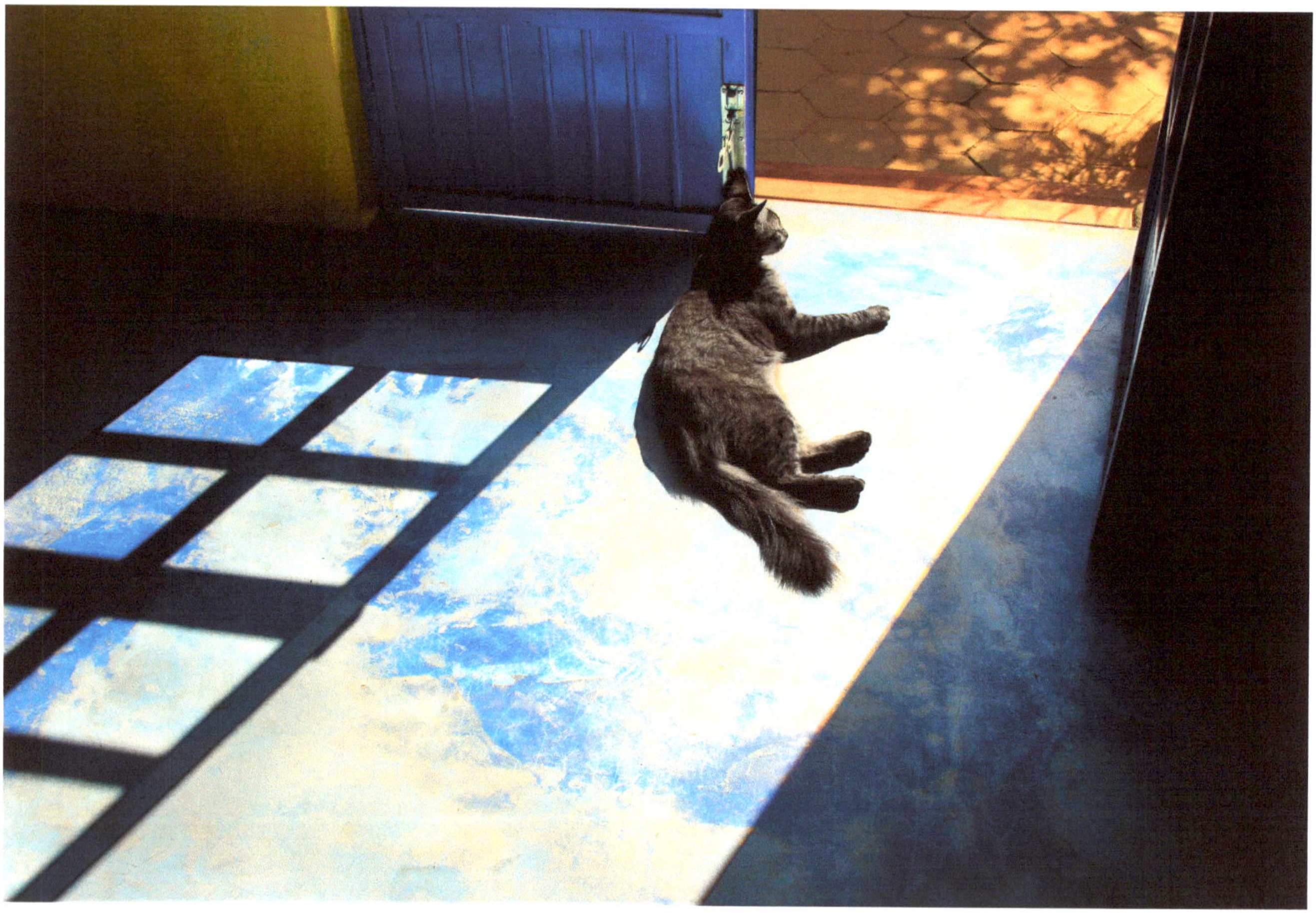

June 2005 150 Todo Santos Cat

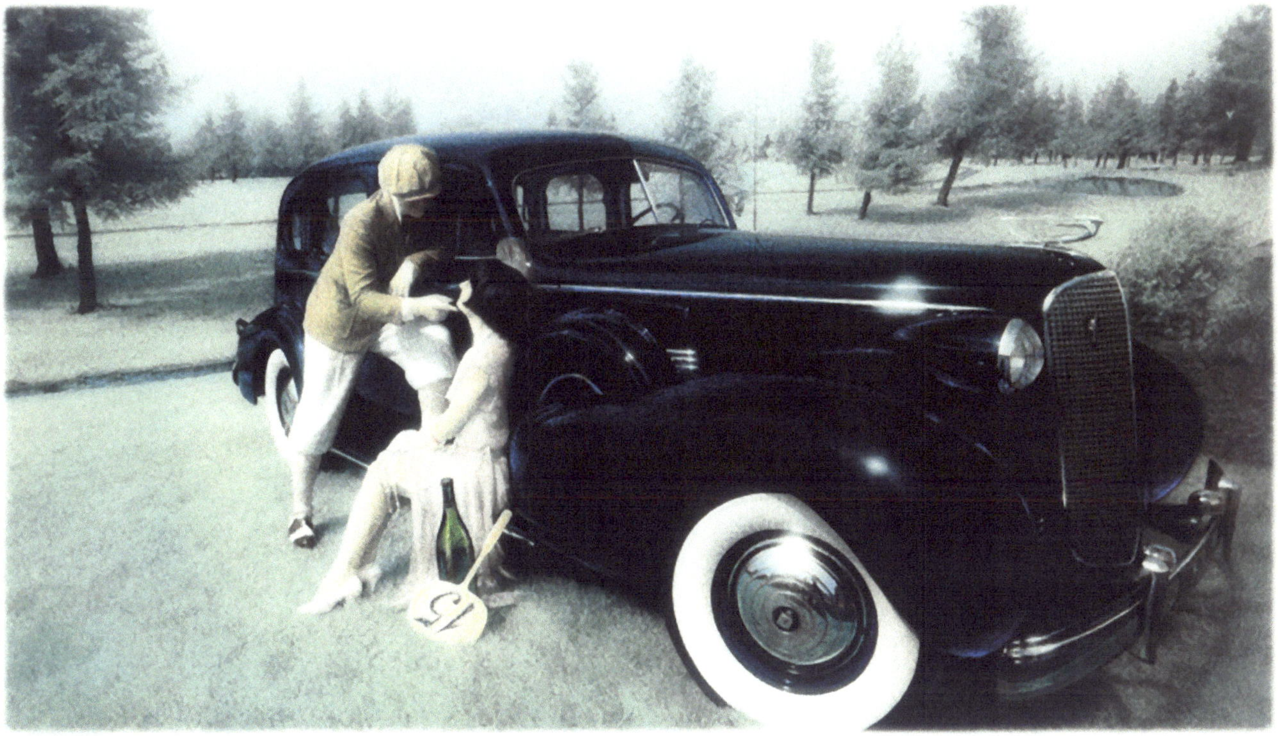

March 2006 **117 Sonoma County Wine Auction Poster**

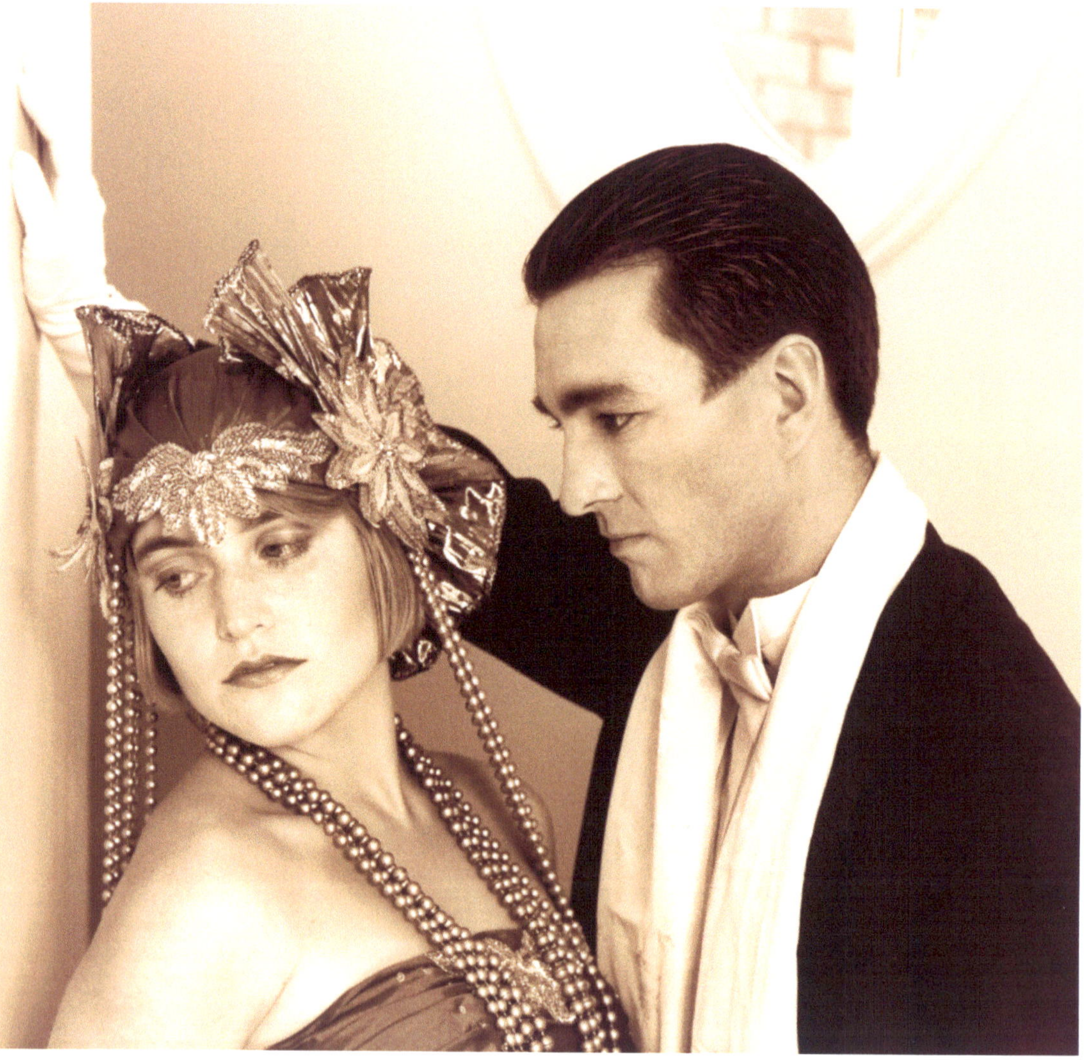

February 1997

128 Aloof

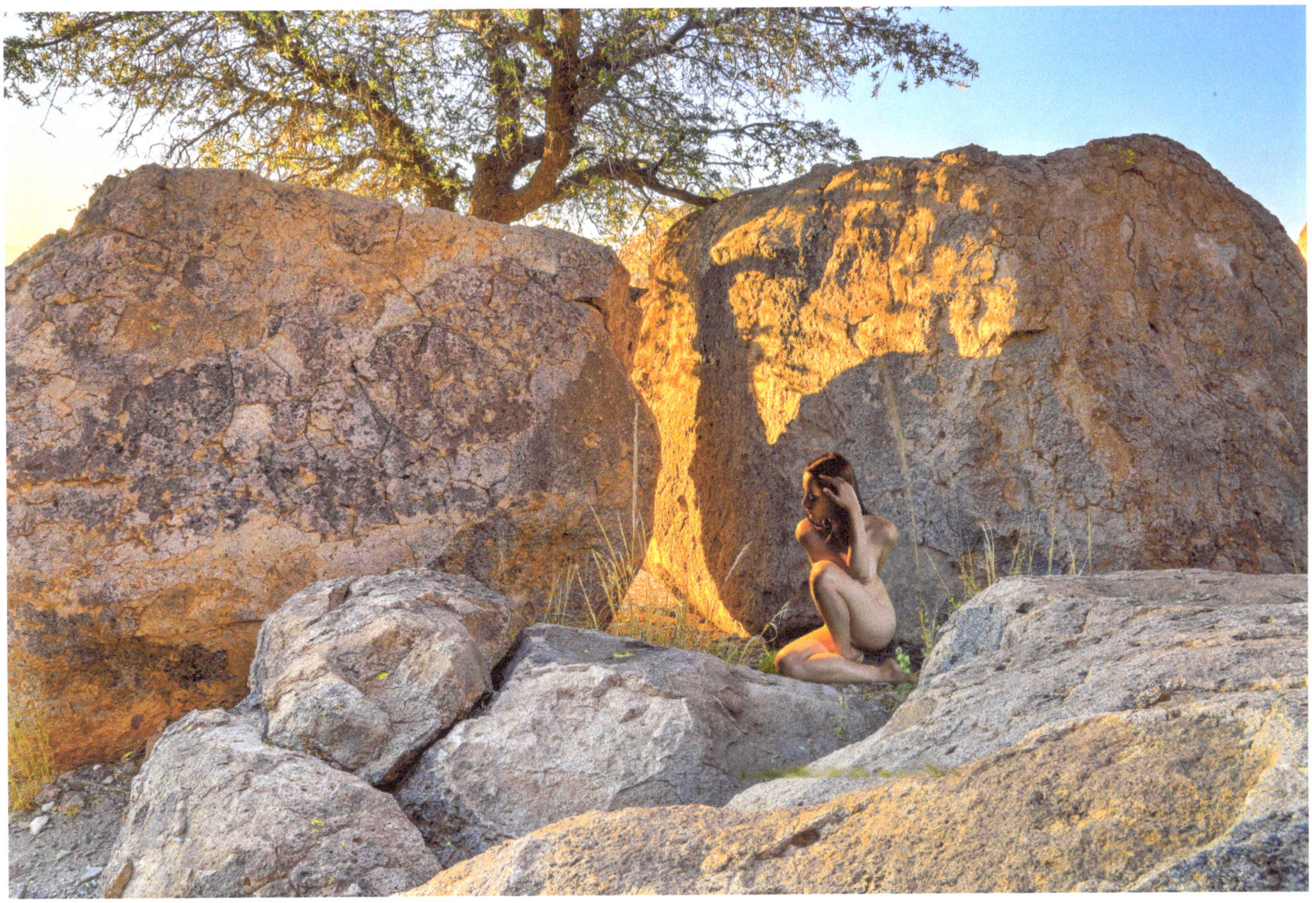

June 2017 285 Warm Desert Sun

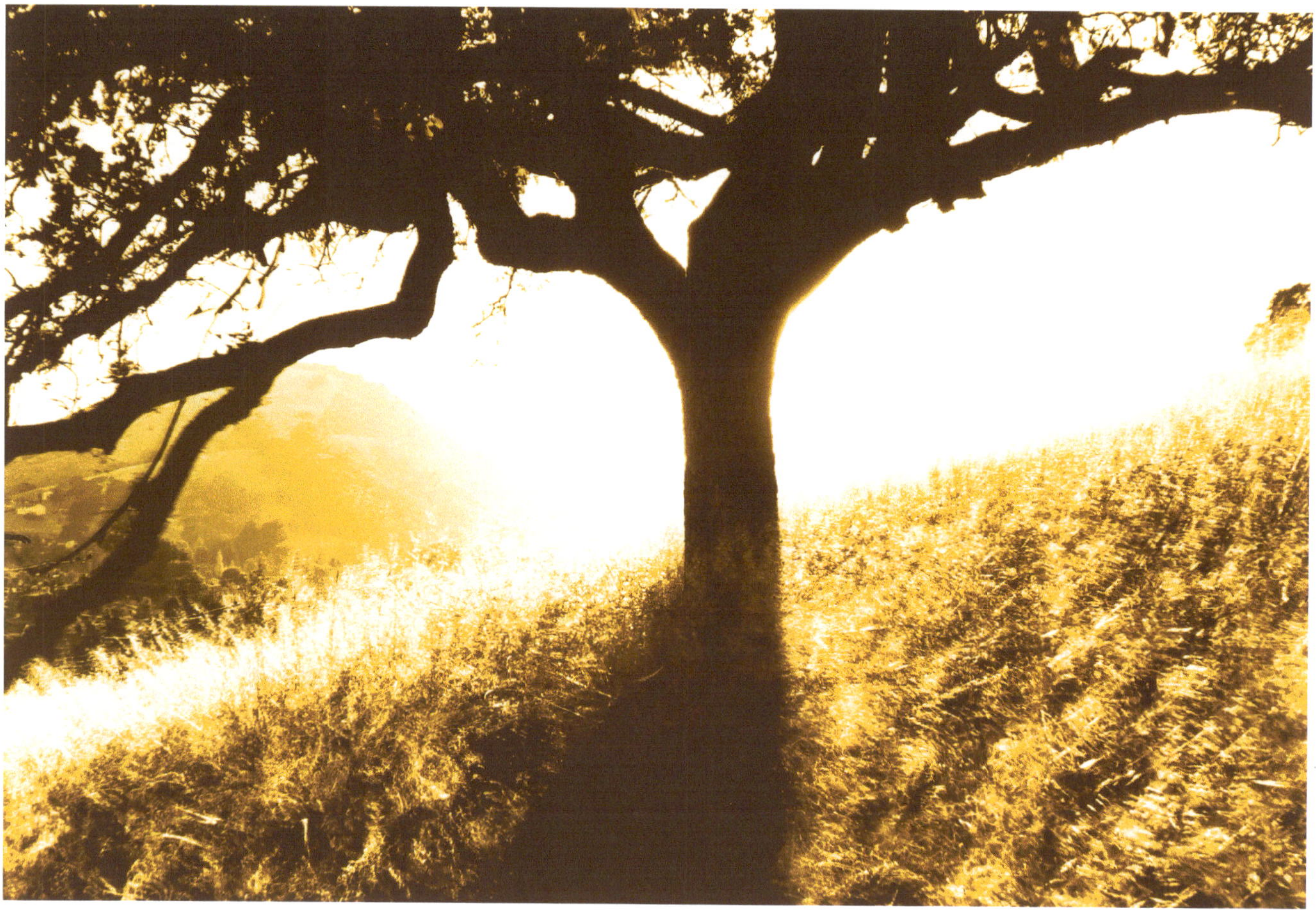

October 1976 126 Oak at Sunset

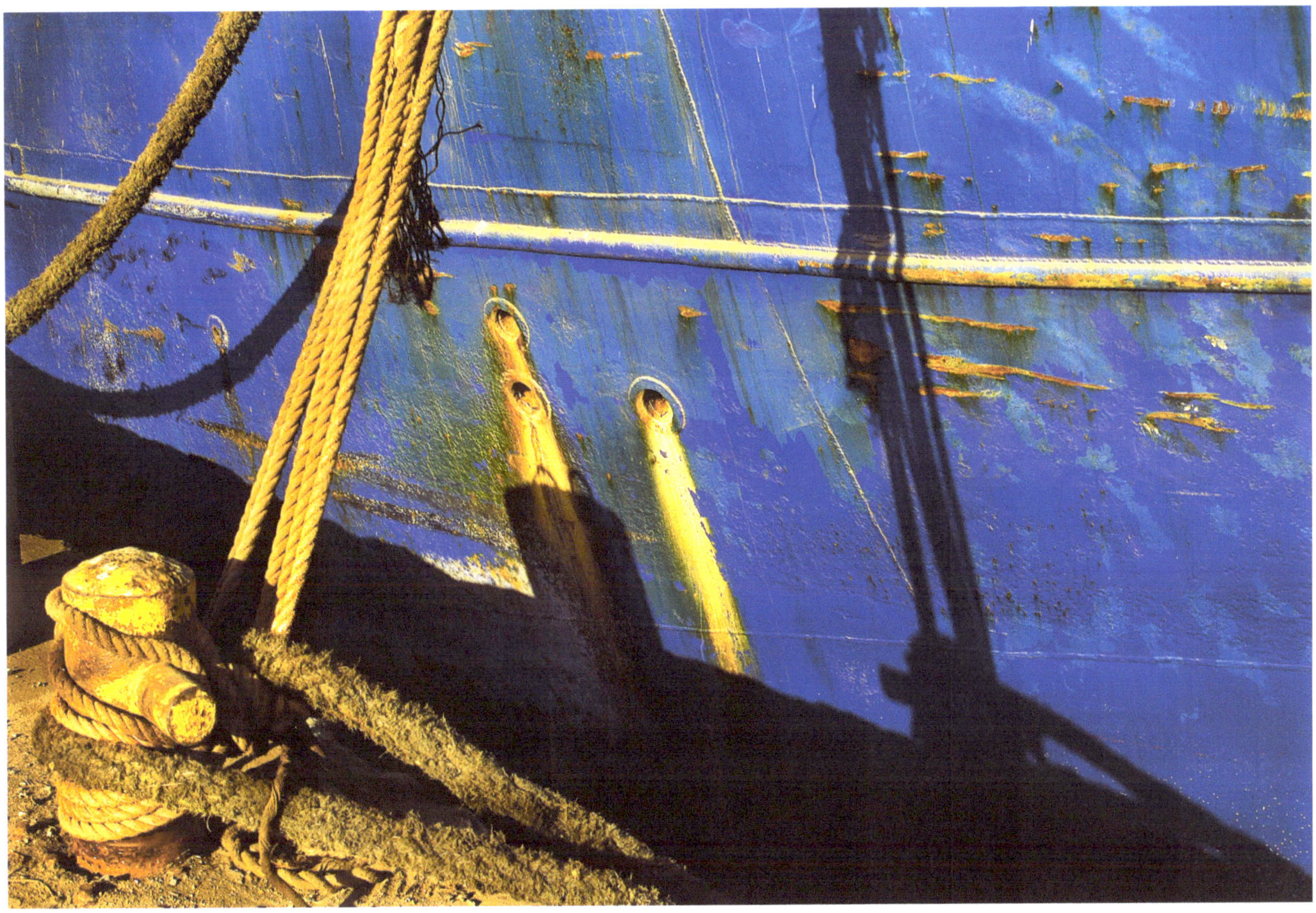

May 1978

135 Rusty Blue Boat

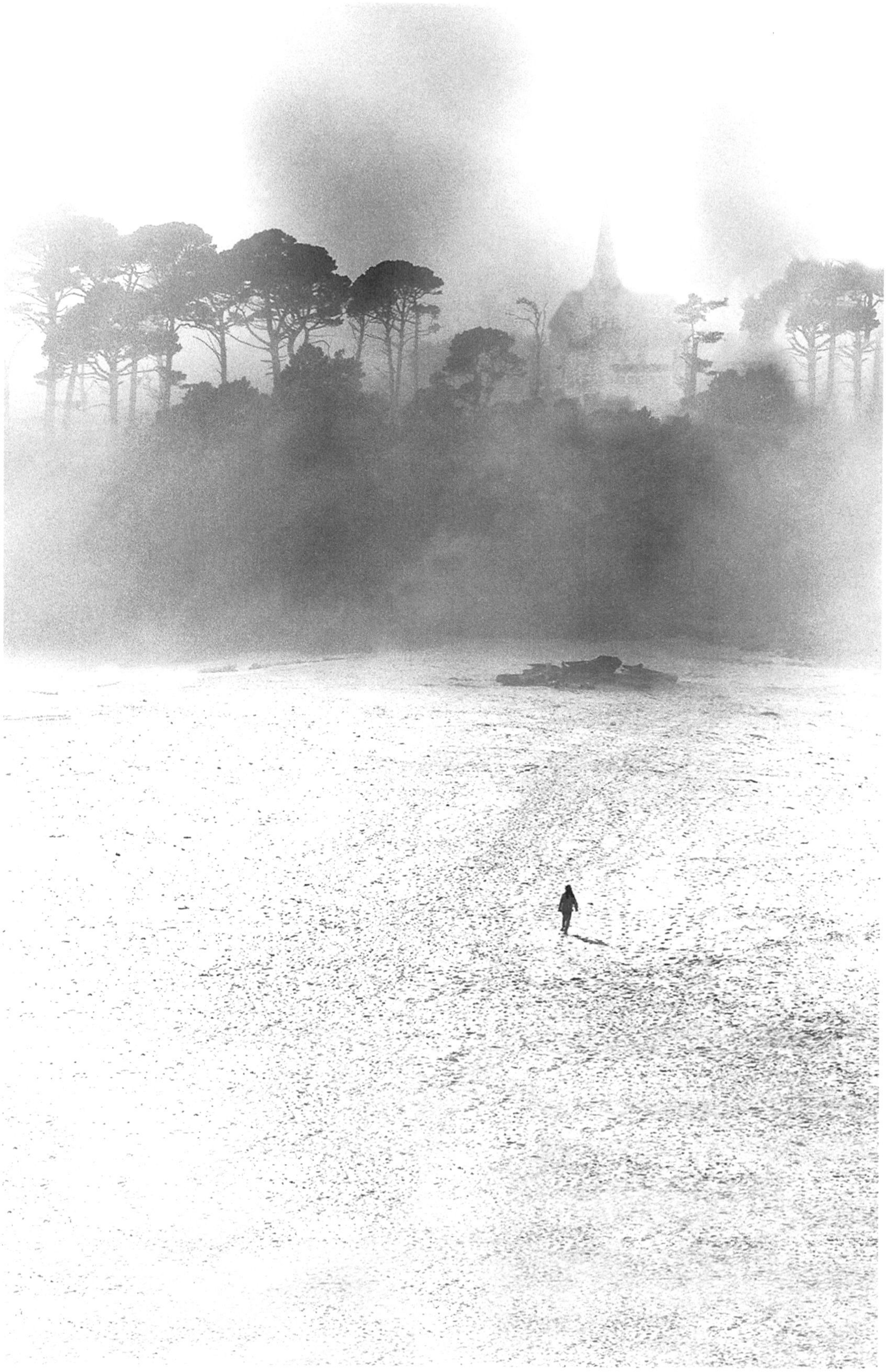

September 1996 129 Church in the Fog

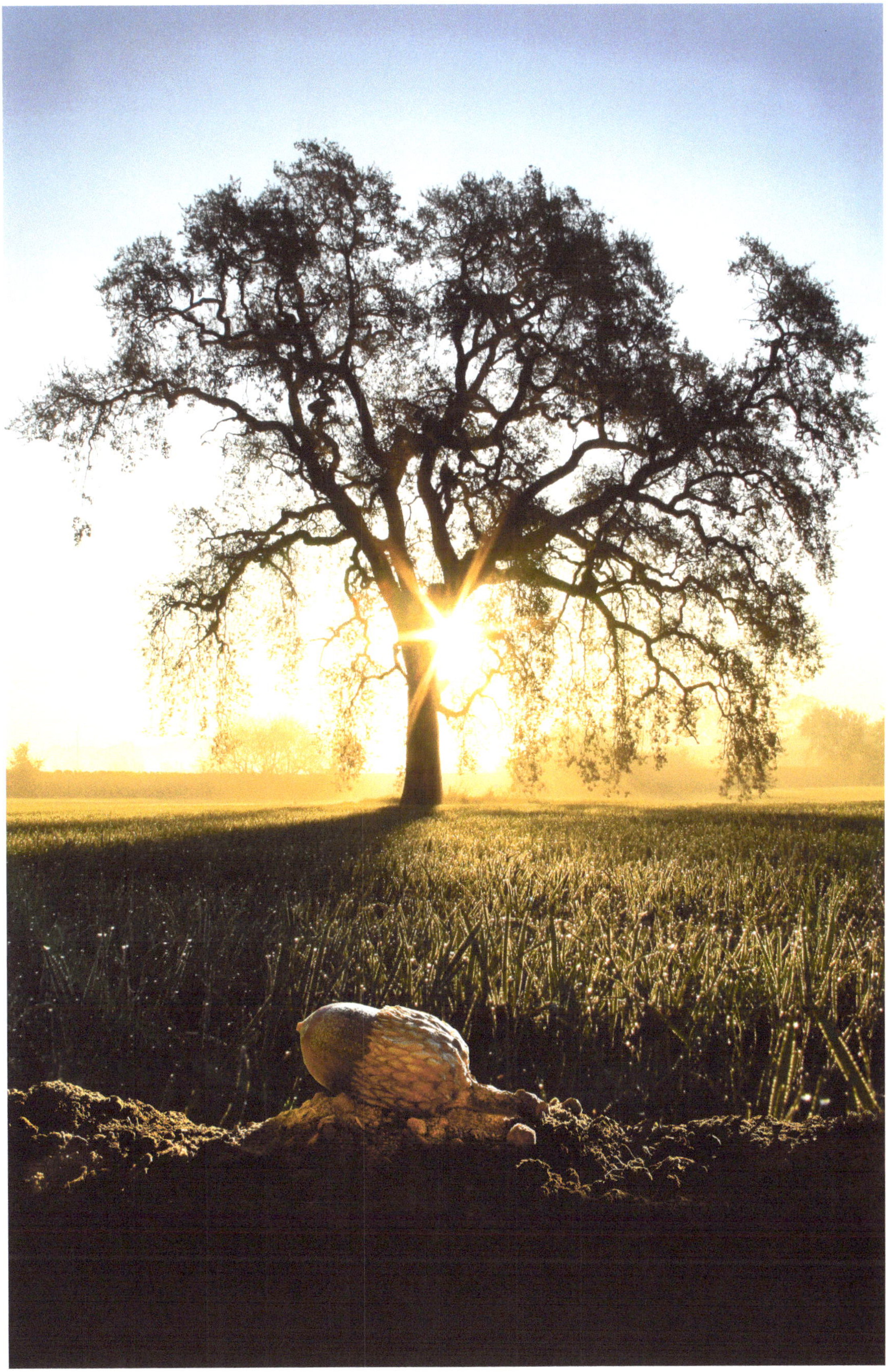

May 2007 252 Acorn to Oak Tree

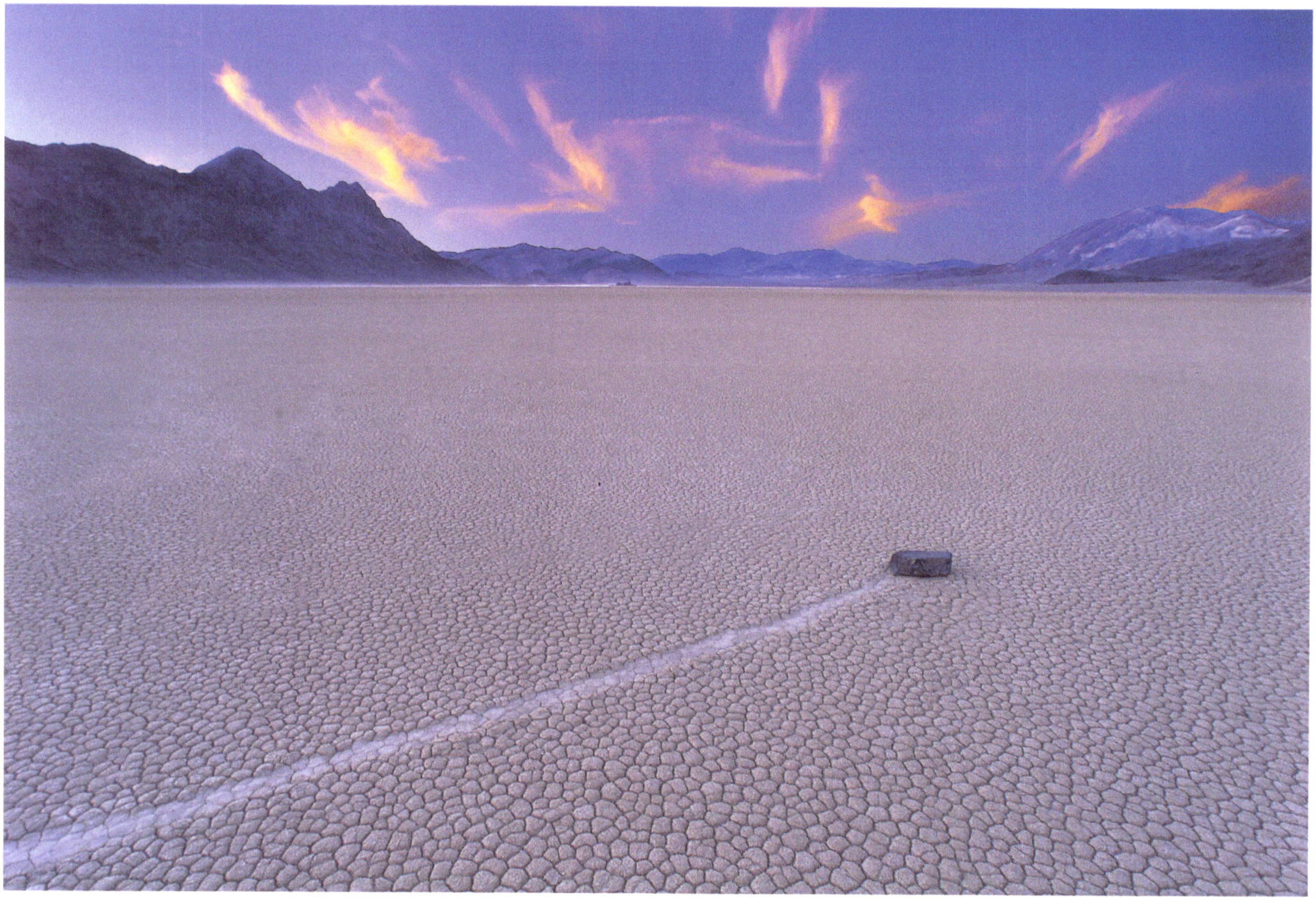

October 2006 170 The Racetrack

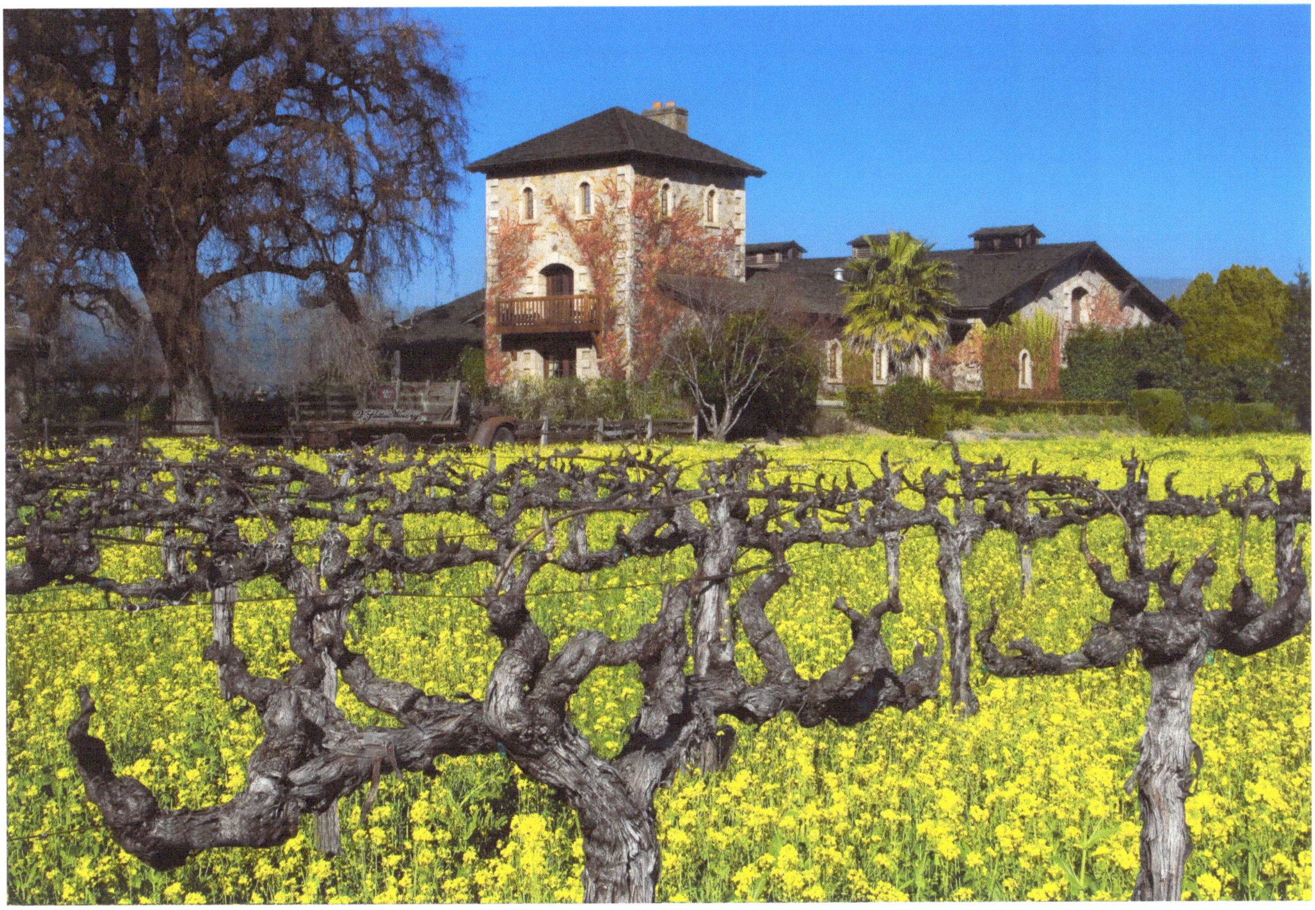

December 2015 79-406 V. Sattui Vineyard

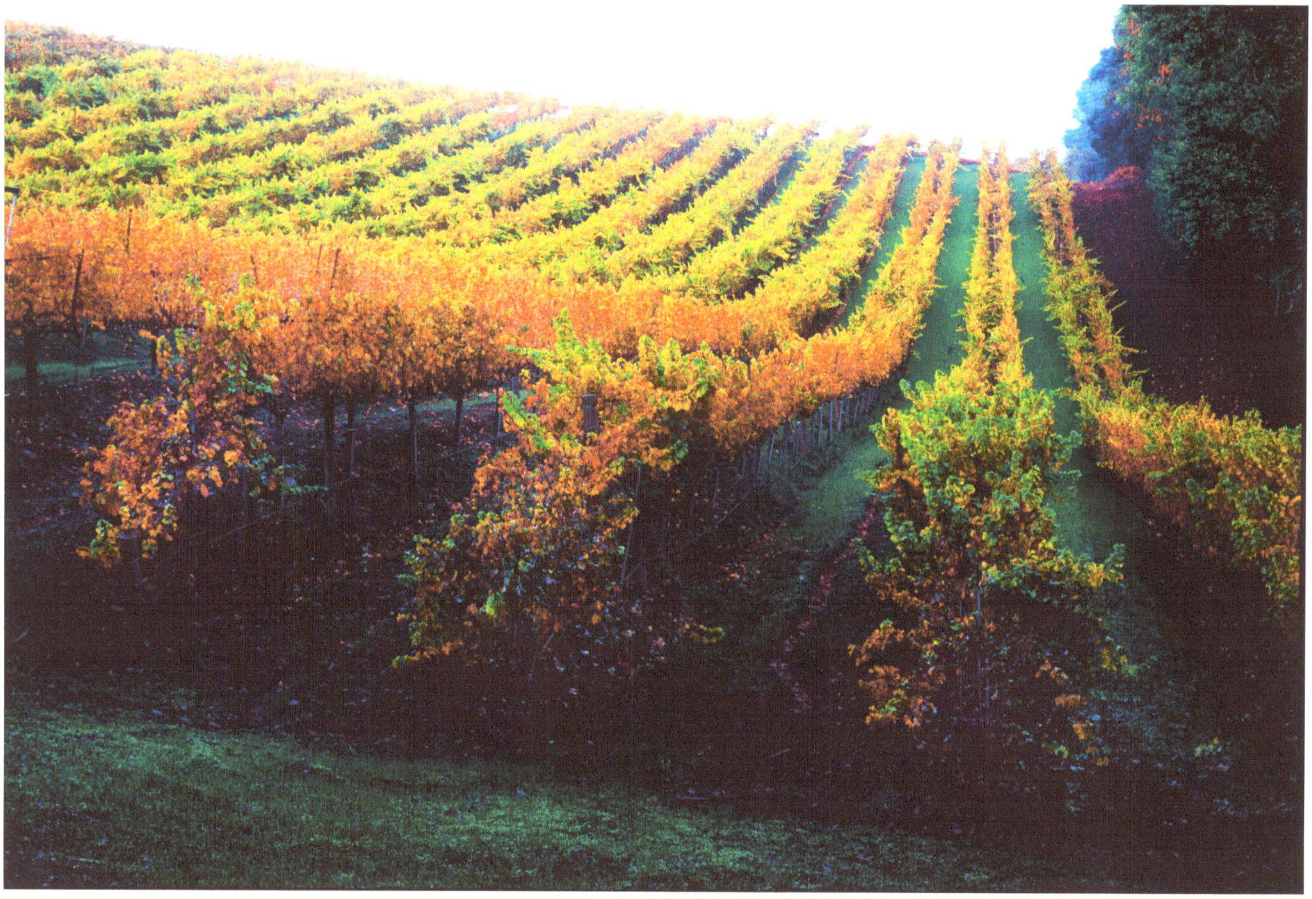

October 2006 347 Glen Ellen Vineyard

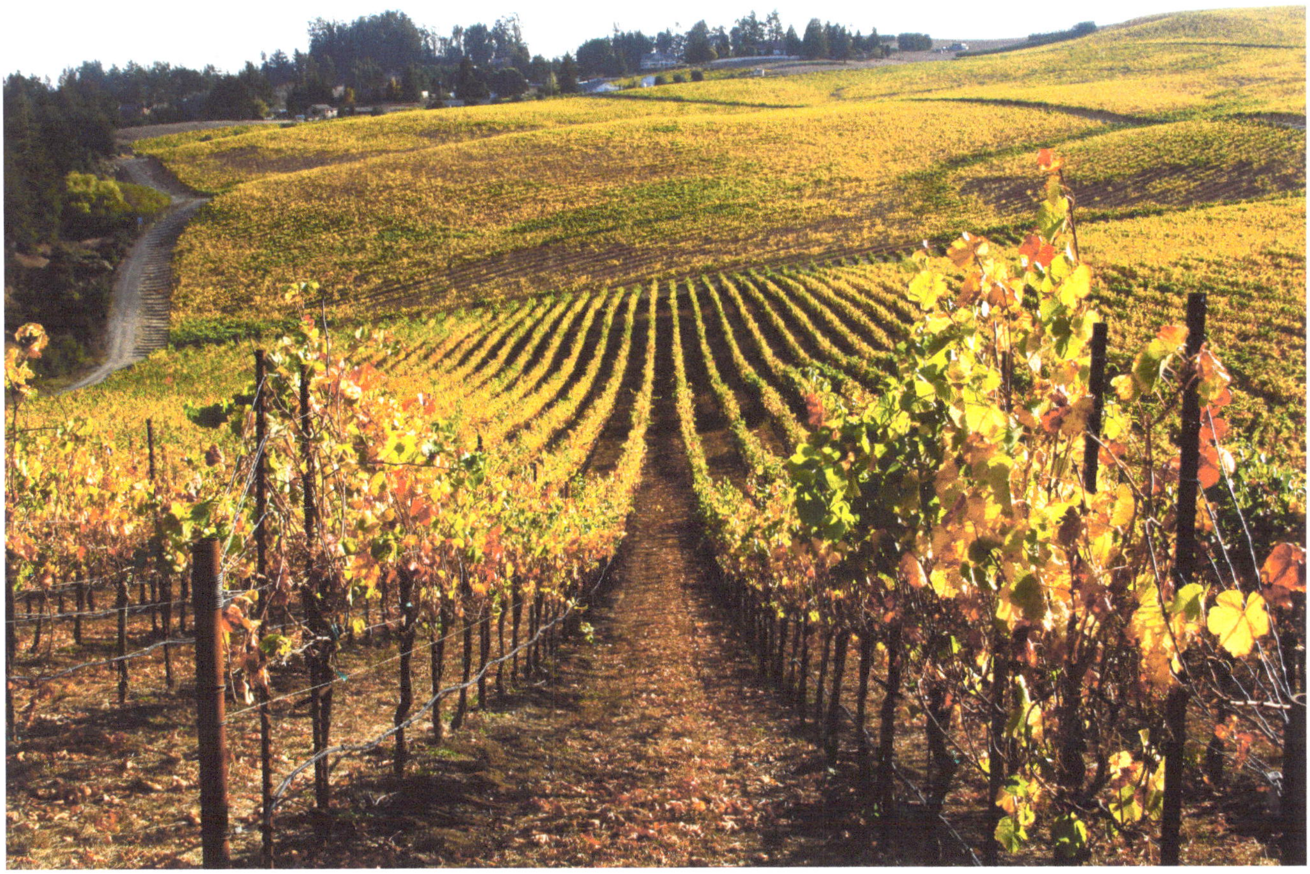

September 2018 252 Cotati Vineyard in the Fall

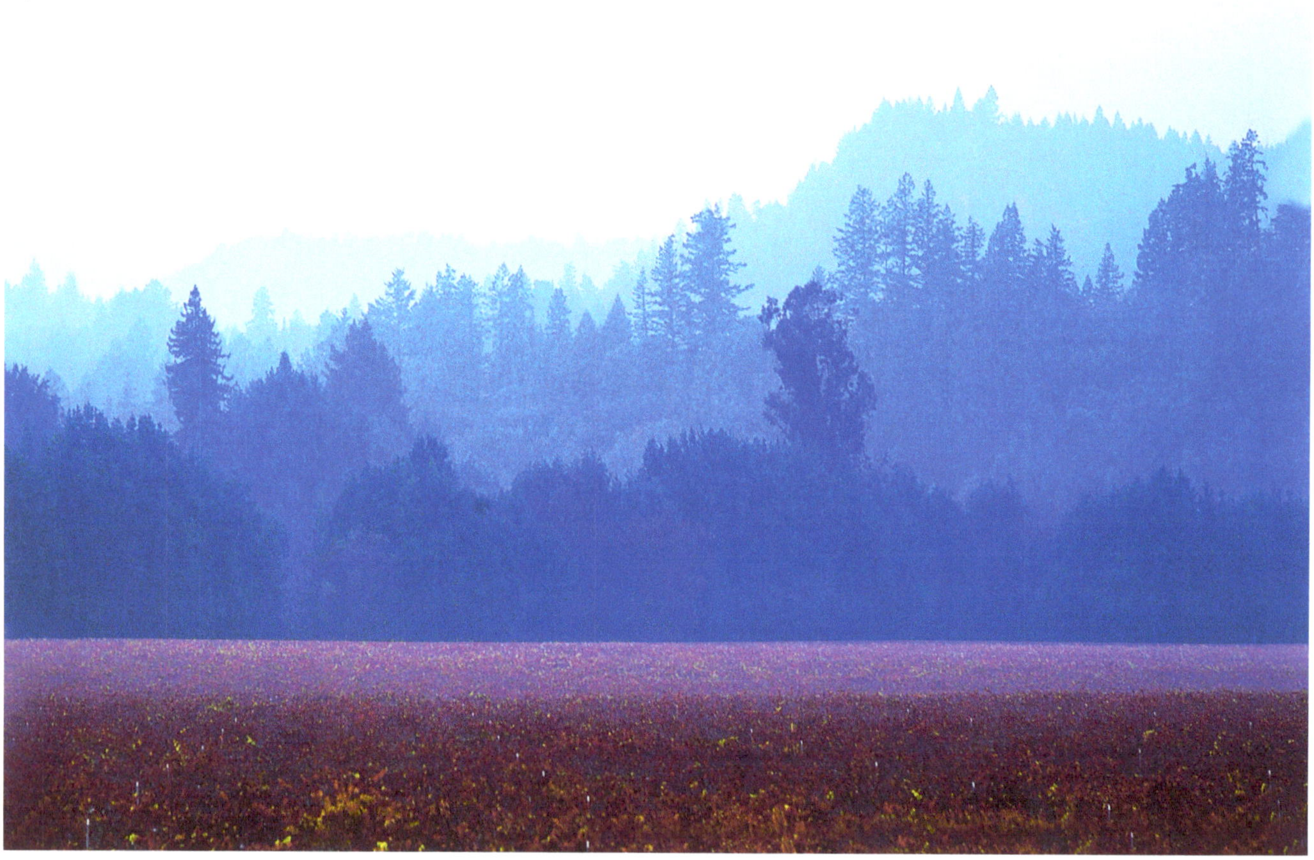

December 2008 353 Midwinter Vineyard

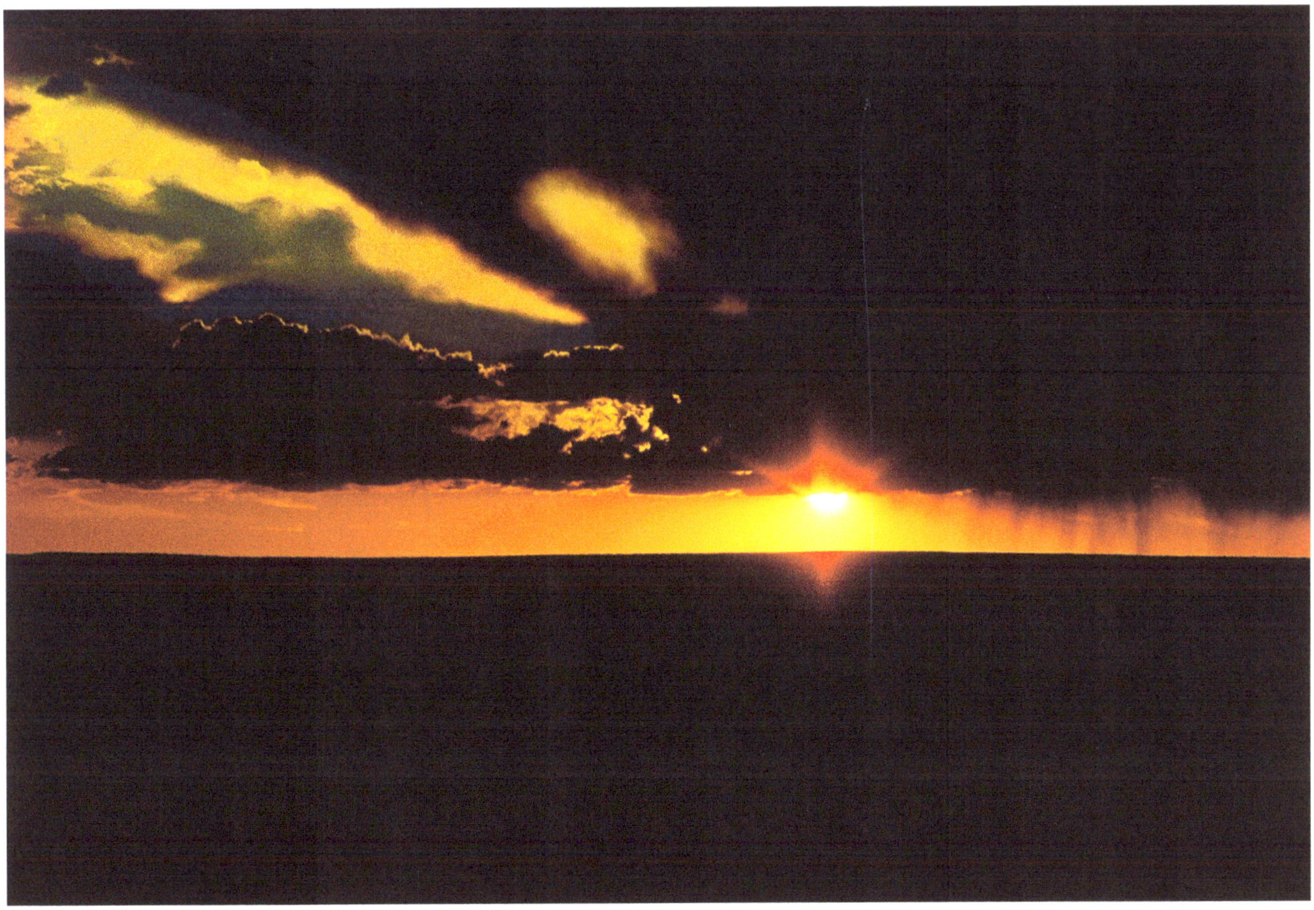

February 1999 333 Rain on the Ocean

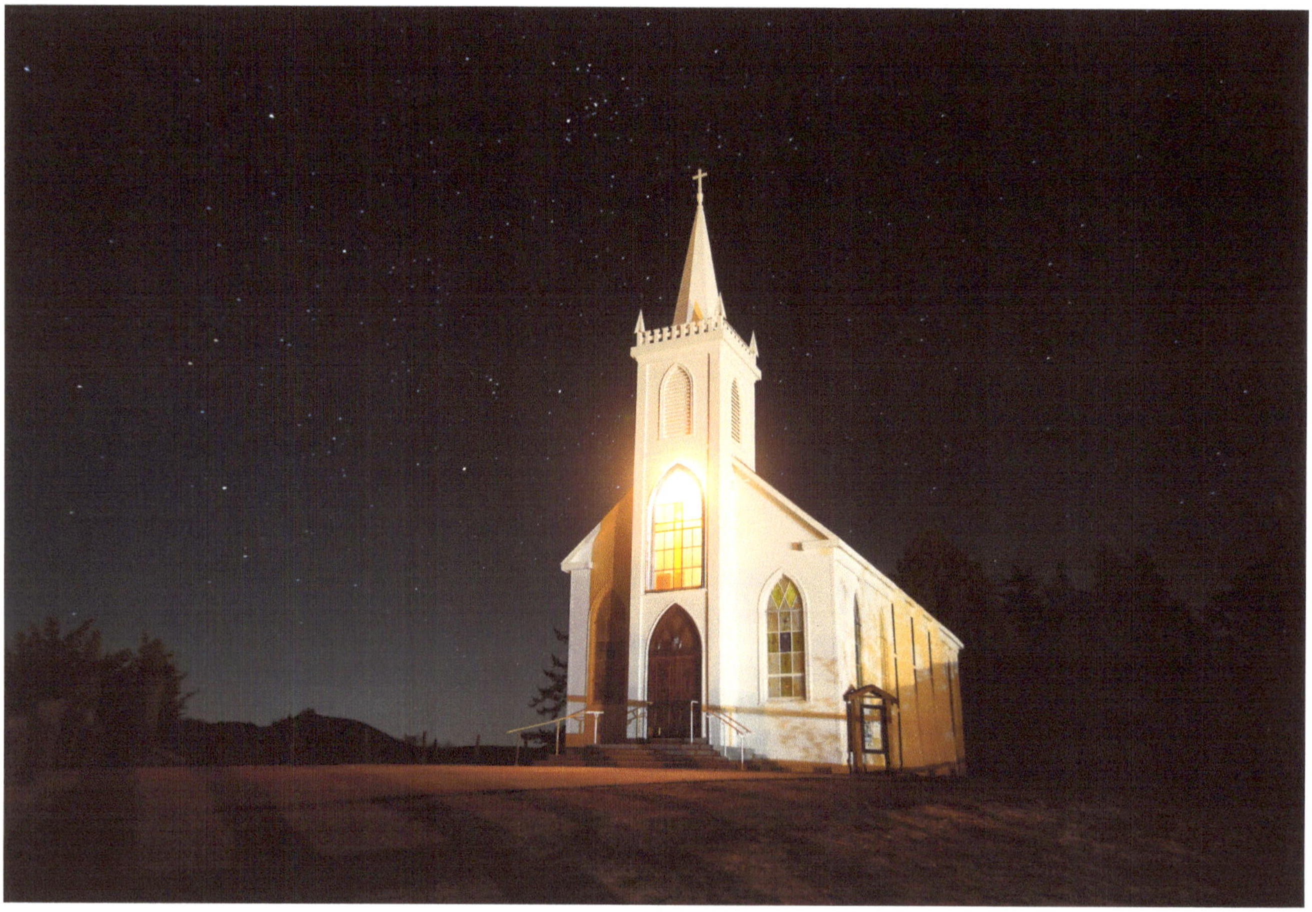

November 2019 374 Bodega Church at Night

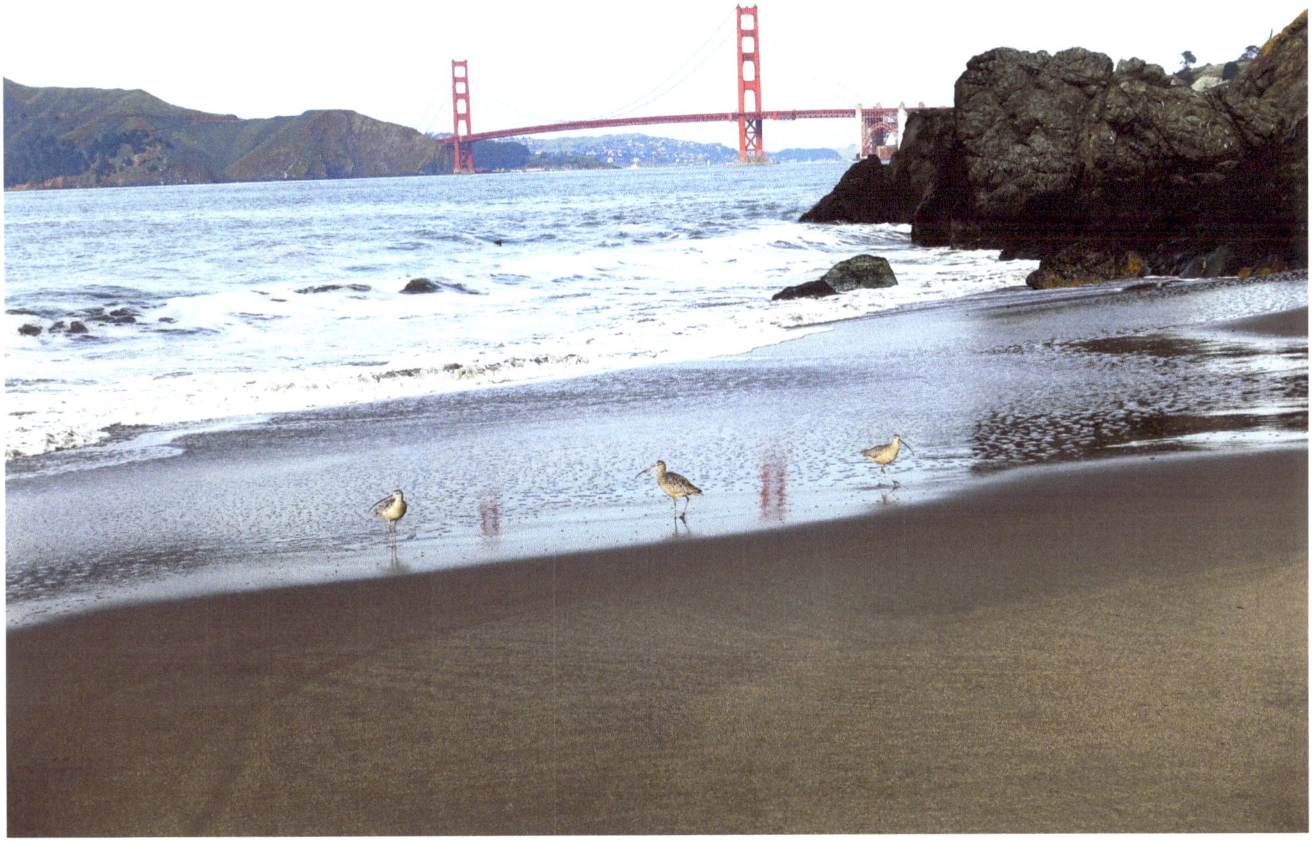

2019 377 Golden Gate Bridge San Francisco

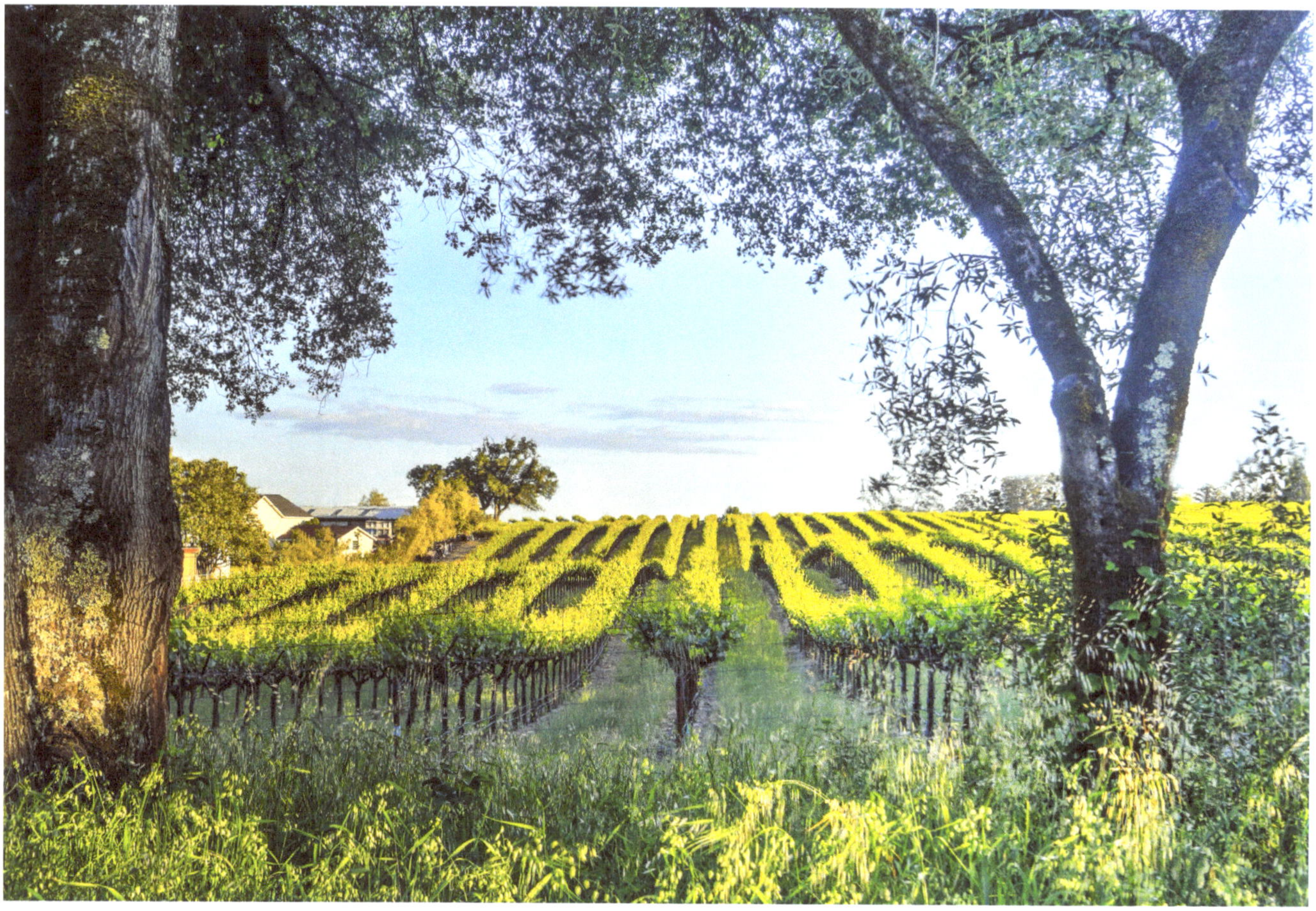

378 Vine Hill Road

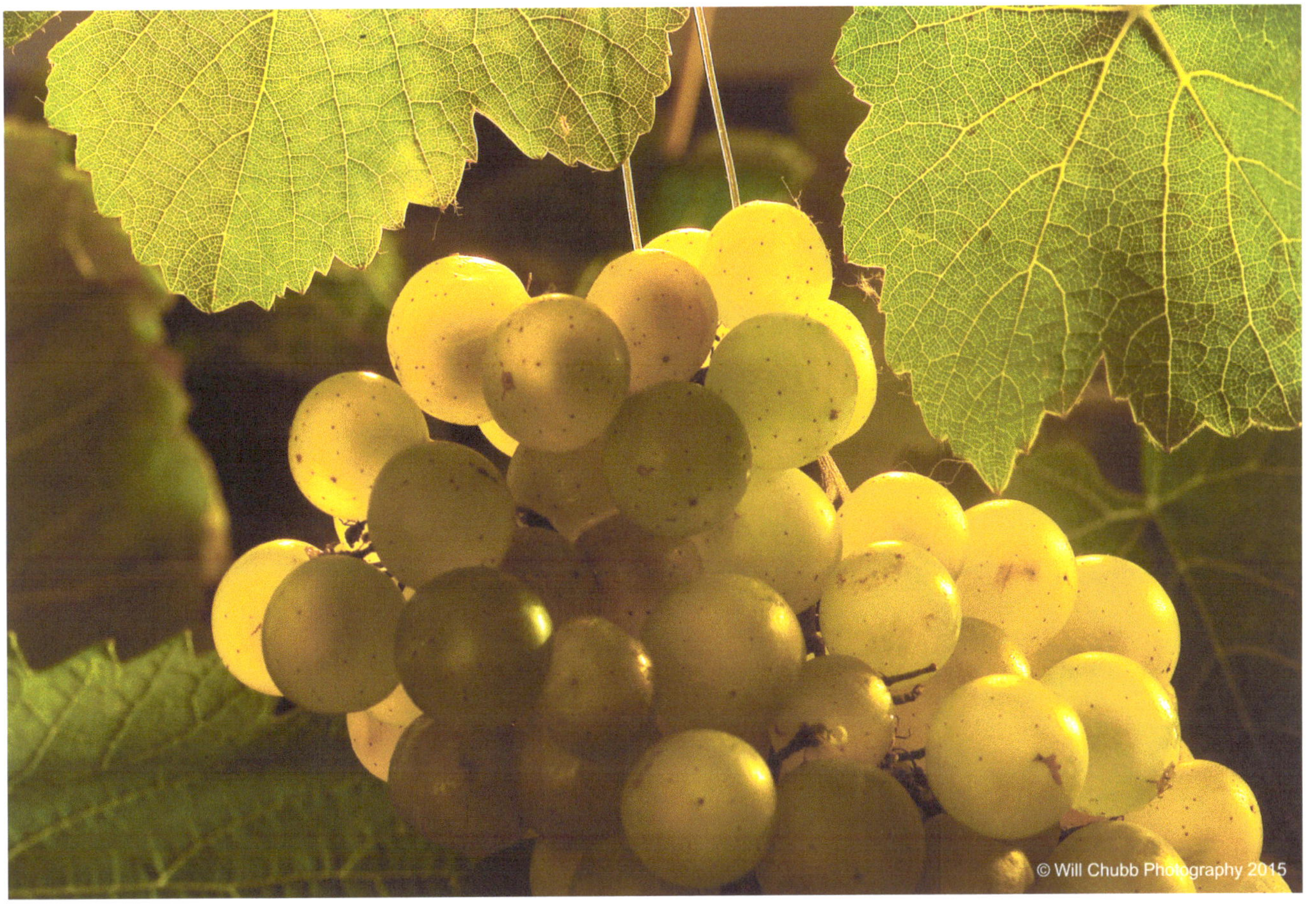

2015 87-405 Lusicious Grapes

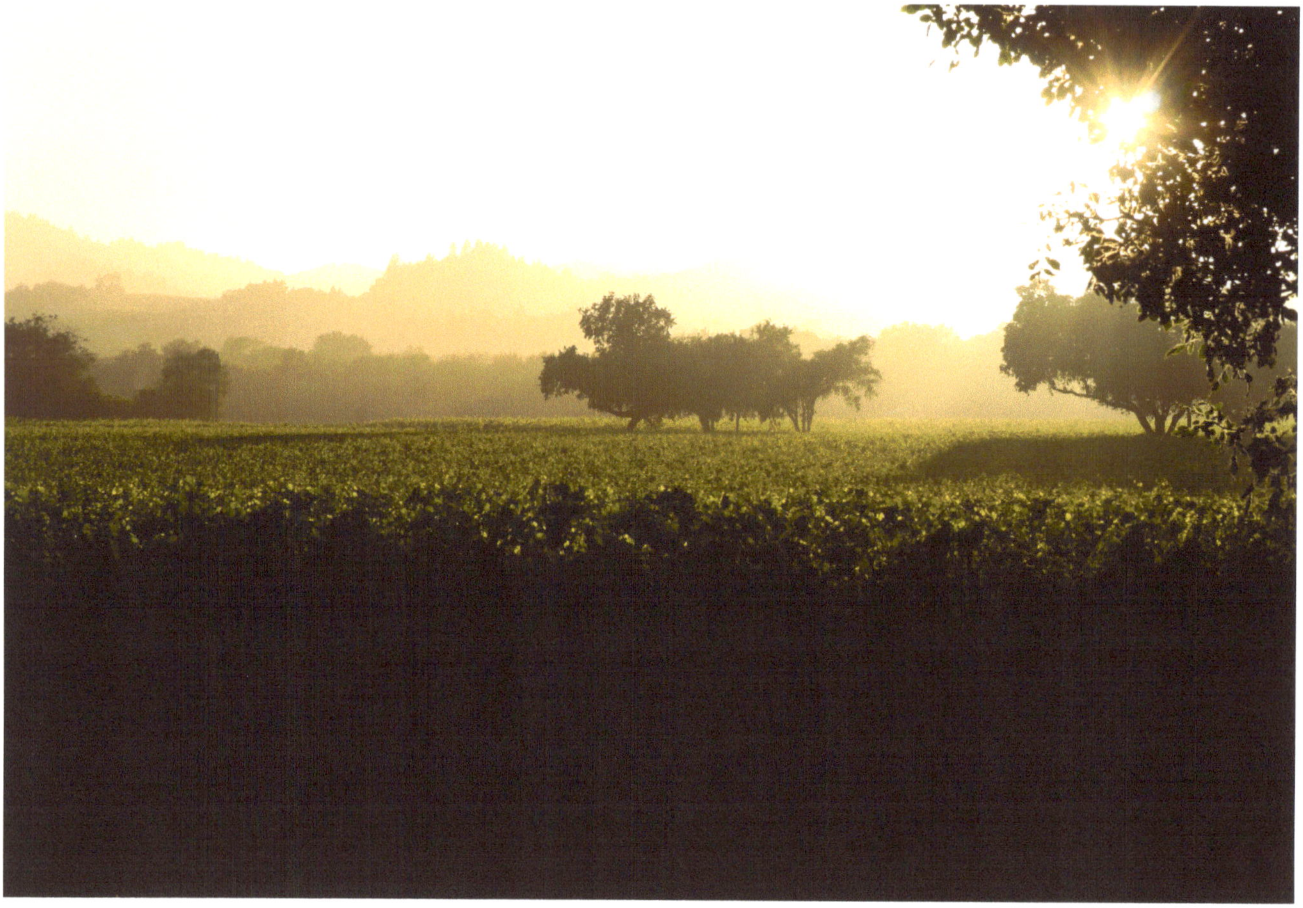

2015 88-403 Sunset in the Vineyard

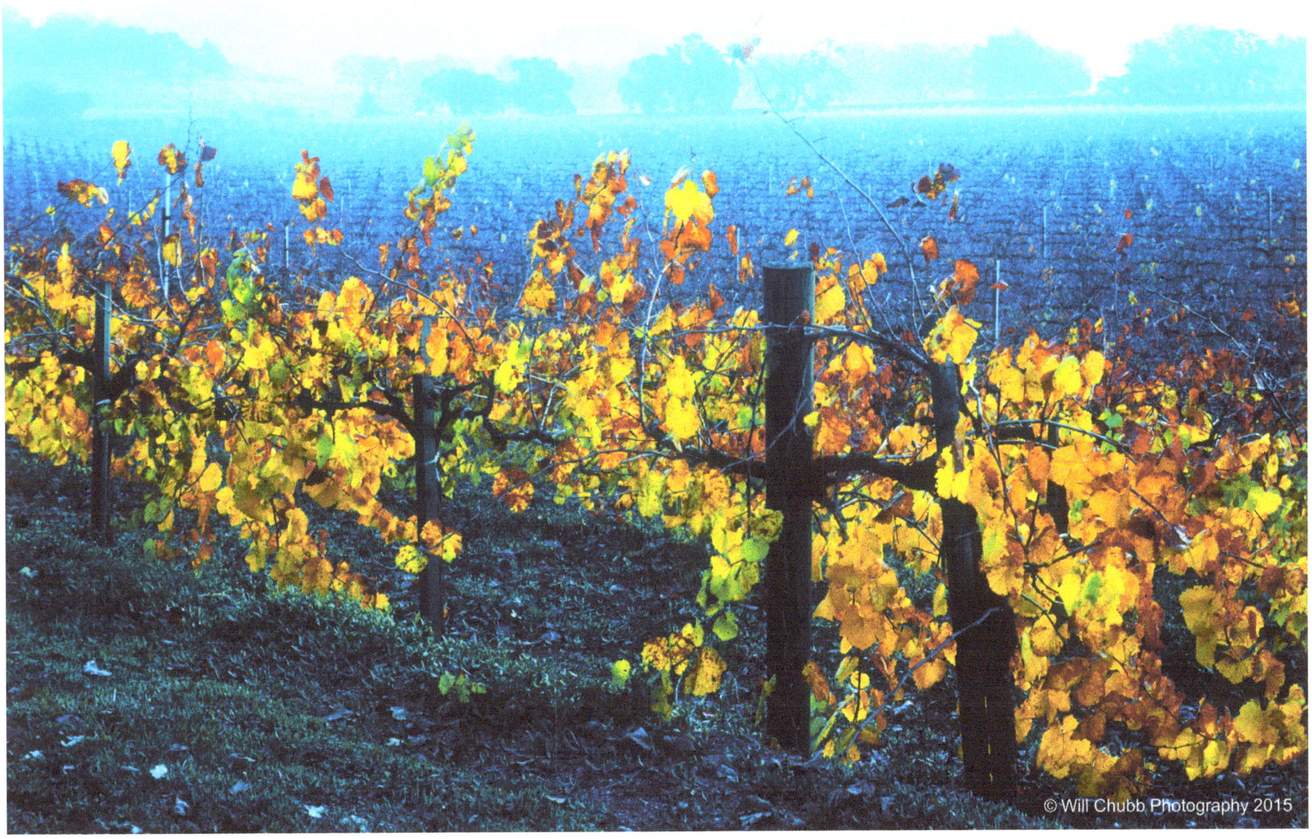

2015

89-404 Late Fall

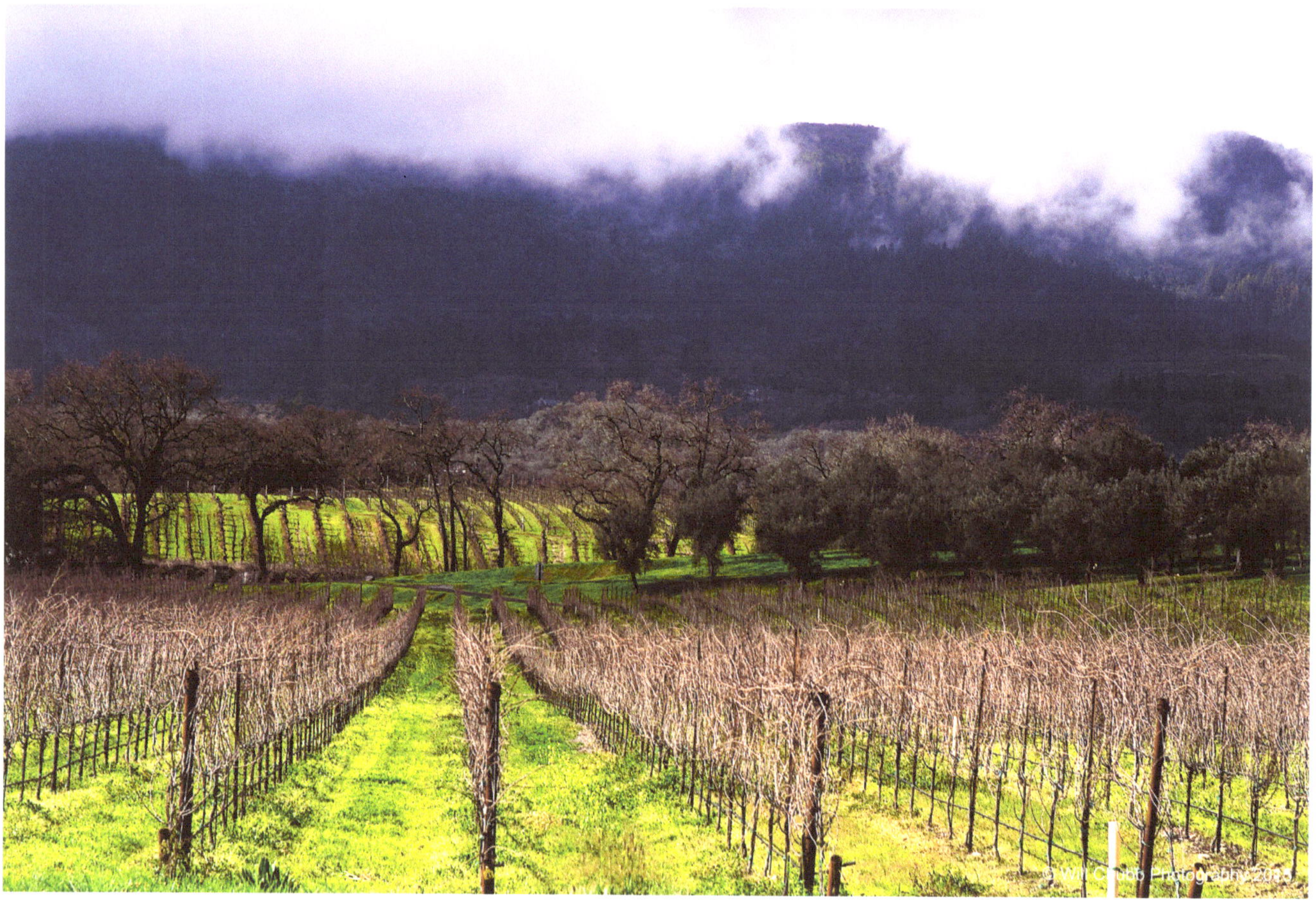

2015 **79-401 Winter Vineyard**

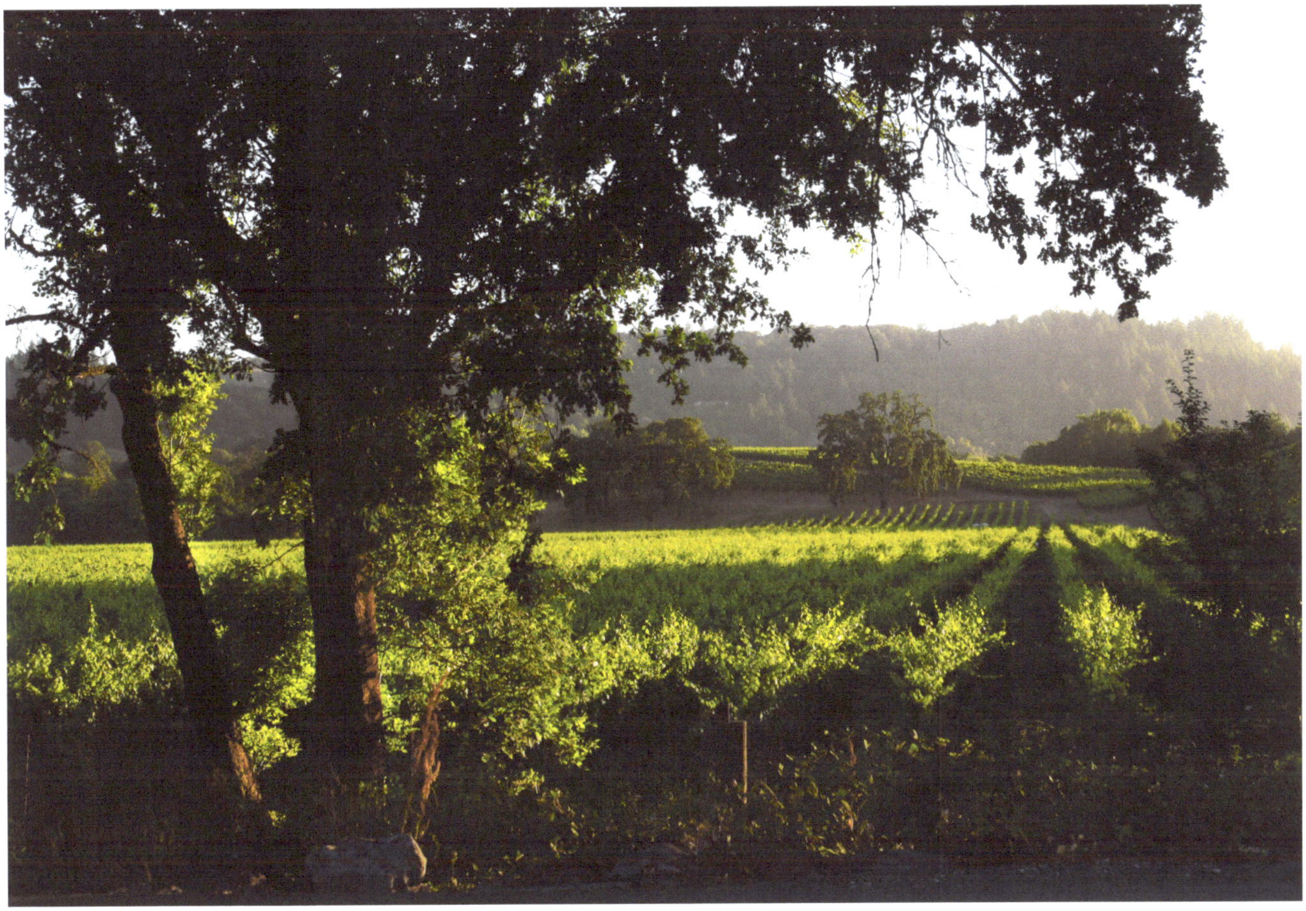

2015 90-402 Vineyard at Dusk

About the Artist

Artist Statement:

Ralph William Chubb (Will) received his BA Degree in Advertising Photography, with honors, in 1968, from the prestigious Art Center College of Design in Southern California. After graduation, he was employed for several years by an Ad Agency in San Francisco. After this he moved to Sonoma County to specialize in photography for the wine industry.

Will has created masterful photographic images for many corporate, small business and personal clients. He has worked with more than two dozen wineries.

He has also had the opportunity to photograph such stars as Joanna Cassidy, Dick Smothers, Suzanne Somers and Bob Cummings. Will's passion is producing fine art images framed and printed on canvas. Go to Will's web site to see the selection of images for sale, including most of the images in this book.

Go to www.willchubbphotograohy.com

Will's Mission Statement: Through my art, it is my intention to inspire those I reach and awaken their own joyful and unique creative spirit. I refuse to die with the music still in my heart. I want to inspire others to get in touch with their "music" as well.

Will was also a firefighter for 30 years with the City of San Rafael Fire Department. He says it's the best job in the world helping people in need. "Also, working shoulder to shoulder with my fellow firefighters was the best," he states. "They are family. For three months the firefighters worked my shifts so that I could be with Linda during her last days."

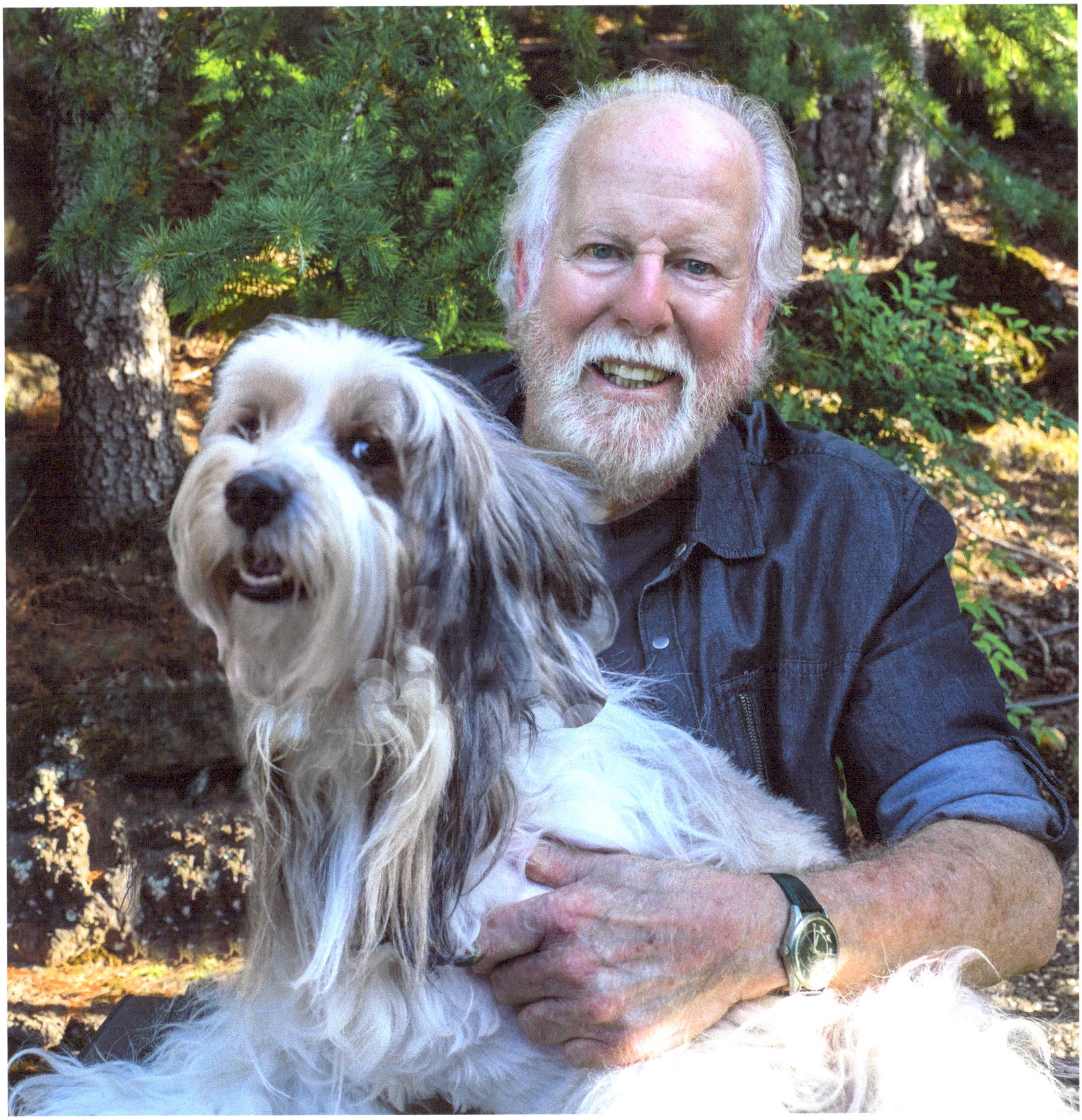

August 2019

Will Chubb and his Buddy, Teddy
Photo by Alan Pitcairn

How to Order Prints

Go to my website:
www.willchubbphotography.com

Select the images you want, and order by the name and number under each photograph. All images are printed on high quality canvas and framed with a simple black wooden frame. Your photographs will be mailed directly to you or if your order is a gift, the package will be mailed directly to your loved one or client. Simply pay using PayPal. Thank you for your interest.

All my best,

Will Chubb

www.ingramcontent.com/pod-product-compliance
Lightning Source LLC
LaVergne TN
LVHW071242210926
848486LV00007B/322
9780578235653